04/2000

The Stakeholder Society

# The Stakeholder Society

Bruce Ackerman
Anne Alstott

Yale University Press
New Haven & London

Designed by Rebecca Gibb
and set in New Caledonia type by à la page,
New Haven, Connecticut.
Printed in the United States of America by
BookCrafters, Inc., Chelsea, Michigan.

Ackerman, Bruce A.
    The stakeholder society / Bruce
Ackerman, Anne Alstott.
        p.      cm.
    Includes bibliographical references and
index.
    ISBN 0-300-07826-9 (alk. paper)
    I. Alstott, Anne, 1963–    . II. Title.
HD2741.A27    1999
658.4′08—dc21                    98-31559

A catalogue record for this book is available
from the British Library.

The paper in this book meets the guidelines
for permanence and durability of the Committee on Production Guidelines for Book
Longevity of the Council on Library
Resources.

10 9 8 7 6 5 4 3 2 1

For Susan

For Russ

# Contents

# Acknowledgments

This book has grown through countless conversations with colleagues at Yale University and beyond. For better or worse, we would never have reached our conclusions without the prod of these (seemingly endless) challenges.

Looking backward, we find that it is impossible for us to recall every helpful contribution. But we must mark some high points. After we finished our first draft, Robert Litan was good enough to invite us down for a daylong workshop at the Brookings Institution in Washington, D.C. We are indebted to each of the scholars who prepared a penetrating commentary on one or another of our early chapters: Gary Burtless, Bill Gale, Kevin Hassett, Ned Phelps, Belle Sawhill, and Gene Steuerle. This careful and comprehensive critique allowed us to gain perspective on our project and rethink our argument from the ground up.

Encouraged by our Brookings experience, we then took our manuscript on a workshop tour. At Yale, we discussed our ideas at faculty seminars in the departments of economics and psychology as well as in the law school. We took to the highway and presented the manuscript at law school workshops at Columbia, Georgetown, and Harvard. This book has been greatly clarified by these encounters.

And then there were many one-on-one (or one-on-two) conversations and E-mails. The ones that particularly stick in our minds involved Barry Adler, Matt Adler, Greg Alexander, Ian Ayres, Jack Balkin, Ben Barber, R. Bhaskar, Boris Bittker, Patrick Crawford, Einer Elhauge, Bob Ellickson, Heidi Feldman, Owen Fiss, Barbara Fried, Herbert Gans, Beth Garrett, Michael Graetz, Amy Gutmann, Henry Hansmann, Dan Kahan, Al Klevorick, Larry Lessig, Jerry Mashaw, Claus Offe, Ned Phelps, Andrezj Rapaczynski, Roberta Romano, Susan Rose-Ackerman, Chuck Sabel, Peter Schuck, Vicki Schultz, Alan Schwartz, Dan Shaviro, Reva Siegel, Reed Shuldiner, Bill Stuntz, Mark Tushnet, Amy Wax, Jim Whitman, Allen Wood, Bill Young, Larry Zelenak, and Eric Zolt.

Our students at the Yale Law School have been among our most astute critics. They took the lead in dissecting *The Stakeholder Society* in our seminar on tax policy and distributive justice. These discussions led to many valuable changes. We are especially indebted to the students who signed on as research assistants: Stacey Abrams, Liza Goitein, Jessica Sager, Phil Spector, and Lucy Wood.

We were particularly fortunate in our collaboration with Mark Wilhelm, then an assistant professor in the economics department at Pennsylvania State University and now at Indiana University–Purdue University at Indianapolis. Mark had already done substantial work with the crucial data sets, and he brought this experience to bear in simulating the revenue and distributional effects of our wealth tax. Mark's careful empirical work helped us bring our wealth tax proposal further into the real world. He did an outstanding job, and we are very grateful to him.

We were also lucky enough to call upon research assistance from two students formally trained in economics. Sarah Senesky, a Ph.D.

student in the economics department at Yale, did an admirable job in producing a very useful study of childhood privilege. And Kristin Madison, a Ph.D. student in Stanford University's economics department as well as at the Yale Law School, prepared a careful study of the present value of social insurance entitlements.

Special thanks also go to Philippe Van Parijs, who, in the spring of 1998, spent hours reading our drafts, attending our classes, and discussing the finer points of liberalism over some memorable lunches.

Dean Anthony Kronman of the Yale Law School gave us generous financial support as well as unflagging intellectual encouragement.

Gene Coakley in the Yale Law Library worked tirelessly to find the voluminous research materials that we requested. Without his help, this book would have taken far longer to complete. Jill Tobey and Diane Hart provided excellent administrative assistance as we conducted research and put together draft after draft.

And last, but never least, John Covell, our editor at Yale University Press, believed in this book from the beginning. We are deeply grateful for his sustained support.

# Introduction

# 1

# Your Stake in America

Americans have always had an uncertain love affair with equal opportunity. We believe in it, we know it really doesn't exist in today's world, and yet we have learned to live comfortably in the gap between ideal and reality. After all, aren't all ideals elusive?

Perhaps unequal opportunity was easier to accept when a booming economy guaranteed that children from every class did better than their parents. Even if lower-class kids still ended up near the bottom, they had a sense of participating in the general upward movement. But those halcyon days are over.[1] Although the economy as a whole continues to prosper, the last generation's vast increase in wealth has utterly failed to "trickle down" to the overwhelming majority of Americans. The indisputable fact is that almost all our newfound abundance has gone to the top 20 percent.[2]

The statistics on income and wages are no less grim. Since the early 1970s, the average family's income has grown little, and the typical male worker has seen his real wages decline. Only the entry of vast numbers of women into the labor force has produced meager gains in median family income.[3] In contrast, real wages for college graduates have continued to go up.[4] By the mid-1990s, the top 5 percent of American families received 20 percent of total income—a larger share than at any time since 1947.[5]

These economic disparities are profoundly shaping the future of the next generation. Rich kids get a big head start in life—they go to the best schools, the best colleges, get generous financial help from Mom and Dad, and eventually receive a tidy inheritance. But things look different at the bottom, where an increasing proportion of children live out their early years. In 1996, children represented 40 percent of all Americans living below the poverty line—but only one-quarter of the total population.[6] We are reaching the point of no return: it is one thing to tolerate a gap between ideals and reality, quite another to allow the ideal to disappear from our moral horizon. Do Americans believe in equal opportunity anymore?

There is only one way to find out, and that is by offering a range of serious proposals that might revitalize our collective commitment. In this neoconservative age, it is all too easy to assert that nothing practical can be done. Isn't increasing inequality the price we pay for progress?

Our answer is no. If America drifts away from the promise of equal opportunity, it is not because practical steps are unavailable, but because we have lost our way.

In developing our vision of the stakeholder society, we also challenge some familiar platitudes of the Left. Instead of focusing on the widening economic gap, American liberals have been increasingly preoccupied with the politics of identity. Insofar as economics has been important, the focus has been on assuring equal opportunity in the workplace. This is a fine goal, but it is not enough. Nor is it enough to redeem the faded promise of *Brown v. Board of Education* and seek new ways of providing a more equal education to all. We must also recognize that increasing inequality of wealth is endangering our sense of community.

We offer a practical plan for reaffirming the reality of a common citizenship. As each American reaches maturity, he or she will be guaranteed a stake of eighty thousand dollars. Our plan seeks justice by rooting it in capitalism's preeminent value: the importance of private property. It points the way to a society that is more democratic, more productive, and more free. Bear with us, and you will see how a single innovation once proposed by Tom Paine can achieve what a thousand lesser policies have failed to accomplish. Through stakeholding, Americans can win a renewed sense that they do indeed live in a land of equal opportunity, where all have a fair chance.

Our vision of economic citizenship is rooted in the classical liberal tradition. It is up to each citizen—not the government—to decide how she will use her fair share of the nation's patrimony. By putting this ideal of free and equal citizenship at the center of our political economy, we challenge two master themes that have dominated discussion throughout the twentieth century.

The first theme is the maximization of social welfare. This goal provides a ready argument for progressive taxation. Because a marginal dollar is worth more to the poor than to the rich, government should tax the rich at higher rates. The same logic implies a safety net for those whose incomes fall below a minimally decent floor. But these progressive tendencies are held in check by a final factor. Excessive redistribution reduces incentives for production and growth. The big tradeoff, then, is between more equality and more wealth to share.[7]

This familiar conclusion is challenged by a second, and recently resurgent, theme. It proceeds from a libertarian model of society: the government does not "own" society's wealth and therefore has no right to redistribute it. Taxes should be low and welfare spending minimal.

People have an equal right to exploit the opportunities that come their way. Freedom comes first, and whenever taxes go up, individual freedom goes down.

We mean to define a third way. Like libertarians, we emphasize each person's right to make the most of his or her opportunities. But we deny that the "invisible hand" distributes these opportunities in a morally defensible way. Like welfarists, we believe in social responsibility. But for us, the central task of government is to guarantee *genuine* equality of opportunity. Americans who begin life with greater opportunities cannot complain when their tax dollars go toward expanding the life-options of the less privileged. Such a program redistributes opportunities more fairly, permitting all citizens to begin life on a level playing field.

Our proposal for a stakeholder society takes one large step toward this ideal. The program we describe is very different from the status quo, yet it is both realistic and politically attractive. Our reforms are unfamiliar because our goal challenges the existing mix of libertarian and welfarist policies of American government. We hope to displace the tired debate between supporters and critics of the welfare state with a new question: How do we achieve genuinely equal opportunity for all?

We reject the idea that there is an inexorable tradeoff between liberty and equality. The stakeholder society promises more of both.

## The Basic Proposal: Stakeholding and Its Responsibilities

As a citizen of the United States, each American is entitled to a stake in his country: a one-time grant of eighty thousand dollars as he reaches early adulthood. This stake will be financed by an annual 2 percent tax levied on all the nation's wealth. The tie between wealth-holding and stakeholding expresses a fundamental social responsibility. Every American has an obligation to contribute to a fair starting point for all.

Stakeholders are free. They may use their money for any purpose they choose: to start a business or pay for more education, to buy a house or raise a family or save for the future. But they must take responsibility for their choices. Their triumphs and blunders are their own.

At the end of their lives, stakeholders have a special responsibility. Because the eighty thousand dollars was central in starting them off in life, it is only fair that they repay it at death if this is financially possible. The stakeholding fund, in short, is enriched each year by the ongoing contributions of all wealth-holders and by a final payback at death.

There are many possible variations on the stakeholding theme. But we have said enough to suggest the broad political appeal of equal opportunity. How many young adults start off life with eighty thousand dollars? How many parents can afford to give their children the head start that this implies?

Stakeholding liberates college graduates from the burdens of debt, often with something to spare. It offers unprecedented opportunities for the tens of millions who don't go to college and have often been shortchanged by their high school educations. For the first time, they will confront the labor market with a certain sense of security. The stake will give them the independence to choose where to live, whether to marry, and how to train for economic opportunity. Some will fail. But fewer than today.

## A Common Bond

Turn back the clock half a century and consider a very different America. For most citizens, World War II had marked a great collective achievement for the nation. Both on the battlefront and on the home front, men and women experienced a sense of genuine contribution to a common enterprise of high moral importance. The military draft created a strongly democratic ethos which endured in American life long after the war was over. This sense of common enterprise was sustained during the next era of economic growth—through the 1960s, most Americans really did share in the growing abundance.[8]

But these bonds have unraveled over the past quarter-century. Citizenship is now a largely formal exercise. Voting rights are important, but confer no sense of individual efficacy. Guarantees against discrimination in employment and the like are too thin to generate an everyday sense of common commitment. With the top 20 percent appropriating the lion's share of the nation's economic growth, most Americans no longer share fully in the free enterprise system. If a deep sense of national community is to endure, the next generation will require new institutions that express America's enduring aspirations.

Consider the fate of the GI Bill of Rights, the last great initiative that targeted young adults. First formulated after World War II, it was designed to provide citizen-soldiers with the funds needed to go to college, start a small business, or buy a home. While its direct benefits went mostly to men, it shared the universalistic aspirations of stakeholding, seeking to redeem America's promise of freedom in concrete terms. But after half a century, the meaning of the GI Bill has changed in the context of a professional military. It has become an employee benefit, not an expression of common citizenship.

Conventional forms of worker protection cannot be expected to fill this gap. Our current social security system reflects the traditional ideal of lifelong employment at a decent wage, with a safety net for occasional unemployment, catastrophic disability, and eventual retirement. That is a pretty picture. But it is no longer a reality for most American workers. The college-educated workforce is doing better than ever, but the least-skilled workers face a labor market that promises high unemployment and poverty-level wages.[9] For this group, traditional social insurance provides very little economic security. And the future promises more of the same: free trade, global capital markets, and technological change are likely to hold down blue-collar wages in the United States.[10] While it may be politically popular for pundits on the Right to deny this fact, it is far more constructive to confront it. How can we reconcile free trade and open markets with real equality of opportunity?

Through stakeholding. Our initiative does not seek to reverse world economic forces. It fully endorses the open economy and the great wealth made possible by the worldwide division of labor. But it insists that the American political community is strong enough to shape this wealth for its own purposes. Is America more than a libertarian marketplace? Can we preserve a sense of ourselves as a nation of free and equal citizens?

As young adults receive their stakes, they will have little doubt about America's answer to this question. As they come forward to claim their eighty thousand dollars, each of America's children will do more than gain the ability to shape their individual destinies. They will locate themselves in a much larger national project devoted to the proposition that all men *are* created equal. By invoking this American ideal in their own case, they link themselves not only to all others in the past who have taken steps to realize this fundamental principle but also to all those who will do so in the future.

To be sure, there are risks as well as rewards. Are twenty-somethings really up to the task of responsible stakeholding? Can they be trusted to invest the money wisely in themselves, their families, their businesses, and their communities? Won't they fritter away the nation's patrimony on drugs and decadence?

We will be discussing ways to structure stakeholding to enhance the prospect of responsible decision-making. For example, no citizen should be allowed free use of his eighty thousand dollars without gaining a high school diploma. Nor should he get all the money at once; the stakeholding fund should provide payments of twenty thousand dollars every year or two as citizens move through their early twenties. And so forth.

But it is better to defer questions of program design for now and consider more basic issues of principle.

## Beyond the Welfare State

We are trying to break the hold of a familiar vision of the welfare state in America. In this view, modern government has succeeded to the traditional tasks of the church—tending to the old, the sick, the disabled. Like the church, the welfare state is concerned with providing the weak with a decent minimum.

Given this statement of the problem, debate centers on how minimal the minimum should be. Even libertarians grudgingly concede that some vulnerable Americans must be provided with some care some of the time; welfarists push the minimum higher.

We reject the organizing premise of this unending argument. Our primary focus is on the young and energetic, not the old and vulnerable. Our primary values are freedom and equal opportunity, not decency and minimum provision. We do not deny that old-fashioned decency has a role to play, and we will try to define its place later on.[11] For now, it is enough to see that stakeholding is intended not as "welfare reform" but as an entirely new enterprise. Our first concern is not with safety nets but with starting points; not with misfortune, but with opportunity; not with welfare, but with economic citizenship.

From this vantage, it is hardly news that America only promises its children the pursuit of happiness and does not guarantee them success. But it is one thing to make a mess out of your life, quite another never to have had a fair chance. The key question, then, is not whether some stakeholders will fail to make good use of their stake. Some will fail, and in ways that they will come to regret bitterly. The question is whether these predictable failures should serve as a reason to deprive tens of millions of others of *their* fair chance to pursue happiness.

We say no. Each individual citizen has a right to a fair share of the patrimony left by preceding generations. This right should not be contingent on how others use or misuse their stakes. In a free society, it is inevitable that different stakeholders will put their resources to different uses, with different results. Our goal is to transcend the welfare state mentality, which sets conditions on the receipt of "aid." In a stakeholding society, stakes are a matter of right, not a handout. The diversity of individuals' life choices (and the predictable failure of some) is no excuse for depriving each American of the wherewithal to attempt her own pursuit of happiness.

Nor is it a reason to transform stakeholding into yet another exercise in paternalistic social engineering. In our many conversations on the subject, somebody invariably suggests the wisdom of restricting the stake to a limited set of praiseworthy purposes—requiring each citizen to gain bureaucratic approval before spending down his eighty thousand dollars. Won't this allow us to redistribute wealth and make sure the money is well spent?

This question bears the mark of the welfarist mindset. The point of stakeholding is to liberate each citizen from government, not to create an excuse for a vast new bureaucracy intervening in our lives. If stakeholders want advice, they can buy it on the market. If people in their twenties can't be treated as adults, when will they be old enough?

Admittedly, there will always be some Americans who are profoundly unequal to the challenges of freedom. It would be silly to suppose that victims of profound mental disability were capable of managing their eighty thousand dollars on their own. More controversially, we would also deny full control over their stakes to Americans who cannot demonstrate the self-discipline needed to graduate from high school. We agree, alas, that more traditional forms of bureaucratic control may be needed to deal sensibly with these tough cases. But we refuse to allow trendy talk of "underclass" pathologies to divert our attention from another and equally pressing problem. Quite simply, there are tens of millions of ordinary Americans who are perfectly capable of responsible decision-making in a stakeholding society but are now becoming the forgotten citizens of our globalizing economy.

We are speaking of the ordinary Joe or Jane who graduates from high school or maybe a two-year college and who then confronts an increasingly harsh labor market. For this enormous group, stakeholding will provide a priceless buffer against the predictable shocks of the marketplace. A temporary economic setback will no longer quickly spiral into a devastating loss of self-confidence or a grim period of deprivation. The stake will provide a cushion in hard times and a source of entrepreneurial energy in better ones.

In emphasizing these ordinary Americans, we do not wish to belittle the importance of stakeholding for those at the top and the bottom of our economic hierarchy. For the top quarter of the population, those graduating from four-year colleges, stakeholding will not only eliminate the crushing burden of student loans. It will also inject much-needed competition among universities for the stakeholding dollar, generating a more responsive and effective system of higher education. For those growing up in the ghettos of America, stakeholding will provide a beacon of hope: stay in school and graduate, and you will not be forgotten. You will get a solid chance to live out the American dream of economic independence.

But stakeholding's message will have a special salience to the broad middle group of Americans, who constitute about two-thirds of the entire population. After all, existing governmental programs already heap large educational subsidies on those who can successfully negotiate the challenges of four-year college; even in today's conservative climate, we have not entirely given up on special programs that address the needs of ghetto youth. But at present, ordinary Americans really are forgotten Americans. After they leave school, they confront the market without much to fall back on. While stakeholding offers economic independence for all, its promise will have special meaning to middle America—which should rally to its support once it has been persuaded that government *can* be made to work again for ordinary people.

This leads us to our larger political objectives. We propose to revitalize a very old republican tradition that links property and citizenship into an indissoluble whole. In earlier times, this linkage was often used for exclusionary purposes.[12] In colonial America, for example, suffrage and office-holding were often restricted to those with substantial property. But during the nineteenth century, a serious effort was made to reverse the linkage. Most famously, the Homestead Act refused to offer up America's vast resources to the highest bidders, but encouraged citizens to stake their claims for a fair share of the common wealth. During Reconstruction, Radical Republicans led a spirited campaign to couple the Fourteenth Amendment's grant of citizenship to black Americans with a stake carved out of rebel property.

This campaign failed, and the closing of the frontier heralded an increasing split between property and citizenship in American thought and practice. Even those genuinely concerned with economic dignity looked elsewhere: socialists would settle for nothing less than the abolition of private property itself; more moderate reformers aimed to build a strong state apparatus capable of regulating the capitalist system. Now that we have had experience with the limitations of both these experiments, isn't it time to consider another path?

We do not join those who would cheerfully sweep away the legislative achievements of the Progressives, the New Deal, and the Great Society. Many of these reforms have withstood the test of time, and others merely require adaptations and refinements. But if we are to confront the emerging problems of our own age, we must once again attempt a fundamental redefinition of the progressive vision. Rather than abolishing private property or regulating it more intensely, we should be redistributing it.

This is the time to make economic citizenship a central part of the American agenda. The task is to enable *all* Americans to enjoy the promise of economic freedom that our existing property system now offers to an increasingly concentrated elite.

## Experiments in Stakeholding

Stakeholding is a simple idea, and one whose time has come. This seems to be the assessment of some astute politicians who have gained great followings through initiatives that bear a family resemblance to our proposal. Margaret Thatcher is a case in point. When she became prime minister of Great Britain in 1979, 32 percent of all housing was publicly owned. Although bent on sweeping privatization, Thatcher refused to sell off these vast properties to big companies. She invited residents to buy their own homes at bargain rates. With a single stroke, she created a new property-owning citizenry, and she won vast popularity in the process.[13]

A more sweeping initiative took place in the Czech Republic in the aftermath of the Communist overthrow of 1989. The prime minister elected in 1992, Václav Klaus, confronted a much larger task than Thatcher's: the state sector contained seven thousand medium and large-scale enterprises, twenty-five to thirty-five thousand smaller ones. How to distribute this legacy of Communism? Klaus saw his problem as an opportunity to create a vast new property-owning class of Czech citizens.

The mechanism was the ingenious technique of "voucher privatization." Each Czech citizen could subscribe to a book of vouchers that he could use to bid for shares in state companies as they were put on the auction block. An overwhelming majority—8.5 out of 10.5 million—took up Klaus's offer and claimed their fair share of the nation's wealth as they moved into the new free-market system. Klaus's creative program helped cement his position as the leading politician of the Republic. More importantly, the broad involvement of citizen-stakeholders played a central role in legitimating the country's transition to liberal democracy.[14]

Thatcher and Klaus conceived of their initiatives as one-shot affairs. But the citizens of Alaska have made stakeholding a regular part of their political economy. Once again, the occasion was the distribution of a major public asset, in this case the revenues from North Slope oil. Rather than using it all for public expenditures, the Republican leadership designed a stakeholding scheme that is now distributing about one thousand dollars a year to every Alaskan citizen. Once again, the system has become broadly popular, with politicians of both parties regularly pledging that they will not raid the symbolically named Permanent Fund.[15]

## Taxing Wealth

The biggest difference between these initiatives and our proposal should be obvious. Brits, Czechs, and Alaskans funded stakeholding out of public property. We look to two other sources. Over the short term—the first forty or fifty years—we rely principally upon an annual 2 percent tax on wealth. Over the longer run, stakeholding will be financed increasingly by recipients' payments at death.

These particular choices deserve their own chapters—and then some. Perhaps you will find yourself unconvinced by our case for the wealth tax and will conclude that some other short-run source of revenue is more appropriate. If so, we would be happy to marry stakeholding with your alternative taxing scheme. But beyond these (important) questions of program design lies a deeper point. In our view, there is no good reason to limit stakeholding to cases involving physical assets like housing or factories or oil. Americans have created other assets that are

less material but have even greater value. Most notably, the free enterprise system did not drop from thin air. It has emerged only as the result
of a complex and ongoing scheme of social cooperation. The free market requires heavy public expenditures on the police and the courts and
much else besides. Without billions of voluntary decisions by Americans
to respect the rights of property in their daily lives, the system would
collapse overnight.[16] All Americans benefit from this cooperative activity—but some much more than others. Those who benefit the most
have a duty to share some of their wealth with fellow citizens whose cooperation they require to sustain the market system. This obligation is
all the more exigent when the operation of the global market threatens
to split the country more sharply into haves and have-nots.

This view gives our proposal a different ideological spin from those
pioneered by Margaret Thatcher and Václav Klaus. Surely there will
be some on the Right who will blanch at the implications of our proposal. But we do hope that many others will come to see its justice. We
expect a similar split on the Left. Some will be deeply suspicious of our
proposal to liberate stakeholding assets from the grip of the regulatory
state, leaving it to each citizen to spend his eighty thousand in the way
that makes sense to him. Others will be more impressed by the justice
of empowering all Americans to share in the pursuit of happiness.

We expect less resistance to the long-run aspect of our funding proposal, which relies on stakeholders making substantial paybacks at
death. This will require us, however, to put some old questions about
inheritance in a new light.

## Expanding the Stake

Our first task will be to explore the many moral and practical questions
presented by the basic stakeholding proposal. But we have a larger
aim as well. We believe that our initiative provides a framework for a
more general reconstruction of the existing welfare state.

To suggest the possibilities, Part 2 focuses on social security and how stakeholding allows Americans to rethink some basic decisions made during the New Deal. In building support for his proposals, Franklin Roosevelt had one overriding aim. He wanted to entrench social security so deeply in our institutional life that it would be politically impossible for his opponents to repeal it. Somehow or other, his program must express the idea that social security was not charity but a fundamental right. What image would convey the requisite notion of entitlement?

Drawing on European traditions, Roosevelt embraced a system that emphasized the workplace. Social security was not charity because workers would earn it by contributing to an insurance fund through payroll taxes. Here as elsewhere, Roosevelt proved himself the master politician of the age: to the libertarians' despair, social security remains a bulwark of economic citizenship. Thanks in large part to social security, the poverty rate among the elderly has plummeted in the past decades, and many more workers can look forward to retirement with a modicum of dignity.[17]

But Roosevelt's enduring political triumph has come at a heavy price. Because "premiums" are paid only at the workplace, nonworkers get nothing in their own right. Of course, many of these people live productive lives. Millions of women spend years out of the paid work force, or in low-paid part-time work, while they rear young children. As a consequence, the insurance metaphor provides them with little or no independent social security. The system ties their economic fate to their husbands'—if they have them. As we shall see, this is only the beginning of many other questionable discriminations and taxation decisions encouraged by the Rooseveltian link between retirement income and the workplace.

Don't get us wrong. Social security is one of the great achievements of American social policy. But as we look forward to the twenty-first century, it is time to move on to a more progressive and more inclusive system. What is required is a new master metaphor to displace the in-surance analogy—and to symbolize the transition from worker citizen-ship to universal economic citizenship.

Stakeholding provides this metaphor. It creates a new way of ex-pressing Roosevelt's idea that a decent retirement is a matter of right, not a question of charity. And it allows us to restructure this right in a much fairer way. Under our expanded proposal, each American citizen not only gets to stake her claim to eighty thousand dollars. She also gets an entitlement to a basic retirement pension. In contrast to the exist-ing system, this citizen's pension would not depend on the vagaries of her work history, her wage rate, or her marital status. Instead, it would be a fundamental aspect of economic citizenship. Each American would receive a monthly retirement check that represented the mini-mum amount needed to live a decent life. Of course, this check would represent a floor, not a ceiling. People who wanted more money in re-tirement would remain perfectly free to invest in private pension plans. But it would be up to each of us to make this decision.

The stakeholding system will also open up a long overdue reconsid-eration of the methods through which we now pay for a secure retire-ment. Once we remove pensions from the workplace, it will no longer seem natural to fund them through payroll taxes. Instead, Americans will begin to see the payroll tax for what it is—a *tax*, and one that hits the working poor hardest. We urge its replacement by a new system that is more in keeping with the principles of equal opportunity at the core of the stakeholder society.

## Stakeholding as a Catalytic Reform

Most reforms, when they are adopted, don't lead anywhere. They may fix a problem, and that is a good thing, but they don't precipitate a larger wave of reconstructive activity.

Stakeholding, by contrast, is a catalytic reform. It can generate further waves of activity that might, over time, lead to the construction of a more just retirement system for older Americans—and much else besides.

Or it may not. The case for our basic proposal in no way depends on anything we say in Part 2. Indeed, we are a bit concerned that the greater complexity of expanded stakeholding might distract attention from one of the greatest virtues of our basic proposal.

And that is its direct appeal to ordinary Americans. Everybody understands eighty thousand dollars and what it might mean in the lives of young adults. Everybody understands a flat tax of 2 percent on net wealth. Because our proposal exempts the first eighty thousand dollars of each citizen's wealth from the new tax, the overwhelming share will be paid by America's upper classes—the very group that has seen its wealth increase over the past twenty-five years. Our basic proposal, then, makes it plain to the general public that something effective *can* be done about America's increasing maldistribution of wealth—and that stakeholding is well within our political reach.

This is, is it not, a democracy where each citizen casts an equal vote, and the majority rules? If we work together, there is nothing that can stop us from building a new foundation for economic citizenship. The effort will require political effort by many, inspired leadership by some, and a certain sophistication by all in dealing with the advertising campaigns launched by those who have so much to lose.

But Americans have managed to overcome larger obstacles in the past. It is past time to begin a new era of reform.

# Part 1

## The Basic Proposal

# 2

# Citizen Stakeholding

Modern policy-talk lives in a time warp. It speaks in languages that have been the object of thoroughgoing philosophical critique over the past generation. With few exceptions, libertarians struggle against utilitarians as if they were the only guys in town. But there are other serious options, and in the past generation, liberal political philosophy has sought to rework the basic terms of debate.

Of course, philosophy is not a game with definite winners and losers. But neither utilitarianism nor libertarianism now dominates the conversation. The weaknesses in each position have led philosophers to define new understandings of "liberalism" and its competitors. This process of ongoing redefinition is nothing new. Over the past two centuries, liberalism has stood for everything from laissez faire to the welfare state. The philosophical task has been to move beyond partisan labels and identify core commitments that organize seemingly disparate agendas.

The new liberalisms that have emerged combine a commitment to individualism with an appreciation of the pervasive impact of economic inequality. While devoted to limited government, they insist that the liberal state should be concerned with more than keeping the markets open for business. It must also assure each citizen a level playing field when he enters the marketplace as an adult. Without this fair start, individual freedom for some is oppression for others.[1]

We do not intend to summarize this complex and ongoing debate. Our aim is to bring it into the real world of welfare-state politics. In contrast to the ready-made policy prescriptions of utilitarian economics and the simple antitax message of the libertarians, the new liberalism has not offered a distinct and workable agenda on taxes and transfers. But we believe that it can and that its promise of greater equality of opportunity can command wide appeal.

We offer, then, a new kind of policy-talk—one true to liberal ideals but also thoroughly practical. The challenge is to marry political philosophy with hardheaded methods of policy analysis based on statistics and social science. Throughout the book, we debate the big questions in the text, but readers can find more elaboration in the notes. The Appendix presents data establishing that our proposals are fiscally sound and well within the nation's budgetary capacities.

## From Critique to Construction

The most appealing thing about utilitarianism is its unabashed striving for a better world. There is so much pain and suffering. Isn't it obvious that we should all work together to maximize collective well-being?

It is a serious thing to say no—it risks the charge of selfishness and callousness. But at the same time, there is something wrong with the utilitarian's picture of society. It makes it seem as though the social value of each individual is merely a function of his contribution to the general welfare. But this can't be right. Consider Nazi Germany, in which Jews numbered 1 percent of the population. Such disproportion places the utilitarian case against racist laws on shaky ground. Obviously, each Jew suffered terribly from discrimination, but this is not enough for a hardheaded utilitarian calculus. After all, the pleasure of the other 99 percent, the Aryans, must also be taken into account—and is it so clear that the average Jew suffered *ninety-nine* times as much as the average Aryan gained from his feelings of racial superiority?

Thought-experiments like this have led contemporary liberal political theory to one of its most fundamental conclusions: utilitarianism, at its core, does not take individualism seriously enough. Each citizen's standing in society should not depend on whether he contributes to others' happiness. We are not just cogs in a collective happiness machine. We are different people, each with rights of self-determination.

This is, of course, the great truth upon which libertarians insist. But they combine this insistence with another false picture of society. They tend to be supremely indifferent to the ways in which social background shapes cultural and economic starting points. It is as if we all emerged as fully formed adults, in the manner of Botticelli's Venus, if only to display a more emphatically commercial disposition.

But this radical anticontextualism is unacceptable. Every individual's personality is a product of dynamic interaction with the cultural and educational opportunities made available in early life. For example, a woman's sense of herself would be forever warped if her parents deprived her of a primary education—and if the state did nothing to make sure that this didn't happen. Thankfully, Americans have recognized such obvious points; a primary education is compulsory in this country. But the libertarian would have us ignore the more subtle, yet still pervasive, ways in which educational inequalities shape the future capacities of children to form and achieve their objectives in later life.

No less important, each person comes to maturity with an economic endowment he cannot be said to deserve. In our society, starting points are irrevocably shaped by parental wealth and position. But nobody deserves his parents. The libertarian picture diverts us from the morally arbitrary distribution of initial economic endowments. It focuses only on the protection of individual freedom to use these entitlements, without too much scrutiny into their moral foundations. At best, libertarians fill this void with a fanciful picture of a "state of nature" in which free individuals stake their claims in a virgin wilderness. But real-world citizens can make claims to true economic independence only through the deliberate political decision to create a stakeholder society.

The philosophical challenge, then, is to construct a liberalism that (*a*) takes individualism seriously, (*b*) recognizes that each individual's starting point in life is shaped by a confrontation with his economic and educational opportunities, and therefore (*c*) grants the state a potentially constructive role in the just distribution of these opportunities.

## Our Focus and Its Limits

We are interested in opportunities, not outcomes. As liberals, we believe that each citizen should be free to shape her outcomes as she thinks best. But as activist liberals, we emphasize the failure of the capitalist system to give each citizen an equal opportunity to exercise this freedom as she goes about the task of shaping her life. By the time Americans reach early adulthood, they have encountered vastly unequal chances to define themselves, realize their talents, and move with financial confidence into the marketplace.

Speaking broadly, we can say that each citizen's basic opportunities in life are shaped by four factors. The first is her inborn capacities—some come into this world profoundly handicapped, while others have a rich variety of talents. The second factor is her cultural and educational opportunities, which depend on a shifting mix of family background and self-conscious state policies. The third factor is her command over material resources during childhood and as she starts out in life as an independent adult. And finally, there is the power of prejudice—an American black interacts with others on terms different from those of her white counterpart, even if her access to other resources is roughly equivalent.

This framework locates our particular initiatives against a broader background. Begin with the dimensions of the problem that we are putting to one side. This book does not deal with the special problems posed by physical or mental handicaps, abusive and inadequate parenting, impoverished and segregated education, or pervasive racial and gender discrimination. Given the compelling importance of all these conditions, we may seem to be suffering from an extreme case of tunnel vision. Our only excuse is that these other problems are the subject of rich literatures, while a vast silence greets our own concern—which is, to put it bluntly, MONEY.

Money matters directly and indirectly. Indirectly, because parental wealth and income shape opportunities throughout childhood—the schools you go to, the friends you make, the role models you encounter. Directly, as teenagers gain more independent control over spending money and finally move out on their own, with or without financial assets.

It is at this point that stakeholding intervenes. The grant of eighty thousand dollars to young adults means something more than the mere possibility of enhanced consumption. It means economic independence. James Meade put the point well: "Extreme inequalities in the ownership of property are in my view undesirable quite apart from any inequalities of income which they may imply. A man with much property has great bargaining strength and a sense of security, independence, and freedom. . . . He can snap his fingers at those on whom he must rely for income, for he can always rely for a time on his capital. The propertyless man must continuously and without interruption acquire his income by working for an employer or by qualifying to receive it from a public authority. An unequal distribution of property means an unequal distribution of power and status even if it is prevented from causing too unequal distribution of income."[2] These concerns shape our inquiry. How much do disparities in income and wealth shape the opportunities available to young Americans as they set out as independent citizens?

## Inequality in America

Begin at the beginning. Although the percentage of children in poverty has fallen over the very long term, it has climbed since the mid-1970s and was 20.5 percent in 1996.[3] In the 1990s, children under six are poorer than any other age group.[4] And just as children's fortunes have been declining, those of the elderly have been on the rise.[5]

Changing social patterns also affect children's prospects. Most married mothers now work outside the home, and their earnings have helped maintain family-income levels despite the drop in men's wages.[6] We do not believe that this transformation is necessarily bad for children, but it can exacerbate inequality of opportunity.[7] Whereas upper-class women can choose whether to hire a private nanny or stay home with their children, poorer families must cobble together a patchwork of often inadequate arrangements.[8] And the growing number of single mothers of all classes cannot rely on a partner for help when child-care plans go awry.[9] Working-class women and women of color, who have long worked outside the home, have faced these problems for years. But recent trends make it an urgent concern for an ever larger number of Americans.

This grim picture does not change when children enter school. Free universal public education represents a solemn affirmation of the ideal of equal opportunity. But despite formal guarantees, there remain tremendous disparities. Richer parents have a much greater range of choice about where to live and whether to send their children to private schools.[10] Among public schools, wealthier school districts spend more than poorer ones, and money undoubtedly buys a broader range of instructional services and better facilities.[11] Students from richer communities consistently outperform those from poorer ones on standardized tests.[12]

Among teenagers, SAT scores strongly correlate with parental income,[13] and high-income students can more easily afford special coaching, remedial help, and private schools.[14] It is no surprise, then, that students with high socioeconomic status are almost twice as likely to enroll in higher education as students at the bottom of the socioeconomic scale.[15] At the end of the day, 51 percent of students from the top quarter of the economic hierarchy earn bachelor's degrees, compared to 22 percent of middle-status students and only 7.2 percent in the lowest socioeconomic quartile.[16]

Unraveling the causes of intergenerational privilege is a notoriously complicated business.[17] Even a society with genuinely equal opportunity would not produce perfect economic mobility or a complete lack of correlation between childhood economic circumstances and adult economic success.[18] Children inherit innate abilities from their parents, and some of those capacities may affect their ability to earn income. (But the correlation between inherited abilities and adult incomes is much smaller than many think.)[19] While parental values and behavior inevitably influence their children's development, we should keep in mind that today's parents also grew up under conditions of significant inequality of opportunity. Even though it is impossible to know just how much economic mobility would increase in an equal-opportunity society, it is obvious that current institutions fall far short of the ideal.

## Education Is Not Enough

These facts suggest the existence of a serious problem, a skeptic might concede, but is it a problem that calls for a solution like stakeholding? If we are committed to equality of opportunity, shouldn't our first concern be the woeful inequalities in the educational system? Why not forget about stakeholding and spend the money on earlier stages of child development?

We certainly favor more money for well-considered initiatives along these lines.[20] For example, only 752,000 low-income children—one-third of those eligible—were enrolled in Head Start programs in 1996. As this level of service cost $3.6 billion, an extra $7 billion or so would allow all poor children to attend—and if we spent $5 billion more, we might actually have a first-class program.[21] Given the stakes, these are piddling sums. Our society's failure to make such basic investments in its youngest and most vulnerable citizens is simply scandalous.

This said, Head Start is not enough. Americans should not pat themselves on the back were they finally decide to cough up the $16 billion a year for an enhanced and comprehensive version of Head Start. A morally serious movement toward real equality of opportunity requires much more. Our basic stakeholding proposal, for example, would cost taxpayers about $255 billion a year.[22] Initiatives of this magnitude can be attempted only once or twice in a generation. Nonetheless, and after considering the alternatives, we believe that it makes sense to prefer stakeholding to more familiar initiatives that would throw vast sums at primary and secondary education.

After all, Americans have been exploring the egalitarian potential of education for a century and a half, and the existing shortfall suggests some sobering lessons. Time after time, we have seen egalitarian initiatives frustrated by the decentralized structure of local self-government.[23] As long as suburbs can insulate themselves from central cities, there is only so much that money alone can accomplish, as the tragic aftermath of *Brown v. Board of Education* has established.[24] The American system of federalism is partly to blame: inequalities in school funding across states are much larger than those within states.[25] And the upper classes have proven themselves adept in channeling federal aid for the disadvantaged into their own local school systems.[26] Worse yet, further decentralization and privatization seem to be the order of the day, rather than a movement toward metropolitan-wide school systems and greater national efforts to provide poorer regions of the country with greater educational resources. We oppose many of these trends,[27] but we see no evidence that the country is ready to reverse gears any time soon. In the absence of a fundamental change, we are skeptical about the egalitarian promise of a massive injection of money into primary and secondary education.

In the meantime, the existing system will continue to generate harsh consequences, especially for the 75 percent of young Americans who do not graduate from four-year colleges.[28] Family income for this enormous group has been stagnating for decades, as college graduates have skimmed off the nation's growth.[29] Thanks to unequal schooling, many of these Americans have failed to reach their full potential. At the very least, they should be provided with their fair share of the nation's property before confronting the full force of the marketplace.

Although stakeholding is not directly targeted at education, it may well help ameliorate some of the underlying inequalities. Keep in mind that each parent will start out adult life with eighty thousand dollars, which can be used to improve children's opportunities. And if the money were put toward a "rainy-day" fund—amounting to $160,000 in the case of a married couple—it may help provide children with much-needed stability in their home environment. At present, unemployment of a single wage-earner can lead to immediate household catastrophe, especially for a family in the bottom half of the population.[30] Unemployment insurance is an important safeguard, but it is temporary and not available in all cases.[31] All too often, children bear the brunt of the ensuing anxiety and dislocation.

But this is only the beginning of a long-term assessment of stakeholding's impact on the socialization of the next generation. From their earliest years, America's children will be told of the stake that awaits them as adults. Especially for children born at the bottom, the stake will stand as a symbol of hope. However grim their present situation, they will know that America has not given up on them. If they stay in school and work hard, they *will* receive the wherewithal to pursue the American Dream. It would be a serious mistake to underestimate the motivating power of this message.

Over the long run, this message of hope may gradually erode one of the principal sources of resistance to more egalitarian initiatives in public education. Sheer racism is not the only cause of America's failure to redeem the promise of *Brown v. Board of Education.* Middle-class resistance is also fueled by the fear that schools will be overwhelmed by lower-class children, who will bring drugs and crime along with them as well as a general disrespect for the value of education.[32] As time passes, stakeholding may help ameliorate these class anxieties. As they prepare to claim their stakes, more poor children will conform to middle-class values, and the transition to better racial and economic integration will thereby be eased. This is a distant prospect, and the case for stakeholding does not depend on it. But we should not overlook the possibility that a national commitment to stakeholding may catalyze a broader movement toward educational equality.

It is much too quick, then, to suggest that stakeholding should await some remote era in which America has made a great leap forward in the provision of equal educational opportunity. Stakeholding can immediately improve children's lives by enhancing their parents' freedom. And, in the long term, the causal arrow may fly in the opposite direction: stakeholding may prove a much-needed catalyst for another round of serious educational initiatives.

This conclusion gains further reinforcement when we turn from our crystal ball to contemplate present institutional realities. As we have suggested, there is absolutely no reason to suppose that a massive movement toward metropolitan government and national revenue-sharing is in the offing. And without such changes, a large-scale assault on educational inequality seems unlikely. Even smaller initiatives like Head Start and child care assistance, although enormously worthy, are not simple to design or to implement.

By contrast, it would be relatively easy to realize the goals of a stakeholder society. To a large degree, the institutional infrastructure is in place even now. We already have the Internal Revenue Service and the Social Security Administration. Although it is fashionable to denigrate these bureaucracies, both agencies are full of competent people whose tasks might easily be broadened to encompass the jobs of identifying eligible stakeholders and paying out benefits.[33] Unlike a comparable educational reform, stakeholding will not require a massive reorganization of the existing institutional framework. It builds on what we already have.

Americans could, in relatively short order, actually achieve the massive step toward equality of opportunity that stakeholding would make possible. This breakthrough, in turn, would give the lie to neoconservative banalities about the inevitability of government failure. If it is established that Americans *can* succeed in redeeming their fundamental ideals by inaugurating stakeholding, many other seemingly impossible initiatives may appear within our grasp.

## Stakeholding as an Ideal

We have been presenting stakeholding as a potentially catalytic reform within the context of existing political and institutional realities. But there is more to be said for our initiative as a matter of principle. Even if the preceding generation had fully respected their children's free and equal status by providing all of them with a first-class education, this would not entitle the elders to distribute their accumulated wealth in morally arbitrary ways.

This basic point distinguishes our brand of liberal individualism from the sort offered up by libertarians. In their familiar view, stakeholding appears as yet another do-good scheme under which the government is taking our hard-earned money and forcing us to make a "gift" to young strangers who have no claim on our benevolence.

But this objection presupposes a false picture of society. Nobody makes money simply on the basis of his own efforts. However hardearned it may be, the wealth gained by every self-made man depends on countless acts of cooperation by others. On the most primitive level, no police force would be big enough to secure private property against criminal depredation without the support of the overwhelming majority. More generally, the free market is a complex social and political creation requiring ongoing acts of self-conscious regulation and adaptation. Given the continuing dependence of the wealthy on the cooperation of their fellow citizens, stakeholding does not involve coercive "gifts" to strangers. It represents a suitable act of recognition by the wealthy of the role played by fellow Americans in creating the conditions for the very system necessary for their own success. Rather than emerging from the state of nature, private property is legitimate only when it is rendered compatible with the larger political order created by free and equal citizens.

This point should resonate with libertarians, for they also seek to create a political order in which equal freedom is a reality. Only their understanding of this ideal is too cramped. As far as they are concerned, people are equally free to make the most of the circumstances in which they are born. But we believe that the moral equality of persons requires stricter attention to starting points. No person is inherently better than any other, and thus everyone has a right to a fair share of initial resources with which to begin and plan her adult life, regardless of whether her parents were rich or poor, frugal or improvident.

Americans have long recognized this basic point in the design of our political institutions. We would think it intolerable, for example, to give rich people more votes than the poor, although this very arrangement seemed entirely acceptable for centuries. We hope that some future society will endow stakeholding with the same fundamental character: just as one person–one vote expresses political citizenship, an equal stake expresses economic citizenship.

Stakeholding enters, moreover, at the precise point at which the existing distribution of property is most questionable from a moral point of view: the point at which the rising generation comes to economic maturity and demands a fair starting point as they begin full participation in adult society. After all, young adults have not been centrally involved in the market processes through which some of their elders prospered while others declined. They were busy at school or were not yet born when the market enriched some and impoverished others. Why, then, should their economic starting points be entirely shaped by their parents' successes and failures? Isn't it especially appropriate to take their standing as equal citizens into account when they are being dealt their initial economic stakes?

This ideal of free and equal citizenship provides the master key to stakeholding. As each American assumes his adult role in a stakeholding society, he will appear on the economic stage as an economic citizen whose fate cannot justly be left to an "invisible hand" that conceals the accidents of family background and the failures of public policy. In claiming his stake, no citizen will be obliged to justify his particular plan for the money to some bureaucratic overlord. He is not only equal but free to pursue the mysteries of life in the way that makes the most sense to him.

Clearly, the grant of eighty thousand dollars doesn't guarantee anybody success in life. This will depend upon each individual's personal ideals and his abilities to achieve them in a competitive marketplace.

But the fact that a stake does not guarantee happiness is beside the point. The unconditional grant makes it plain that Americans are willing to put their money where their mouth is—to guarantee each citizen the wherewithal needed to pursue happiness on his or her own terms.

We do not suppose that our proposal suffices to achieve the ideal of equal opportunity. Not only educational reform but the special problems posed by serious physical or mental handicaps are beyond the scope of our initiative. And even within the limited domain of the marketplace, our proposal must be structured to take economic incentives into account.[34] For all its limitations, our proposal does represent a serious step forward—and at a time when so many other forces seem to be pushing us backward.

## The False Promise of Maturity

But why is it so important for each American citizen to start off adult life with a substantial financial stake in the country?

At one level, our point is uncontroversial. Nobody denies that decisions made as a young adult profoundly shape the course of later life. Nor is it really controversial to state that the movement beyond the teenage years generally has a sobering effect. The realities of earning a living, leaving home, and making some initial mistakes cumulate into an understanding of limits and the recognition that choices have consequences. This is what it means to be an adult.[35]

To be sure, adulthood is a sometime thing. Everybody falls short, and lots of people fail to live up to their own standards. Young adults will often make decisions they will later regret. But this is true throughout life. It is not as if forty-year-olds were immune from folly and shortsightedness. Even if a certain wisdom comes with age, there is a countervailing point: it becomes harder and harder to reshape your life as time goes on. If a liberal society is to vindicate the value of individual autonomy, it must consider carefully the conditions under which young adults confront basic choices.

This is not true today. Public policy deals with childhood under the rubric of education and with old age through social security. But we do not focus upon early adulthood as a distinct phase of life. Some aggregate numbers give a sense of the imbalance. In 1994, Americans spent $265 billion, or 4 percent of the GDP, on public primary and secondary education, and $477 billion, or 7 percent, on Social Security and Medicare.[36] Young adults, on the other hand, are basically on their own once they leave the classroom. Stakeholding would fill this void by directly providing them with $255 billion each year, or about 3.4 percent of 1996 GDP.[37]

From the liberal point of view, the consequence would be a massive increase in effective freedom. Our present arrangements impose an unnecessary moral dilemma: just at the moment we expect young adults to make responsible life-shaping decisions, we do not afford them the resources that they need to take a responsible long-term perspective. Forced to put bread on the table and pay the rent, almost all young adults are squeezed into short-term thinking as they confront an open-ended future. Call this the false promise of maturity.

The problem is less acute for the top 25 percent who are graduating from four-year colleges.[38] Thanks to subsidized loan programs, this elite can borrow against future earnings to make sensible choices for the long run. But even they face crushing debt repayments that force them into short-termism. And the problem for the typical American is far worse. Banks don't give large loans to twenty-one-year-olds for a reason—without track records, it is impossible to distinguish good risks from bad. As a consequence, any serious long-run investment—from starting a new family to establishing a new business or gaining more education—wars with the financial imperatives of daily life. Given the current life-cycle imbalance in resources, it is remarkable how much future-oriented behavior goes on, especially among the upper classes. But innumerable studies recount the enormous amount of alienation among ordinary working Americans as they confront life with no prospects for serious self-improvement.[39]

The problem will only get worse during the next century, and for two reasons. The first is longevity. When parents regularly live to age eighty or ninety, the next generation will receive inheritances when they are no longer young adults.[40] Such bequests are not opportunities to start a business or raise a family. They will come when they are least significant for life-shaping decisions—at fifty or sixty years of age. Loving parents recognize this and may sometimes give young adult children substantial gifts, particularly for education.[41] But this tendency is checked by a great deal of uncertainty about a parent's own longevity and an understandable reluctance to play the part of King Lear.[42] A second factor is the decline of the family farm or business. Fewer family businesses means that fewer parents can informally transfer resources to their adult children as they "prove themselves."

In response to these trends, the propertied classes are investing much more heavily in their children's schooling. Rather than transferring money, they are counting on high-priced educations to secure their offspring a solid place in the information society.[43] This investment in human capital will be sociologically central, but it should not divert attention from the increasingly dysfunctional character of old-fashioned inheritance. Although inheritances of substantial property occur only at the top of the socioeconomic pyramid,[44] such bequests will increasingly be divorced from one of their classic functions—to provide young adults with an initial stake. And of course property inheritance never did discharge this function for the great majority of young adults.

From this angle, stakeholding is a more democratic and more effective substitute for a declining institution: providing a social inheritance to the rising generation just when it needs it most.

## The Immaturity Objection

But aren't young adults too immature to handle such large sums of money? Won't they waste it on foolish extravagances or fall victim to con artists?

Let's break this predictable objection down into bite-sized pieces. There is an obvious short-term problem. At present, most teenagers are not educated to undertake serious economic responsibilities. In countless ways, society sends them the message that the grown-up world of investment and entrepreneurship is not for them. But this sharp dichotomy between teenage years and adulthood is not one of the eternal verities. Coping with sexuality and the moral ambiguities of modern life will predictably remain principal preoccupations of teenagers. Yet there is nothing to stop us from building more bridges between teenage culture and the economic world that awaits.

The advent of stakeholding will have a revolutionary impact on education in this country. For the first time, high school students will have an intense and practical interest in fundamentals of economic planning. Classes named "How to Manage Your Stake" will be as eagerly attended as those in driver's education—a universal rite of passage into the real world. While the normal motivational problems of high school instruction will not disappear, even the bored student will see a compelling need to pay attention. If anything, the practical importance of money management will motivate interest in basic skills like math and reading, not to mention economics. More broadly, stakeholding will serve as a reference point for countless conversations from early childhood, as parents and others impress their charges with the importance of economic maturity when the time comes to enter the marketplace as an adult.

At least in part, what we're calling the immaturity objection may be a classic case of self-fulfilling prophecy. Because most teenagers don't expect to have stakes in the near future, they have little reason to prepare themselves for serious long-term planning. By taking young adults seriously, the stakeholding society will encourage teenagers to take themselves seriously.

This cultural dynamic will not occur overnight. During the first generation of stakeholding, we will have to rely heavily on more institutional solutions. Most important, we should require each stakeholder to graduate from high school before gaining full control over his eighty thousand dollars. Dropouts would receive an annual market return of four thousand dollars or so on their stakes.[45] But they could not invade the principal except for a limited set of purposes—buying a house, going back to school, or paying extraordinary medical expenses. These limitations would dissolve whenever they obtained the equivalent of a high school diploma.[*]

We would also structure the stakeholding transaction to encourage responsibility. Because most Americans graduate from high school at age eighteen or so, there will typically be a three-year gap before stakeholding payments begin at the age of twenty-one. We should use this period to its maximum educational advantage. Within ninety days of graduation, each American should be required to claim his or her stake by submitting a diploma and other necessary documents to the stakeholding office, which will respond by sending the young man or woman a quarterly statement of account.[46] The first statement will explain that an appropriate sum has been invested in Treasury bonds in the stake-

---

[*] There are some obvious corruption possibilities here. Private academies might spring up to offer watered-down curricula leading to easily earned diplomas sufficient for stakeholding. Public schools might also abet easy graduation in order to take some pressure off state welfare rolls. There is also a danger of aggressive students intimidating individual teachers into giving them passing grades.

If these abuses proved serious, the federal government might be obliged to institute a national examination for high school graduates before they could qualify for their stakes or to require the states to come up with satisfactory exams of their own. Because we favor such an exam on independent grounds, we think that this would be another happy consequence of our proposal.

holder's name. While the recipient will initially be unable to gain access to "his" money, he will see it grow, quarter by quarter, at market interest. At the same time, he will doubtless be inundated with advice—good, bad, and indifferent—on the best way to handle the funds once he can get his hands on them. For all the noise, one message will emerge over the din: "This is a key decision in your life. Don't blow it."[47]

We would encourage this investment perspective further by giving a distinctive structure to the transaction as the stakeholder approaches her moment of truth. Rather than allowing her to cash out her Treasury bonds all at once, she will be allowed to gain control over her investment portfolio only in twenty-thousand-dollar increments over a four-year period. When the first quarterly statement arrives after her twenty-first birthday, the stakeholder will be given a range of options for her first twenty thousand dollars, ranging from rolling over her Treasury notes to diversifying into mutual funds to buying individual stocks to taking the money in cash. After mulling over her choices for three more months, she will exercise her first option, and she will go through the same exercise in each of the next three years.[48]

This will make stakeholding an ongoing source of conversation and comparison: "Look at the way Joe Blow is wasting his money! Doesn't the fool recognize . . ." "No, I think you're wrong. Joe knows what he's doing . . ." The extended payout will also allow each stakeholder to learn from her own mistakes and invest subsequent installments more wisely.

### The Misuse Objection

No set of precautions will magically prevent some Americans from blowing their stakes. But they will help raise a fundamental question of principle in the public mind. Young adults are now put in the moral double bind that we have called the false promise of maturity: they are held fully responsible for their long-range choices without the material base needed for responsible long-term planning. With stakeholding clearly structured to remedy this problem, millions of young adults will prove by their actions that they are indeed capable of redeeming the promise of maturity. Given this practical demonstration of individual responsibility, will it seem right to repeal the program merely because some young adults are misusing their freedom?

Admittedly, the misuse will come in a variety of shapes and sizes. Some will be duped by out-and-out fraud. This is regrettable, but it happens to people of all ages. The best response is a serious public commitment to fighting fraud generally, not the punitive removal of stakes from the entire population.

Another sort of misuse has its origins in class anxieties. Would the working class, not to mention the very poor, be particularly susceptible to short-run temptations? We doubt it. After all, they have been forced to learn the value of every dollar. In contrast, the children of the upper middle class have lived a charmed life as teenagers, and some will fail to appreciate the seriousness of stakeholding. While they will undoubtedly receive better financial advice than their lower-class peers do, they may be less hardheaded and more prone to underestimate their downside risks.

Of course, some poor Americans do face multiple social problems—inadequate education, drug or alcohol abuse, a propensity to violence—that leave them ill equipped for handling the financial responsibility of their stake. But, despite pervasive media images, the size of the so-called underclass is actually quite tiny. Although measurement and definition are inevitably imprecise, this group amounts to less than 4 percent of the population, even at its upper bound.[49] And most of these people would be excluded from full control of their stake by the requirement of high-school graduation.

If anything, our program is likely to be too restrictive rather than too inclusive. In recent years, the high school graduation rate has hovered around 75 percent, with an additional 10 percent obtaining high school equivalency diplomas in their twenties.[50] If these numbers remained constant, 15 percent of the population would fail to gain full control of their stakes. But we expect that, as a side benefit of stakeholding, the high school graduation rate will rise, as capable youths who now drop out finally discover a good reason to stay in school.

Yet another misuse lies in the eyes of the beholders. Stakeholding decisions will undoubtedly reflect the plurality of American values. Some citizens will disdain and condemn the choices of others, who will respond in kind. But as liberals, we deny that this familiar kind of mutual recrimination should serve as the basis for sound social policy. Our liberal instincts are further engaged when we contemplate the kinds of social judgments that would be required to define "wasteful spending." If a woman uses her stake to stay at home with her small children for five years, is she a slacker? If a young man opens up a beachside concession renting umbrellas and lounge chairs, is he a beach bum? The possibilities for moral condescension are endless—as are the possibilities of evasion of any legalistic definitions.

But the rejection of paternalism still leaves us with a serious problem. Some individuals will undoubtedly use their stake in ways that, decades later, they will deeply regret. We concede this but emphasize that the flip side of the problem exists today. Too many forty-year-olds look back to their twenties with bitter regret at the chances that they never had but that were readily available to others higher up on the economic scale.

We propose to shift the balance of regret—it is impossible to abolish it. Or perhaps it is best to distinguish two kinds of regret. One is remorse at one's failure to make the most of the chances that one did have. The other and deeper regret is never having had a fair chance to engage life as a responsible adult. In a liberal society, everyone should have at least one chance to seize the brass ring of opportunity.

## The Coercion Objection
But perhaps there is a deeper objection here, and we can sum it up in a single word: coercion. Haven't we merely created a smokescreen of

supposedly free choices that hides the social and economic coercion that will overwhelm stakeholders as they consider their options? Consider a twenty-four-old woman whose lover spends her stake on his own endeavors, all the while assuring her, "Don't worry, honey, I'll take care of you for the rest of your life." Or the impoverished stakeholder who has little choice but to use his stake to weather a period of unemployment or to supplement his meager earnings. In what sense do these stakeholders have any really meaningful choices?

If this critique suggests that the only freedom worth having is unlimited freedom, it is impossible to satisfy. There is no such thing as a coercion-free society. Whatever decisions we make, we must confront the facts of scarcity and mortality, recognizing that our options are dramatically limited by our circumstances. For all of us, the only possible freedom is the freedom to choose among a restricted set of options.

Once this is recognized, the claim of coercion seems inflated. Stakeholding vastly increases the choices available to the young and distributes them more fairly. To be sure, it only takes one large step toward equal opportunity. Some young adults will have markedly superior educational and other social advantages that will help protect them from a variety of overreachings. But the answer to this is to take further steps to realize justice, not to restrict the freedom of the poor and otherwise disadvantaged.

Perhaps the coercion critique is implicitly grounded in a more pessimistic view. Poor people have been so oppressed during early life that they simply cannot function as free men and women capable of shaping the larger contours of their lives. They live for the moment and lack the cultural resources needed to adopt a long-run view and take responsibility for their decisions.

We reject this view.[51] It is based in part on self-fulfilling prophecy: at present poor people *correctly* understand that they lack much control over their futures and so, unsurprisingly, may opt for more short-term satisfactions within their effective control.[52] But because stakeholding expands the range of long-term opportunity, the disadvantaged will have greater reason to take the longer run seriously.

What is more, everyone encounters difficulties in shaping a life plan, and it is arbitrary to suppose that only poor folk are unequal to the task.[53] Freedom is always a gamble. Nor is it always clear who is acting foolishly and who wisely.

When all is said and done, we value individual freedom for its own sake. And so, we think, do most other Americans.

## Liberal Community

A later chapter makes these themes more concrete by showing the big difference that stakeholding might make in the lives of ordinary Americans. But for now, we shift our focus from the individual to the larger community and consider what our initiative might mean for America's sense of itself as a nation.

We intend to question a sharp dichotomy that threatens to become one of the banalities of the age. Too often we are told that Americans must choose between a stronger sense of community and a stronger commitment to individual freedom.[54] In this familiar view, our recent infatuation with individual rights has eroded our sense of association with the larger group. To restore equilibrium, we must radically change our political conversation and reaffirm the collective values that bind us together in concrete communities.

We disagree. Given the diversity of life and creed in today's America, a communitarian politics of virtue will be divisive at best, oppressive at worst. It is simply silly to suppose that elected politicians, of all people, could lead a sensitive moral dialogue that would invite the religious and the secular, the gay and the straight, the city slicker and his country cousin, to a profound and tolerant understanding of each others' way of life. Far more likely is the intensification of culture wars and sporadic efforts to legislate morality and repress deviance. Rather than bringing us together as Americans, the politics of virtue will drive us farther apart.

Stakeholding takes a very different path toward community. It seeks to foster individual freedom, not smother it. By making freedom's promise universal and concrete, stakeholding appeals to all Americans, regardless of their different aspirations, to join together. As members of the rising generation come forward to stake their claims, they will be doing more than affirming their individual right to shape their own particular destinies. They will also be affirming their identity as citizens of a great country devoted to freedom and equality. Throughout the rest of their lives, these Americans will endlessly consider how their stakes contributed to their individual pursuits of happiness—and at the same time reflect on their good fortune in enjoying the precious rights of American citizenship.

Except for the most hardened cynics, this will lead to a deep and sustaining loyalty to the country that made stakeholding a concrete reality. Rather than dismissing the Declaration of Independence as boastful words on paper, stakeholders will hear in Thomas Jefferson's proud phrases a description of their own lives and will seek, as best they can, to repay their own debt by passing on their great heritage to the future.

This is the kind of loyalty that befits the free men and women of America. It will yield a voluntary sense of obligation, not one that is coerced by politicians in the name of virtue. As more and more citizens enjoy the fruits of stakeholding, the country will be better and better prepared for the next crisis.

And make no mistake about it. Our present prosperity and military hegemony will not last forever. There will come a time when America will once again call upon its children to sacrifice greatly in support of its ideals.

How will they respond?

# 3

# The Stake in Context

It is time to bring stakeholding down to earth—to consider the tough choices required to transform our idea into an operational reality. For starters, there are key questions of eligibility. Who precisely should be allowed to stake a claim? Resident aliens? All citizens? Criminals?

Having drawn the circle around eligible stakeholders, we consider crucial matters of program design. Instead of forcing everybody to wait until age twenty-one, we think that high school graduates should be allowed to spend their stakes immediately on their college educations. This single step will in turn revolutionize the existing system of higher education in this country—and for the better, we think. Then there is the matter of setting the size of the stake: why eighty thousand dollars and not half or twice that amount? We finally turn to the problem of transition to the new regime: how gradually should we phase in the program?

It would be foolish to explore every nook and cranny of programmatic detail. But a head-on confrontation with key issues will give real-world substance to stakeholding, allowing a better appreciation of its strengths and weaknesses. Reasonable people will disagree with our answers to particular questions. This is all to the good, as long as these disputes do not defeat the entire project. There is a danger of this happening, but the only remedy is a sense of perspective—remembering to keep our eyes on the whole as we argue about each particular part.

After some substance has been put on our proposal, the next chapter provides a more concrete sense of the ways in which stakeholding will alter the real-life choices confronting a variety of young Americans. Eighty thousand dollars will mean different things to different people—that is its beauty. In providing a kaleidoscopic view of its potential significance, we hope to gain your empathetic understanding of our ultimate goal—which is to revitalize the liberal ideal of an independent, responsible, property-owning citizenry.

## Immigrant Stakeholders?

Imagine a twenty-one-year-old English tourist arriving at Kennedy Airport, hailing a taxi for New York City, and making his way directly to the closest stakeholding office—only to leave empty-handed. While nobody will have trouble denying the tourist a stake, it is easy to think of harder cases. How strong a connection to America should be required?

Begin with longtime resident aliens. As long as they decline to take the oath of citizenship, we should exclude them from stakeholding. We see no reason to extend them rights of economic citizenship if they do not voluntarily assume obligations of political loyalty.[1]

A harder question is whether all American citizens should qualify. There are two problem cases. The first involves people who make their claim based on the accidents of birth. Suppose that a French graduate student gives birth to a baby boy while studying at Yale in New Haven and shortly afterward returns with her child to Paris, where they live for the next twenty years. A day before the boy turns twenty-one, he takes the plane from Paris to New York to make his claim at the stakeholding office. Under the Fourteenth Amendment, he qualifies as a citizen by birthright. Should he be entitled to take his eighty thousand dollars and return immediately to Paris?[2]

A second case involves citizens by naturalization. Our hypothetical immigrant arrives in this country as a teenager and takes his oath of citizenship the day before he turns twenty-one. He immediately proceeds to the stakeholding office to make his claim. Should it be accepted?

It is tempting to err on the side of generosity, but we urge restraint. Let's start with the naturalization case. In 1996, of the more than 1 million immigrants who took the oath of citizenship, 10 percent were under the age of twenty-five.[3] If extending a stake to all of them would lead a majority of American voters to support a more restrictive immigration policy, we confront a hard choice: is it better to admit a smaller number of immigrants and grant them eighty thousand dollars apiece, or admit a larger number and deny them stakes?

Like it or not, political realities force us to take this tradeoff seriously. We believe that it is much more important to keep the door open than to provide stakes to the few who might manage to squeeze in. American citizenship is a priceless boon for millions living in oppressive or impoverished circumstances around the world, and it is imperative that as many as possible find a place of hope in this country. As a consequence, we would not allow a twenty-one-year-old to naturalize and claim a stake on the same day. We would restrict this right to those with deeper roots in this country.

Our line would track an important psychological distinction. When teenagers arrive in America, they come with vivid memories of life in the old country. While they will naturally resent their failure to qualify for a stake, they will be in a psychological position to reflect on the many other advantages that they have acquired from citizenship, contrasting their old lives in Russia or India or Mexico with the great possibilities opened up by their new situation. In contrast, when immigrants arrive as small children, America is the only land that they really know, and they will be unable to console themselves by making similar comparisons. For them, exclusion from stakeholding will seem an utterly invidious act of discrimination by the only country that they can call their own.

This seems an important difference, and one that should count in a world where America's commitment to the open door cannot be taken for granted. As an interim measure, a citizen should be required to live for at least eleven of his twenty-one years in this country before qualifying for his eighty thousand dollars.[4] Once stakeholding is firmly in place, this distinction might one day be overcome. But we fear that too generous an embrace of immigrants at too early a stage would be counterproductive: either the open door would swing closed or the prospect of showering riches on newcomers would be used as a political weapon to destroy the general appeal of stakeholding.

Our restrictive approach also has implications for the treatment of birthright citizens. Surely the young immigrant taking the citizenship oath is a much more attractive candidate for stakeholding than the guy with a round-trip ticket to Paris. Probably the Parisian himself would agree that he is cynically manipulating a legal loophole—although this may not stop him from taking the money and bragging about it. This is the sort of abuse that can easily discredit the entire program.

It is also much more likely that birthright citizens with few links to this country will spend their stakes beyond America's borders. This factor is particularly important in a liberty-affirming initiative like stakeholding. One crucial feature of the stake is that it comes with no strings attached: once a stakeholder gets the eighty thousand dollars, he can do anything he wants with the money—including taking off for some remote corner of the world far away from the sight of the American flag. Within this structure, the only feasible way to save the Treasury from the most cynical abuses is by imposing a residency requirement on birthright citizens: it is one thing for somebody with deep roots in the country to decide to take his stake and head off for parts unknown, quite another for somebody with deep roots elsewhere to take his eighty thousand and spend a small part of it on a one-way ticket back home.

We have, then, come to the same place via two different paths. For naturalizing citizens, a residency requirement makes sense as part of a realistic effort to keep the doors open for future generations of immigrants. For birthright citizens, it makes sense to prevent cynical raids on the Treasury. It would be invidious—and probably unconstitutional—to impose different residency requirements for different classes of citizens.[5] If an eleven-year residency is demanded of naturalized Americans, it should apply to the rest of us as well.[6]

## The Stake as a Deterrent: Carrots and the Criminal Law

Traditionally, criminal law has treated young wrongdoers as if incarceration were the only alternative to less oppressive forms of control. But stakeholding provides another tool, with distinctive advantages and dangers.

First, the advantages. Once stakeholding begins, youngsters will suddenly have something to lose other than their freedom. The criminal law of a stakeholding society can threaten them with the loss of some or all of their eighty thousand dollars. To be sure, this threat will influence the actions of only those youngsters who can look ahead. And the younger they are, the less responsive they'll be to the threat. Even with foresight, younger criminals might impose a heavy discount rate on the relatively distant prospect of losing funds at the ripe old age of twenty-one. Thus it would be silly to "punish" a twelve-year-old by declaring his stake forfeit. But this sanction would carry greater force for an eighteen-year-old.

It would also have a more general educative effect. Impoverished communities would be full of stories about good guys who stayed honest and were now claiming their eighty thousand, while others tossed away their stakes by dealing drugs.

But there are dangers in an overly enthusiastic embrace. It would be all too easy for politicians to brandish their new tool as a blunderbuss. Rather than using the withholding of stakes as a substitute for incarceration, demagogues might simply add forfeiture as an automatic consequence of every conviction. Worse yet, they might expand the list of felonies in order to deprive minors of their eighty thousand when they would not think of imposing a comparable fine on older wrongdoers. The dangers of abuse are magnified by the notorious racial disparities in the administration of the criminal law. It would be tragic to allow stakeholding to become another monument to racial injustice.

Nonetheless, both stakeholding and the criminal law share a common foundation in liberal notions of individual responsibility. As a stakeholder, you are responsible for shaping your life plan, and if it involves criminality, you are justly held to account. There is nothing categorically wrong in using the stake to support the principles of responsibility at the core of the criminal law.

At the same time, we should not allow the criminal law to cheapen the meaning of stakeholding. It would be all too easy to treat the stake as if it weren't "really" the property of the young wrongdoer and to take away thirty or forty thousand dollars for a trivial offense, explaining that a stake is a privilege, not a right. But the entire point of stakeholding is to move beyond the rhetoric of the welfare state.

A great deal of thought will be required for a sensible integration of stakeholding into the criminal law. Here are a few guidelines. First, stakeholding sanctions should be reserved for serious offenses and those where an economic deterrent seems particularly appropriate—trafficking in drugs, for example. Second, these penalties should generally serve as an alternative to prison. The aim should be a more humane, cheaper, and more effective system of deterrence: why throw a twenty-year-old into jail when you can hurt him just as much by depriving him of his first stakeholding payment of twenty thousand dollars? Third, stakeholding sanctions should come in graduated doses. Except in the most heinous cases, nobody should lose all of his stake for a single offense. Once a convict has lost all hope of getting any of his eighty thousand, the deterrent value of stakeholding has been exhausted. Finally, and in the same spirit, stakeholding should be used for rehabilitation. Generally speaking, youthful offenders should be given a second chance to reclaim their stakes by keeping clear of crime for a substantial period. Although they may have forfeited some or all of their eighty thousand as teenagers, they should be able to reestablish themselves as stakeworthy citizens through years of law-abiding conduct.

## The Stake and Higher Education

Having defined the outer bounds of eligibility, we turn to consider more carefully the conditions under which stakeholders should gain access to their money. Up to now, we have been speaking as if the normal American will be claiming his stake in twenty-thousand-dollar payments between the ages of twenty-one and twenty-four. But any sensible proposal should carve out a large exception to enable Americans to use their stakes to finance their higher educations. Nowadays, about 60 percent of high school graduates go on to more formal training.[7] Almost 10 percent earn two-year associate's degrees and about 25 percent finally graduate from a four-year college.[8]

We believe that stakeholding can yield a vast improvement in the status quo—when judged both in terms of justice and the likely quality of the educational experience. But this can happen only if we design the program appropriately: rather than insisting that stakeholders wait until the age of twenty-one for their first twenty thousand dollars, we should allow them to draw down their accounts before then to pay for higher education. More precisely, college-bound stakeholders should be able to withdraw up to twenty thousand per year for four years, as soon as they graduate from high school. In contrast, other Americans will not be able to pledge their stakes to pay for purchases made before they reach twenty-one.[9]

Consider some basic facts. Students, parents, and federal and state governments spend more than $130 billion per year on higher education.[10] States pay 31 percent of the total, largely by funding public colleges.[11] The federal government provides another $13 billion or so, largely in the form of student grants and loans.[12]

These subsidies have indeed helped more and more Americans make it to college.[13] But there remain huge disparities in effective access.[14] Nearly 40 percent of low-income high school graduates do not move on to postsecondary education, but only 21 percent of their middle-income peers stop at this stage; the number dwindles to 7 percent among high-income families.[15] Even when low-income students do make it to college, they are much more likely to delay enrollment and much less likely to earn a degree in the end as compared to their richer peers.[16] Poorer students also are more likely to attend two-year, rather than four-year, institutions.[17] These numbers become especially poignant when one recognizes that poor children, once they have graduated from a four-year college, earn, on average, as much as those from wealthier backgrounds.[18]

Stakeholding cannot directly compensate for differentials in early education and childhood experiences. But it can guarantee access for all college-ready students regardless of their parents' income and wealth. Federal grants to lower-class students have not kept pace with tuition inflation, and much aid now takes the form of loans rather than grants. As a result, the financial burden on students and their parents has grown, not shrunk, over the past fifteen years.[19]

Lower-class students confront hardships unknown to their better-off peers. College kids from the upper middle class take generous parental support for granted, but those from below are constantly required to juggle schoolwork and jobs in ways that can easily overwhelm self-confidence. Indeed, the endless rounds of scholarship applications and intermittent failures to pay tuition take a toll by themselves. Statistics confirm that students in two-year colleges are even more hard-pressed: a much higher percentage live at home, hold a job, and work more hours.[20]

For this large group, stakeholding would work a genuine revolution. It would allow college-bound students to focus their energies on academic work and compete with their peers on more equal terms. By enabling these students to gain early access to their stakes, the program would also signal the importance of advanced schooling in the emerging information society.

No less important, it would inaugurate a new era of healthy competition in higher education. Every student would enter the market with significant resources and an incentive to shop carefully. No longer would state universities or community colleges have a captive pool of in-state or low-income students who are without other options. These people could now choose a school in another community or across the country or even overseas. In contrast, the bulk of government money now goes to institutions rather than to students, which is exactly backward. The current system limits individual choice, but stakeholding will promote it.

Of course, the transition to a new system could not happen overnight, and there are many important details to work out. But as competition takes hold, the price of a college education will change as two effects begin to operate. Prospective students will have much more money than before, encouraging all colleges to raise tuition or cut financial aid. But this tendency will be checked by an opposing dynamic: colleges will be competing for the stakeholding dollar much more intensively, both with one another and with other kinds of enterprises. This last point is particularly important. In contrast to traditional education programs, stakeholders can spend their money elsewhere if the price of college rises too much.[21]

We cannot predict how the market will shake out—how many old institutions will survive, how many new ones will be created, or what the competitive tuition for different types of schools will be. But one variable will be crucial: the extent to which American governments respond to stakeholding by restructuring more traditional forms of subsidy.

Looking backward, Americans can justly take pride in the creation of a vast system of public universities and the complex network of federal programs that have provided grants and loans to tens of millions over the years. These initiatives have opened the door of opportunity for millions of middle- and lower-income students.

But stakeholding dramatically changes this traditional equation. With college-bound students already guaranteed eighty thousand dollars, even the most hallowed programs will undergo a period of agonizing reappraisal. This is all to the good, for there is every reason to believe that the outcome will be leaner, but more sharply focused, educational initiatives.

Begin with the $40 billion a year currently spent by the states on public colleges.[22] A lot of this money could be replaced by stakeholding funds, but there are still some reasons for states to continue direct institutional support. Most obviously, students may balk at funding academic research that does not directly pay off in classroom instruction. Yet this research can yield large dividends to the region, the nation, and the world. Students may also respond to an overly narrow understanding of the job market and fail to appreciate the importance of areas of instruction—most notably, the liberal arts—that deserve sustained public support.

Apart from these special areas of enduring need, the appropriate level of general support for public universities will remain an open and politically contested question. In 1996–1997, four-year public colleges charged an average tuition of only $6,534—too big a bargain when prospective students come to the table with eighty thousand dollars.[23] But this hardly implies that public universities should inflate their tuition levels to the $18,071 now charged by the average private college.[24] Citizens can reasonably disagree about appropriate tuition levels in the new world of stakeholding, and different states will answer this question differently. This is what federalism is for.

National policy should take its cue from the emerging pattern of subsidy decisions in the states and heightened competition in the marketplace: in spite of the great increase in funds made available through stakeholding, have any legitimate interests been left out in the cold? We can think of a few serious candidates for continued aid, although their claims will certainly add up to a lot less than the $13 billion currently charged to the federal budget. Most obviously, recently naturalized citizens could make a compelling case for a special scholarship program, because they would face much higher tuition levels without receiving stakes. So too would older students, who had already passed the age of eligibility before stakeholding was enacted into law. We would also support a program for specially gifted students going on to graduate school, who might have already exhausted their eighty thousand dollars on college and its related expenses. And surely private scholarship programs will be required to keep admission to elite colleges open to all.

But the overall tendency of educational policy should be clear: more freedom for young adults to choose their colleges and complete their educations without constant and debilitating financial hassles; more competitive pressure on colleges to provide quality teaching and a supportive environment for learning; more narrowly focused government and private support for programs and students whose interests are not adequately served by the emerging system.

## Leveling Up

Stakeholding will mean a lot to graduates of four-year colleges. But it will mean more to the much larger group who don't want to go that far in their educations. At present, the nation's two-year community colleges provide much smaller subsidies to their students than do more traditional universities.[25] But under the new system, students at two-year colleges will have the same buying power as their more academically inclined contemporaries. To be sure, these stakeholders will be utterly unwilling to spend their entire eighty thousand on a couple of years of post–high school education. But their stakes will create new incentives for serious programs directed at their distinctive concerns. Over time, two-year colleges will emerge from the shadow of their bigger brothers and build their students' skills and self-confidence with increasing imagination and vigor.

We have left the best for last. Consider the millions who decide that college—even a two-year college—isn't for them. These are today's forgotten Americans. Many of them have already been denied the decent high school education that should be every citizen's birthright. Now they are tossed gently into the marketplace unaided, while their upwardly mobile peers are given federal scholarships and state-subsidized tuitions.

This is wrong. Joe Six-Pack is every bit as much of an American as Joe College. And for the first time, his claim to equal citizenship will be treated with genuine respect. Because these high school graduates are not going to college, they will have to wait until their twenties to gain access to their stakes. But we do not think that this delay will prove very controversial. Most high school graduates would themselves concede that they need some seasoning in the school of hard knocks before they can be trusted with eighty thousand dollars.

Some of our readers may want to require young adults to wait until age twenty-five or so before they get any of their money. We would be happy to compromise as long as our basic principle remains intact: the decision to go to college should not be required for an American to gain his country's support for the pursuit of happiness. All Americans have a fundamental right to a fair share of the nation's resources as they accept the full responsibilities of adult life.

This principle suggests one more refinement in the stakeholding program. To ensure that the noncollege group does not lose out financially because of the three-year delay, their stakes should earn interest in the meantime. Instead of four payments of twenty thousand dollars beginning at eighteen, they should get four payments of $21,225, beginning at age twenty-one. The difference is three years' interest on each delayed payment.[26]

This is also the point to anticipate an obvious danger. While high school graduates must wait until their twenties to claim their stakes officially, won't aggressive merchants figure out ways to get them to sign away their rights before they reach twenty-one? "Get your Mercedes 'for free'! Just sign this contract containing mumbo-jumbo and we will seize your money at the stakeholding office."

It is tough to imagine an easier way of casting doubt on the program. But it would be too draconian to respond by making it legally impossible for underage stakeholders to obtain any credit at all. Many teenagers are workers, parents, entrepreneurs with assets and income that currently allow them to borrow a good deal of money. They should continue to be eligible for as much credit as they would have gotten in the absence of stakeholding.

To implement this principle, the stakeholding statute should segregate stakeholding dollars in a special account. Creditors could not ordinarily reach these assets to satisfy debts incurred by stakeholders before they came of age.[27] But after that age, stakeholders would be free to write checks from their account for purchases as well as investments. This would allow underage stakeholders to continue borrowing against other earnings and assets but would notify creditors that they could not count on the stake for repayment.[28]

## Why Eighty Thousand Dollars?

We have thus far been speaking of the false promise of maturity that confronts the typical young adult in modern society: on the one hand, she is held responsible for life-shaping decisions, but on the other, she lacks the economic resources to make them in a responsible way. In setting the size of the stake, we should keep this basic moral dilemma in mind. The stake should be big enough to provide each citizen with a cushion against market shocks and to enable her to take a long-term perspective as she determines the most sensible ways of investing in herself, her family, her career, and her community. This logic suggests that small sums—say, ten thousand dollars per person—are inadequate, but how high should we go?

The comparison between Joe College and Joe Six-Pack helps us set the standard. As we have seen, eighty thousand dollars is enough to pay for four years of tuition at the average private college in the United States.[29] While colleges may raise tuition a bit in response to stakeholding, market forces will tend to keep these increases in check.[30] This means that typical college-bound youngsters will be in a position to graduate debt-free (more or less) if they get good summer jobs or can rely on some parental support.[31] Liberated from the crushing burden of debt, they will confront the future with a precious independence.

Four years at college will not magically eliminate the need for hard choices about career, family, and the meaning of life. Nonetheless, the skills and self-understandings that these students will gain will place them in a fair position to take responsibility for these choices. At the very least, they will not be locked into dead-end jobs or locked out of the vast range of cultural opportunities open to them as citizens of the twenty-first century. In a rough-and-ready way, a college education serves to redeem the promise of maturity in contemporary society.

But if this is so, eighty thousand dollars should also set the standard for the three out of four Americans who don't earn bachelor's degrees.

As equal citizens, they too are entitled to confront their adult years with their heads held high while preparing themselves for the future as they see fit. We will shortly be considering the concrete ways that stakeholding will allow ordinary Americans to gain control over their lives. But for now, the moral challenge is plain: if eighty thousand dollars suffices to provide the top quarter of the population with effective economic independence, shouldn't all other Americans obtain equivalent resources?

Perhaps not, detractors may say. Perhaps the costs of financing such a generous stake would cripple the economy. Or perhaps it will force us to starve other social programs that promise a more effective assault on unequal opportunity. We believe that these predictable responses lack substance, and we will soon be describing a funding system that is well within our economic means as a society.

But for now, we will take up a single concern that does not require lengthy economic analysis and that has cropped up with surprising frequency when we have presented our ideas before audiences: won't the prospect of an eighty-thousand-dollar grant lead to a vast increase in the birthrate, which will break the bank in the long run?

We strongly doubt it. Certainly the promise of eighty thousand dollars at maturity ensures every child a good start in life—and this prospect may encourage some parents, previously worried about the financial burdens of raising their families, to consider going ahead and having another child. But this positive point has to be placed in a larger context. Most obviously, child-rearing will remain very expensive, in both money and time. Even a moderate-income family will spend $200,000 or more to raise that extra child—not to mention all the extra years of diaper-changing.[32] Parents must weigh these immediate costs against the discounted value of eighty thousand dollars twenty-one years hence.[33] Then there is the fact that when the child finally reaches maturity, the stake goes to her directly, not to the parent—and the child may not spend the money as the parent would like.

This independence effect is an integral part of the case for stakeholding, and many farseeing and altruistic parents will see its value. But it will also prevent greedy parents from casually treating their children's stake as if it were their own.

Finally, there is suggestive evidence from Western Europe, which has responded to declining birthrates by adopting aggressively pro-natalist policies. In contrast to our proposal, Western European governments do not require parents to wait a generation before seeing their children get some money. Instead, the European system of family allowances pays large sums directly to young parents with large families. Nonetheless, these policies have failed to raise the birthrate.[34]

We agree that our initiative might well change the moral climate over time in ways that may subtly encourage higher birthrates. Parents will know that, even if the worst befalls them, their children *will* have a shot at the American dream. And this new confidence might well encourage them to take the plunge into the unknown that comes with starting a family. But it would be a mistake to overestimate the importance of this point when so many other cultural and economic factors are at work.

## Women and Minorities

By itself, stakeholding will not automatically lead husbands to share child care equally, persuade bosses and coworkers that women can be welders, or dissolve harmful stereotypes about African Americans. Nonetheless, it will make a difference in the short run and contribute to the erosion of pervasive cultural vulnerabilities in the long run.

As a matter of dollars and cents, minority group members will be the big winners from stakeholding. A recent study found that one-third of all households, but 61 percent of black ones, have absolutely no net financial wealth.[35] While middle-class blacks earn about 70 percent of middle-class white wages, they own only 15 percent of white middle-class wealth.[36] As a consequence, blacks will not pay much of the wealth tax that we shall propose to fund our initiative.

The effect on women will be subtler but cumulative. For the foreseeable future, they are likely to continue to bear the primary burden of child care and to confront a labor market poorly adapted to the demands of child rearing.[37] When women respond by opting for part-time work, they are now often consigned to a second-class "mommy track" with limited prospects of advancement.[38] While stakeholding will not bring this system to an end, it will provide women with new tools. Even though eighty thousand dollars is "only money," it will give women more real independence in everyday life, allowing them to negotiate better deals for themselves at the workplace and at home.

But perhaps this rosy scenario masks hidden dangers, critics may object. Women may think that they're better off if, say, they use their stake to take extra maternity leave or cut back their work hours while their children are young. But wouldn't such decisions suggest that they are victims of "false consciousness"?

By retreating from the workforce to tend to their kids, these skeptics would continue, women may be forfeiting long-run earnings potential.[39] In the end, they may wind up even more dependent on a husband or boyfriend for support. If so, the independence that stakeholding promises is a cruel illusion. A better program would devote the same resources to subsidized day care, work-training programs, and other initiatives to help women get into the workforce and stay there for the long term.

We don't buy this argument. We recognize that deep-seated gender-role expectations have irrevocably shaped women's (and men's) ideas about what women should want from life. We certainly support educational efforts to challenge these stereotypes. But we refuse to dismiss the genuinely felt aspirations of today's women as false consciousness. No less than men, they deserve nothing less than the real freedom that stakeholding offers. Traditional gender expectations may limit women's bargaining power, both within and outside the family.[40] But over time, the clear message of equality embodied in the universal eighty-thousand-dollar grant may also begin to affect men's perceptions of women and women's perceptions of themselves.

Despite these very real advantages, we do not suggest that our initiative can serve as the be all and end all of the struggle for real equality of opportunity. It is only one tool among many, and we would be happy to embrace other programs that targeted vulnerable groups more specifically for special assistance. Nonetheless, we think it would be a serious mistake to bring concerns about affirmative action to the design of our proposal—adding twenty thousand dollars, say, to the stakes of minority members.

Such a step would deflect stakeholding from one of its great aims. Especially at this time of deep cultural division, Americans require some contexts reminding them of the commitments they share. Stakeholding fills this desperate civic need. When each citizen comes forward to make her claim, it ought to be enough for her to say that she too is an American, involved in the common enterprise of redeeming the great words of the Declaration of Independence. This is a time for women and men, blacks and whites, to join in a mutual recognition of their standing as free and equal citizens, without distracting references to the differences and injustices that still tear them apart.

## The First Stakeholders

And then there is the matter of transition. How to get from here to there?

We favor a gradualist approach that targets a particular cohort of eighteen-year-olds to serve as America's first stakeholders. On his or her eighteenth birthday and once a year thereafter, every stakeholder would be sent a statement of account showing eighty thousand dollars to be paid over four years, provided that the stakeholder graduates from high school and stays out of trouble. The college-bound could draw on their stakes immediately to pay tuition and living expenses, but the others would have to wait for three years before receiving their first payment.

This delayed phase-in would help respond to an obvious transition problem of the first magnitude. At present, most teenagers have little reason to prepare themselves for the responsibilities of managing eighty thousand dollars. This will change over time as parents, teachers, and friends spend endless hours telling them of the perils of blowing their stakes. We believe that, after hearing years of such talk, most young Americans will surprise the skeptics and make responsible use of their new-found freedom. But there is a very real danger that the first stakeholders will treat their money as a gift from out of the blue and discredit the program by wasting it on a splurge or frittering it away through mindless consumption. A three-year delay will give the first stakeholders a chance to internalize their new prospects and to weigh their new opportunities carefully. At the same time, the three-year lag will give the IRS a chance to phase in and fine-tune the tax measures needed to fund the stake.

There is something to be said for an even more gradual approach. Rather than targeting a single group of eighteen-year-olds, it might be wiser to begin by providing "fractional stakes" to a broader cohort of teenagers ranging between, say, fourteen and seventeen. Under this approach, kids of fourteen would eventually claim eighty thousand dollars, whereas fifteen-year-olds would get sixty thousand dollars, and so on, leaving eighteen-year-olds empty-handed. This fractionalist phase-in avoids the arbitrariness in granting a full eighty thousand to the first crop of stakeholders while their slightly older brothers and sisters get nothing.

Another way to respond to the problem would be through the creation of a large "transitional fund" for the needs of those born a little too early. This special fund should award training grants and scholarships that compare favorably to those available under the preceding regime. That way, those who just missed out on stakeholding might console themselves with the thought that they had nevertheless done better than had their immediate predecessors.[41]

Undoubtedly, many other transitional problems will arise. But there is no reason to think that they will prove unmanageable or so costly as to overwhelm the long-run benefits of life in a stakeholder society.

# 4

# Profiles in Freedom

We have been telling our story with statistics, but there is another way of putting stakeholding in context. We invite you to imagine what eighty thousand dollars might mean in the real lives of real people you know. Then try to move beyond your own friends and neighbors to imagine other lives at greater distance. To help in this, we offer a few American profiles of our own devising. Bill and Brenda represent millions of hard-pressed young couples in the twentieth through fortieth percentile of Americans.[1] Mike and Mary Ann come from the better-off group in the fiftieth to seventieth percentile. Then we consider people both higher and lower in the economic order. Bill, Brenda, and the others are fictional, but their life situations represent reality for many Americans.

For all of them, stakeholding will have revolutionary implications. At present, the average young family has a net worth of about $11,400, cars included.[2] Fewer than half own a home, usually a heavily mortgaged one.[3] In the bottom half of the income distribution, the typical young household has a net worth of only a couple of thousand dollars—or less.[4] Although an overwhelming percentage of these families call themselves "middle class," they are at a terribly vulnerable moment in their lives. A small economic misstep can have large consequences. The anxieties of everyday life generate enormous tensions.

The stake will not work magic. It will not make it easy to confront crucial life decisions about marriage, children, education, and career—nor will it guarantee happiness. But it can transform the character of these crucial decisions. Too many now seem as if they are almost inevitable responses to the forces of economic necessity. In a stakeholding society, they will be hard choices among real alternatives.

Our profiles are constructed in a simple way using today's statistics on education, income distribution, marriage, child-bearing, and so on. Although stakeholding may change these numbers over time, we have not tried to predict such shifts. We simply sketch currently realistic portraits and then ask what difference stakeholding would make.

## Bill and Brenda

Bill and Brenda are a young married couple in their mid-twenties.[5] Like 32 percent of their contemporaries, they graduated from high school but did not go on to college.[6] Their working-class high school wasn't particularly inspiring, and they weren't inclined to see college as the key to their dreams. Instead, they found work similar to that of other young high school graduates.

Bill has had a series of jobs as a construction laborer. When construction slows during the winter, he often works as a clerk in a hardware or auto-parts store.[7] Bill's income varies, since he sometimes spends months unemployed.[8] In a good year, he can make as much as twenty thousand dollars, but in a bad year he earns very little.[9]

Brenda works as a home health aide.[10] She receives assignments through an agency and serves as a companion to mostly elderly clients. She helps them with the tasks of daily living they can no longer handle themselves. A typical assignment might last from a few weeks to six months, and although the work is exhausting and sometimes depressing, she earns eight dollars an hour—better than the five dollars or so that she might make as a grocery cashier or fast-food worker. The work is pretty steady, although there are occasional periods of down time between assignments. She routinely earns fifteen thousand dollars a year.[11]

When they are not working, Bill and Brenda spend their time in church activities, hobbies (Bill is a talented amateur auto mechanic and has a collection of old cars that he is fixing up), and taking care of their son, Peter, who is four.[12] Until now, Bill's mother has been minding Peter while his parents are at work, but Grandma's arthritis is worsening, and she is having a hard time keeping up with an active grandson. Bill and Brenda are worried about how they will afford the tuition at a day care center.

Bill and Brenda save money by living in a rented apartment in a run-down neighborhood. But their family is quickly outgrowing the two-bedroom unit, and they would like to buy a house, although they haven't saved much for a down payment and they fear that their income is too irregular to qualify them for a mortgage.

They are also worried about Peter's education. They can tell that he is enormously bright, and they want him to have the best opportunities. They would like to put Peter in an excellent preschool this year, but the tuition is expensive.[13] Over the longer term, the best local option is parochial school, which also costs something. Or they could move to a better neighborhood with better public schools—but the catch is that most "good" neighborhoods have few apartments.

Although Bill and Brenda try hard to be frugal, money is a constant problem. In lean times, it is sometimes a challenge to meet the rent and to pay for heat, food, and doctor's visits for Peter. (Brenda has health insurance for herself through her agency, but the monthly cost of family coverage is too high.) Even in good times, they clip coupons, drive old cars, and buy clothes at the discount store.[14]

To this point we have said nothing about the stake, in order to sketch Bill's and Brenda's concerns today. But now assume that stakeholding became a reality and that Bill and Brenda each received eighty thousand dollars (plus interest, since neither went to college). How would their choices change?

Let's assume that Bill and Brenda choose a conservative investment strategy for their money, one that yields a 5 percent nominal return each year (much less in real terms, given an inflation rate of 3 percent or so).[15] By their mid-twenties, they have a principal balance of nearly $170,000 and are getting about $8,500 a year in interest from their stakeholding account, which they are spending for furniture, car repairs, and living expenses during hard times.[16] Just this year, they invaded their stake and spent an extra ten thousand dollars to cover costs during one of Bill's longer lay-offs.[17] The decision caused them great anxiety. They know that their remaining $160,000 offers a lifetime opportunity—but what to make of it?

Bill would like to get out of construction and into a more secure and better-paying job. He has tried to get work as an auto mechanic, but employers tell him that he needs some formal training in the latest high-tech methods. So one option is for Bill to enroll in a training course and apprenticeship for a year or two. Another is for Brenda to go back to school. In two years at the community college, she could earn an associate's degree in nursing and qualify for a higher-status job with better pay. Their stakes would allow Bill and Brenda to pay tuition and living expenses while one of them is in school and out of work. And over the long term, a better job for Bill or Brenda would mean extra security for the family.

There are other options. Unemployment is a frequent reality for Bill. Just this year, when the construction industry slumped, the stake was a godsend. Without it, the family would have had to make ends meet solely on Brenda's income and a modest—and distressingly short-term—unemployment check. Having that cushion may also allow

Brenda and Bill to take some time for their family, too. They would very much like to have a second child, and the stake makes it possible for Brenda to take a few months' unpaid maternity leave.

Buying a small house is another possibility. Their stakes would allow them to put a sizable down payment on a modest house, with a remaining mortgage that they could afford.[18] And moving to a better neighborhood would ensure Peter a higher-quality education. Peter's care is another issue. Their stakes could help them buy day care for their son and send him to a decent preschool.

Brenda's father is urging the young couple to take another route: to save all their money and avoid spending any even during hard times. He warns, "You never know what life holds," and reminds the pair that they have many long years to go until retirement.

Of course, Bill and Brenda cannot do all of these things at once— even $160,000 will go only so far. They have some hard choices to make. They could take Brenda's dad's advice and bank their money as a rainy-day fund. They could continue to spend a couple of thousand here and there—some maternity leave for Brenda, preschool and parochial school for Peter, extra money when Bill is out of work. Or they could take the leap and make a bigger investment—a house or a training program that might have a major long-term impact on their security, but at the cost of depleting their one-time stake.

We cannot predict which choices they will make, much less how their decisions turn out. We do believe that the vast majority of Brendas and Bills—and their children—will have more self-confidence and more real security. But even if they fail, they have had the taste of *real* freedom to make their own decisions about how best to live their lives.

## Mary Ann and Mike

Mary Ann's and Mike's choices are not so different, even though they are several steps up the economic scale. These twenty-five-year-olds are also struggling with foundational questions about marriage, children, and career that will shape their adult lives.

Mary Ann graduated from high school and went on to the local community college, where she earned an associate's degree.[19] She would like to finish college and become a teacher. But she didn't like the idea of taking out big loans, which she would then have to repay on a teacher's salary. She now works as an executive secretary at a local bank, earning twenty thousand dollars a year plus health insurance.[20] Mike graduated from high school but decided not to go to college. He's doing pretty well, though. As a unionized truck driver for a national supermarket chain, he earns as much as thirty-five thousand dollars a year, including some extra pay for overtime.[21] He would love to buy a truck of his own, work as an independent contractor, and build a bigger business over the long term.

Mike and Mary Ann have two children.[22] Cathy is three, and Jenny is just six months old. Both are in family day care with a neighbor down the street. Mary Ann went back to work when Jenny was ten weeks old, but she's exhausted these days from juggling work and family. Mike helps out with the children, but his hours are unpredictable, so Mary Ann bears most child care responsibilities—getting the kids to and from day care, taking them to the doctor, and so on. The baby has been sick this winter, and Mary Ann has already missed more than a week of work. Her boss has warned her that she can't take any more time off. Like a lot of young mothers, Mary Ann is feeling overwhelmed.[23] She would like to stay home with the children at least part-time, but she and Mike worry that they can't keep up their standard of living without her income.[24]

They are currently living in a rented townhouse but would like to buy a home. They have saved about ten thousand dollars toward the down payment, but that isn't enough, and neither set of parents can afford to help them out. In fact, Mike's parents have very little money and are approaching retirement without much except a modest social security check. Mike and Mary Ann anticipate that they will end up helping to support his parents after they retire.

The stresses of life have left their marriage more than a little shaky. Mary Ann's mother, who has gone through a divorce herself, is urging Mary Ann to go back to college now so that she will have a solid career if the marriage fails. She doesn't want her daughter to have to choose between a bad marriage and life on her own with two small children on a secretary's income. Teachers don't make much more at first, but they have job security, their incomes grow over time, and they have their summers free. Mike opposes the idea of college, saying that Mary Ann would be foolish to go back to school with two little children at home.

Suppose now that stakeholding has been introduced. In contrast to Bill and Brenda, Mike and Mary Ann have already spent a substantial part of their stakes. Mary Ann spent thirty thousand dollars on community-college tuition and living expenses. Mike spent fifteen thousand of his stake on their dream wedding and honeymoon trip to Asia. (His parents warned him against this "extravagance," but Mike knew that it was the trip of a lifetime.) Since then, though, they have reinvested their money without touching the principal. Today, Mary Ann has accumulated nearly $58,000, and Mike has about $78,000, for a total of $136,000 that earns $6,800 a year for them in the conservative version of the stakeholding account that they selected for themselves.[25]

What are their choices? Mike wants to use the money to pursue his dream of starting his own trucking business. The $136,000 would be enough to get a bank interested in providing enough capital for a two- or three-truck operation. He is tired of working for someone else, and he is sure that he can run his business efficiently and undercut the competition. But to do that, he would need Mary Ann's stake as well as his own.

Mary Ann is torn. Her mother warns her to keep her stake for herself. Mike says, "Honey, let's invest in our future *together*. If you don't want to help me start a business, let's at least use our money for a down payment on a house." Mary Ann might go along or choose to keep what's left of her stake. If she keeps her own money, she might spend it on college, save it in case they get divorced, or use some of it now to allow her to cut back her work hours. Not an easy choice.

For Mike and Mary Ann, too, the stake means real freedom—of a kind beyond their reach in today's America. Freedom brings hard choices, with real consequences. But isn't that what life is all about?

## Looking Ahead: Judy and Debbie

Judy and Debbie are young sisters, only two years apart. They live with their divorced mother, Meg, in a high-crime, low-income area. Meg wants the best for her children, but she knows that she is struggling against the odds. The local schools are little more than warehouses. The neighborhood's unemployment rate is in double digits, particularly among the young. Some turn to dealing or using drugs, and others drop out of school to have babies. Judy and Debbie might be white or black or Latina; they might live in an inner city or in a poor rural area.[26]

To this point, we have been telling our stories as if the stake has simply dropped from heaven unannounced. But now let's consider what the promise of stakeholding might mean for Judy and Debbie as they grow up. As we have emphasized, stakeholding cannot solve the multiple problems that confront the most disadvantaged. Nonetheless, Judy and Debbie will grow up hearing about stakeholding and what it means to their older peers. Those who stay in school and keep away from drug dealers and gangs will claim their stakes proudly at age twenty-one—and their friends and neighbors will hear about it. Others will falter. They will lose their stakes to repeated criminal convictions or drop out of high school and settle for a modest annuity instead of full control over their money.

When Judy and Debbie are youngsters, Meg uses the promise of a stake and the experience of her friends' children to reinforce her exhortations that her girls stay on the right path. Debbie, the elder, succeeds with flying colors. She graduates from high school at eighteen and heads to college. Nowadays, a talented but poor student like Debbie often ends up in a community college.[27] The tuition is low, and she can save money by living at home. To be sure, a better school with higher tuition may offer a package of grants, loans, and work-study jobs to get her through.[28] But Debbie might be wary of taking on big debts *and* working her way through school, simply in order to get better credentials.[29] In contrast, the stake will let Debbie choose a college based on its programs, not on its location and degree of state funding. Aiming for a career in business, Debbie chooses to go to an out-of-state college that offers low tuition and a solid business school. Four years later, she emerges at age twenty-two with a bachelor's degree, several good job offers, and no college debt. She is on her way up.

Judy, the younger sister, hasn't done so well by age twenty-two. She was always impressed by Debbie's example, but she got pregnant at sixteen and dropped out of school to keep the baby, whom she named Joey.[30] Her boyfriend, Stan, is still around but can't pay much in child support, even when he has a job.[31] For the past six years, Judy has been living with her mother and working at a series of minimum-wage food-service jobs.[32] Even when Judy has a job, she faces constant money problems. Her annual earnings of about ten thousand dollars are stretched thin by paying for food, clothing, and medical care for herself and her son, and if it weren't for Meg's help, she and Joey would be facing even tougher times.

Just this year, Judy has started to rethink her life. For one thing, she received her first dividend check from the stakeholding fund.[33] The money is a welcome addition to her meager budget, but it is also a reminder that if she were to finish high school she could take control of her own stake. The other triggering event is that Joey is about to start school—in the very same crumbling first-grade classroom that Judy once sat in. Judy wants better opportunities for herself and her son.

The first hurdle is earning her high school equivalency diploma. Judy studies at night while Meg watches Joey, and by age twenty-four the diploma is hers. She walks proudly into the stakeholding office to document her achievement. The next decision, though, is equally tough. Meg warns her to invest the money: "Don't throw away this second chance you've worked so hard for." Her sister Debbie urges her to go to college. Joey wants a house with a swing set. Stan, who didn't graduate from high school, is suddenly more attentive and mumbles something about getting married. Judy is not so sure: it is *her* stake.

We leave Judy facing a multitude of possibilities: if she marries Stan, he might waste her money; if she gives him the cold shoulder, she faces the hard life of a single mother. If she goes to college or to vocational school, she must choose her studies carefully and budget well, because the eighty thousand dollars (plus interest) will buy only one chance, and she already has family responsibilities. If she spends the money on private school for Joey, she cannot use it for herself. And so on. Our basic point remains. For Judy as for the others, stakeholding means recognition as a real citizen, whose pursuit of happiness is entitled to respect. Her choices, successes, and failures are her own.

These profiles are representative of a broad spectrum of Americans. But they do not begin to do justice to the complexities of life in this vast country. Consider three young women each putting forty thousand dollars of their money into a Meals on Wheels operation. Or a young man going to work in an older fellow's garage and buying him out five years later. Or a group of skilled craftsmen going out on their own in a new partnership. Or a GI who gets through college on today's GI Bill and still has his stake to get him started in civilian life.

Or the son from an upper-middle-class family who bitterly breaks with his parents, perhaps because he is gay when they are straight or he is a born-again Christian when they are not. Or a young woman, harassed at work by an overbearing boss, who gains the financial means to quit her job and run the risk of a few months' unemployment before finding a better one.

But we are not writing the great American novel. We leave the next story up to you.

## The Culture of Stakeholding

Now take the next step and consider how all these stories will interact with one another over time. Soon enough, everybody will be telling everybody about somebody he knows who . . . New words and phrases—"What a stakeblower!"—will gain currency and influence.

A new culture will emerge—one that will seriously challenge existing patterns of self-understanding. The stories surrounding stakeholding will provide a dramatic alternative to the icons of teenage culture that so dominate at present. Rather than glorifying instant gratification, the new stories will champion the longer view: its heroes will be young men and women who understood the life-shaping possibilities provided by the stake and made the best of them; its dunces will be the kids who refused to grow up and blew their stakes on childish stupidities.

At the same time, the emerging culture will greatly enrich the stock of stories that we now tell ourselves about young adulthood. These are presently dominated by tales of yuppies' success on Wall Street or in Silicon Valley—and for good reason, since the lives of the great mass of Americans have been stagnating over the past quarter century. With yuppiedom so obviously out of reach for most people, millions grimly resign themselves to decades of quiet desperation. To be sure, there are exceptions: some twenty-somethings find meaning in volunteer service for their community or church, but most are so hard-pressed by work and family that they can do little more than turn on the television for glimpses at a never-never land of sports stars and sex symbols. Apart from the occasional TV sitcom, there is little in pop culture that remotely displays their own lives in a sympathetic way.

This will not be true of a stakeholding society. The world will come alive with real-world stories starring people like themselves—making hard choices and taking the consequences. Rather than grim resignation, the order of the day will be responsible decision.

Our repeated invocations of the Declaration of Independence are more than rhetorical gestures. We are taking up Thomas Jefferson's deeper challenge: can we reconstruct his vision of an America as a property-owning democracy full of freedom-loving individualists?

Stakeholding cannot end poverty, cure cancer, or make life easy. But it can promise more real freedom for all, and this promise will itself help create a new generation of Americans more equal to freedom's challenges. There is undoubtedly something utopian about this aspiration, but it is a dream worth fighting for.

# 5

# Payback Time

Real freedom and equal opportunity don't come cheap. Using conservative assumptions, we estimate that the cost of our initiative in 1997 would have been about $255 billion—a little less than what we spent on national defense.[1] This is a big number, but as a nation we have made comparable commitments in the past. Would America have been a better place after World War II without the GI Bill of Rights? At that time, wealthy taxpayers were a lot poorer than they are today, and they were paying far heavier taxes, yet they did not seek to evade their obligation to give the rising generation a fair start in adult life.[2]

To be sure, the GI Bill represented the payment of a debt for the sacrifices that our soldiers made during the war. Today the ties that bind older to younger are less obvious—but no less important. Day after day, our society demands countless small acts of voluntary cooperation as well as many larger personal sacrifices. If the younger generation is denied a fair start, how can the rest of us expect them to reciprocate as the need requires?

We begin with moral fundamentals: what obligations, if any, do we owe succeeding generations of Americans? After defining some principles, we consider how they might govern a stakeholding society. Over the long run, stakeholders themselves should play an increasingly central role in financing the system. As the first recipients begin to die out, they should be expected to pay back their initial eighty thousand dollars, with interest, into the stakeholding fund. Family members should be allowed to claim large inheritances only after the stakeholder has paid back the eighty thousand that helped give him a start in life.

If any young adult finds this future obligation too onerous, he can escape it by waiving his claim to the stake. But once he stakes his claim as a citizen, fairness requires him to pay back his debt to his fellow Americans before making other substantial bequests. Working out this position will require us to consider lots of fascinating themes and variations. But we do not expect our general approach to be too controversial.

More controversial, perhaps, will be our views on the crucial question of the short term: because very few stakeholders will be dying any time soon, how are we going to finance the initiative over the next half century? Chapter 6 proposes a 2 percent annual wealth tax to fill the fiscal gap. Wealth taxes, especially on real estate, serve as the foundation of local public finance in this country, and they are quite familiar in Europe.[3] But American government on the national level has relied on income and payroll taxes to finance redistribution. Our suggestion of a wealth tax may seem, then, more novel than it really is.[4]

Even so, it *is* novel, and so it suffers under a special burden of justification. We begin by emphasizing that one could reject a wealth tax but still embrace stakeholding. All this requires is some other plan for coming up with the money. Most obviously, one might increase income taxes or cut expenditures—or both. Or one might consider a fiscal favorite of conservatives, who have been agitating for a national sales tax to replace the income tax.[5] Taken by itself, this last proposal strikes us as a bad idea, as a sales tax hits the poor harder than it does the rich.[6] But as a possible source of new revenue for stakeholding, the idea has greater promise, for the progressive character of our program would outweigh the regressive character of the sales tax, leaving poorer citizens far better off in the aggregate.[7] We are not purists and would be happy with half a loaf. Nonetheless, we think that a wealth tax is the best available option.

Chapter 7 concludes the fiscal side of our argument by considering predictable objections. Every new tax generates the same old cry: it will kill the economy. Rich people are always happy to remind you of the story about killing the goose that lays the golden eggs. But is it just a fairy tale?

Not only has our economy boomed, and busted, under very different levels of taxation; recent empirical research also suggests that the link between tax rates and economic growth is far weaker than the prevailing political rhetoric implies. We conclude, then, by exposing the emphatic certainties of antitax rhetoric to the indeterminacies and complexities revealed by serious economic analysis.

## Obligations to the Future?

Each generation has the next in its power. We can lay waste to the planet or scrimp and save in order to transform our grandchildren's world into a technological cornucopia. The decision is up to us. But it doesn't necessarily follow that we should consider ourselves morally free to make any decision we like. Are there principles of public morality to which America should be committed in making this fundamental decision?

Perhaps not. We can well imagine some hardheaded libertarian consigning the entire question to the "invisible hand." It is up to each

American to decide on her own what she should do with "her property," both during life and after death. If most property owners choose to mark their passage into the beyond by committing all their earthly possessions to the flames, the next generation would have no just cause for complaint. It would simply be tough luck.

To be sure, this is not an aspect of libertarianism that even fierce partisans take pains to emphasize. They are prone to praise the market system as a machine for growth without reflecting on the deeper implications of their philosophy. But the truth is that the market does not guarantee growth by itself. The market depends on the prevailing preferences of property owners. And if the rich ones don't give a damn about the future, libertarians have few conceptual resources enabling them to argue that the rich have done a grievous wrong.[8]

So much the worse for these callous folk, or so goes the dominant utilitarian response. Rather than taking the narrow view of an individual property owner, the utilitarians say, we should adopt the position of a concerned citizen attempting a truly impartial view of the situation.[9] From this vantage, the interests of young Americans of the year 2050 should count equally with those of us who happen to be around right now. In Jeremy Bentham's famous formulation: each should count for one, and none should count for more than one. As a consequence, utilitarians would have no trouble with the "bonfire" method of estate planning that exposed the callous indifference of the hardheaded libertarian. They would strongly support legislation banning such utility-minimizing activities: while the older generation might well experience some frustration in foregoing their bonfires, this pain is readily outweighed by the satisfactions gained by keeping the property around for use by their successors.

When we turn to harder cases, the utilitarian calculus depends on a complex balancing operation. Speaking broadly, it begins by comparing the relative wealth of earlier and later generations. Because the marginal utility of money generally declines as people grow richer, a relatively poor generation shouldn't scrimp to enable its relatively rich successors to get even richer.

But other things aren't necessarily equal. If, for example, great technological miracles are just around the corner, extra savings might generate massive returns. Under this scenario, the enormous extra gains in welfare accruing to the rich generation in 2050 might morally offset the extra welfare losses suffered by poorer folks in the year 2000.[10] The nature of our collective obligations depends quite heavily on predictions about the future that are difficult to subject to serious empirical critique.

This is a significant disadvantage, the utilitarians must ruefully concede, but consider the alternative: isn't it better to make guesses about the future than to blind oneself to the problem, as the libertarians do?


## Liberal Trusteeship

We find something lacking in both sides of this debate. Like the libertarians, we reject the idea that justice is a matter of designing an enduring happiness machine. Each of us is a free and equal citizen whose rights should not depend on social engineering, however benevolent the engineer may be. At the same time, we reject the libertarians' nonchalance toward the future. While it falls to us to determine the collective fate of our grandchildren, we may not look upon their claims with indifference or disdain. Temporal priority does not imply moral superiority. We should, instead, be prepared to explain to them how we have taken their status as fellow citizens into account in our deliberations.

We propose a principle of trusteeship that speaks in terms of individual rights, not aggregate welfare. We must take the claims of equal citizenship for tomorrow's Americans seriously—as seriously as we take our own. If we wish to sustain a civic bond with our successors, we have no right to arrange the future for our convenience and let our

successors fend for themselves. At the very least, we have an obligation to provide them with the same fundamental rights that we have
provided for ourselves. Call this the principle of liberal trusteeship.[11]

To consider its long-term implications, begin with a thought-exper-
iment. The year is 2010, and America has just adopted stakeholding as
its response to growing economic inequality. As the debate moves to
basic questions of program design, the status of future generations
comes into view. After all, the country is not engaging in a one-shot exercise in benevolence. Stakeholding is not only for the year 2010 but
for as long as Americans continue to find inspiration in the Declaration of Independence. Shouldn't this commitment to the future be in-
scribed into the very terms of the stake itself? Each stakeholder should
take her eighty thousand dollars under conditions of trusteeship.
While the stake is her property during her lifetime, her control should
not extend beyond the grave. If a stakeholder is successful and dies
with millions in the bank, she should not be allowed to forget the
eighty thousand dollars that helped give her a start. Instead, she must
first repay it into the stakeholding fund, with interest, before she may
give large bequests to her children or to charities.

Here as elsewhere, we are insisting upon the priority of citizenship
over the claims of other relationships. Success in the marketplace does
not trump the stakeholder's obligations to future citizens. Nor does
her desire to perpetuate the economic dominion of her family for generations to come. Dynastic ambition is not a good reason for forgetting
one's debt to one's country and refusing to do a fair share to provide future citizens with an equal start in life.

This principle of stakeholding trusteeship will, we think, prove to
be one of the least controversial aspects of our program. Even libertarians will have a hard time rejecting it. After all, nobody is forcing
anyone to take the eighty thousand dollars. If someone finds the trust
too offensive, he can simply refuse to claim his stake. But for the rest
of us, this payback obligation will seem an obvious implication of our

membership in a republic that existed long before we came onto the scene and will endure long after.

When cashed out in monetary terms, trusteeship will carry a big price tag. Thanks to the wonders of compound interest and increasing longevity, a stake of $80,000 received in 2010 implies a payback obligation of about $250,000 (in real dollars, after inflation is taken into account) when the typical American dies sixty years later in 2070.[12] And if human nature remains the same, stakeholders will respond with a characteristic ambiguity. On one hand, most will appreciate the justice of repaying this large sum to the stakeholding fund. But on the other hand, many will try to weasel out of their debt. Rather than dying with substantial estates, they will be sorely tempted to make an end run around the stakeholding fund by giving large gifts to their children and others before they die. If nothing were done to prevent this, the integrity of the program would be threatened. It will not be enough, then, to apply trusteeship principles to bequests; it will also be necessary to regulate large gifts made before death.

This must be done sensitively to take account of the realities and values of family life. Parents, both rich and poor, have a fundamental right to share their lives with their children. While this means that children of the rich will enjoy the material fruits of their parents' success while growing up, this is perfectly fine—provided, of course, that the state takes an active role in providing a genuinely rich set of educational opportunities for others less advantaged. Liberalism has always favored leveling up, not leveling down.

Trickier problems arise when children become grown-ups. By the time they claim their stake, young adults will have typically left home to establish a certain independence from their parents—indeed, the eighty thousand dollar stake will undoubtedly encourage this. On the parents' side, stakeholding will also serve as a marker. Even today, most parents believe that their financial obligations to their children end when their children leave school.[13] Stakeholding will reinforce this belief. For the overwhelming majority of parents, it will seem absurd for their children to call upon them for more money when they have eighty thousand dollars apiece at their command. Except for the top 1 or 2 percent, intrafamily exchanges will become limited to holiday or birthday presents and the like. Only those at the very top are likely to consider eighty thousand dollars too little for a suitable start in life.

This is the point at which the principle of liberal trusteeship becomes important. If equality of opportunity means anything, it means that the rich must restrain themselves. At the very least, parents should be taxed substantially if they wish to shower their adult offspring with large financial advantages. While these gift taxes will predictably affect only a small minority at the very top, serious regulation is required in order to avoid a more general demoralization with the system.

We will return to the practicalities of translating these principles into workable estate and gift taxes. But for now, consider the next question of principle: how should we deal with the problem of stakeholders who die without sufficient funds for paying back their stakes?

## The Trusteeship Tax

As the first generation of stakeholders passes away, their successors will confront one of three fiscal possibilities. Depending on the first generation's response to the payback obligation, their aggregate contributions to the stakeholding fund may match the stakeholding requirements of the coming generation, they may generate a surplus, or they may leave the fund with a shortfall. The first possibility marks a steady-state solution. Each generation claims its stake and recognizes its trusteeship responsibility to its successors, leaving enough for the next generation to begin the process again. The second, or surplus,

scenario would allow either an increase in the average stake or a modification of estate and gift taxes to allow for more bequests to children
and charities.

The third possibility raises more serious problems. It is most likely
to arise if the first generation responds to the payback obligation by increasing consumption during their lives, leaving less to their children
and less to the stakeholding fund. Under this scenario, the payback requirement will not allow the first generation to fulfill its trusteeship
obligations, and so further steps must be taken to assure the fiscal
soundness of the stakeholding fund.

This is the function of the second prong of our long-range program.
Call it the trusteeship tax. Rather than waiting until stakeholders die
before calling upon them to replenish the stakeholding fund, why not
require them to pay a supplementary tax during their lifetimes so as to
guarantee the fund's solvency?

At this point, we expect, libertarians will begin squirming: "It was
one thing to impress a trust on the original eighty thousand dollars that
I received from the government. But now you're proposing to take the
*real* money that I have accumulated from other sources. I always knew
that, once you stakeholding guys got into power, you'd begin to use
your pet program to squeeze more money out of me. But it's up to me
to decide whether I give my money to the Americans of the future or
not. If I choose to spend it on something else, that's what freedom is
all about. You guys are nothing better than thieves!"

We have reached a moment of genuine moral disagreement. We
agree with our libertarian friends that each citizen, after paying her
taxes and fulfilling her other obligations, should generally be free to
spend her money as she sees fit. It is up to her, and not the community,
to determine the meaning of her life and the proper use of her resources.

But we deny that any of us can treat the interests of future citizens as if they did not raise authentic civic obligations. Our hypotheti-

cal libertarian has cried "thief" one time too often in condemning the trusteeship tax. Just as the polity rightfully intervenes against the garden-variety thief, so too may it rightfully intervene to prevent the present generation from robbing the future. After all, the rising generation did not participate in the process through which our hypothetical libertarian gained her wealth in the marketplace. Many had not been born at the time of her greatest market triumphs. Even though she might have fairly gained her property in competition with others of her generation, this does not mean that she can escape her fair share of trusteeship taxes.

Rather than telling future Americans to fend for themselves, she should recognize them for what they are—fellow citizens of an enduring republic. Each American is a link in a chain that extends beyond her own lifetime; the first link was fashioned by the opening words of Jefferson's Declaration, and each of has an obligation to give these words real meaning for our successors. Like it or not, our libertarian friends cannot expect their fellow citizens to allow them a special exemption from this collective obligation.[*]

## Beyond the Wealth Tax?

But this conclusion only gets us to the really interesting questions. It is not yet clear what kind of trusteeship tax is best suited to serve the backup function that we have identified. To see the problem, return to

---

[*] Taking this libertarian objection to its extreme, childless stakeholders might also claim a special exemption from the trusteeship tax. After all, they do not have any children, so why should they pay for stakes for other peoples' progeny? This question dramatizes the libertarian's peculiar blindness to the reality of civic obligations. A childless American remains an American—a citizen who enjoys the priceless legacy of legitimate government handed down by his predecessors and has an obligation to reciprocate by handing down this legacy to the future in a revitalized condition.

the likely scenarios that will greet Americans in the year 2060. As the first generation passes from the scene, some citizens will have more than enough money to pay back their quarter of a million dollars, but many will go to their graves penniless, leaving the fund uncompensated for their initial eighty thousand dollars.[14] Ideally, shouldn't our trusteeship tax be structured to encourage these people to save, thus minimizing the fiscal consequences of their final shortfall?

The problem raises a relatively unexplored issue of public morality: how should more successful citizens respond to the predictable failures by others to fulfill their obligations? After all, the Thirteenth Amendment does impose some limits, and we do not urge the resurrection of debtors' prisons. All in all, it is better to view payback failures in the same way that we have learned to look at bankruptcies. Obviously, bankrupts have not done something commendable; depending on the facts of their cases, many may be worthy of moral censure; but it is not as if they were ax murderers.

So, too, in the case of men or women who die penniless. It is hard to condemn their failures to fulfill their trusteeship obligations without knowing a lot more about their lives. Perhaps some of them never had a decent education—remember, our basic stakeholding proposal focuses only on young adults and does not seek to remedy the injustices of earlier life. Perhaps somebody trained hard to become a keypunch operator, only to see demand for her services plummet. Or perhaps she blew the money in Las Vegas.

Given the rough justice that is inevitably tax law's fate, it is too quick to raise the banner of "double taxation" in objecting to the fact that the economically successful will invariably pay more. As we have emphasized, it is better to view them as participating in a collective venture, in which the entire generation has an obligation to discharge its trusteeship obligations to its successors. And because the failure of some to live up to this obligation is so predictable, it seems fair to ask for more from the more successful.

Whatever form the trusteeship tax takes, it marks a decisive break with libertarian understandings. Stakeholding is not simply a governmental loan program with a favorable rate of interest. If it were, we might want to limit participation to those citizens who can demonstrate good prospects for making the money to pay back the loan. But we reject any such exclusionary notion in favor of a collective commitment to equality and freedom for all, not just for some. As long as stakeholding serves as a mark of citizenship, we cannot allow the most privileged to avoid the trusteeship tax merely because they have paid back their stakes. They must share in the citizenry's collective responsibility as well.

But how to measure this share? Depending on your answer, you can choose among three tax bases. The advantage of a sales tax—also called a consumption tax—is that it would squeeze the most out of those who will ultimately die penniless. Even the poor have to buy food, shelter, and clothing. And a consumption tax is a particularly good way to target the improvident, who, by definition, have consumed a lot and saved very little over their lifetimes.

The second possibility is an income tax. The appeal here lies in its more progressive base. It exempts the poorest citizens, who are just getting by at a subsistence level. And it also collects more from wealthy savers, for the tax must be paid whether citizens spend or save their incomes.[15] The corollary, though, is that the income tax takes less from spendthrifts and more from savers.

The third option is a wealth tax, which would place the burden entirely on savers. Because wealth is more concentrated than consumption or income, the wealth tax would be the most progressive of the three.[16] But the rich savers who pay the wealth tax are also the very people who will fulfill their payback obligations. Why should these people pay even more?

Our own choice among these tax bases would depend on the extent to which America moves toward social justice during the next half cen-

tury. Begin with an optimistic scenario: not only does the next generation go for stakeholding, but it also redeems its commitment to a first-
rate education for all of America's children—from Head Start to high
school. Under this scenario, a diminishing number of failed paybacks
could be fairly attributable to systemic injustice. Dying with a bank-
rupt estate would increasingly suggest a self-conscious effort to take a
free ride on others' conscientious efforts to fulfill their trusteeship
obligations at payback time. Within this evolving context, we might
well favor a trusteeship tax based on income or consumption.

But for the foreseeable future, we are likely to remain far away
from real equality of opportunity. And under these conditions, the
best form of trusteeship tax is a wealth tax.

Or so the next chapter will argue.

## From Principles to Practicalities

Before turning to the case for wealth taxation, we consider the practical problems involved in making the payback principle into a workable
system. Fortunately, we can build on our existing tax system, which already contains the basic tools.[17] It imposes heavy gift taxes on rich parents who seek to provide their offspring with overwhelming financial
advantages. It also recognizes that there is something special about inheritance. While Bill Gates is free to spend millions on a futuristic
mansion during his lifetime, his effort to pass on the same amount to
his children is subject to special and onerous estate taxation.

A particularly valuable feature of present law is the way that it inte-
grates gifts during life and bequests at death. Individuals cannot avoid
estate taxes by making lifetime transfers. Instead, they are permitted a
lifetime exemption of $650,000 against both the estate and the gift tax.[18]
Any gifts and bequests above that amount are taxed at rates of up to 55
percent. In addition, each parent can give each child an annual gift of ten
thousand dollars before he begins to use up the $650,000 exemption.

The payback obligation can fit comfortably within this basic framework, although it would require revision of key policy decisions. Most obviously, stakeholding requires rethinking the $650,000 exemption. Citizens should not be allowed to give so much money away tax-free before they begin to repay their stakes. We would not insist, however, that they begin paying back with the very first dollar. Most people have a few heirlooms of high sentimental value but relatively low market value. They should be allowed to pass them on during life or at death without much trouble. A lifetime exemption of fifty thousand dollars should be more than enough to satisfy this need.[19]

At this point, the claims of stakeholding rightly come to the fore. The initial grant of eighty thousand dollars, after all, represented a collective commitment to equal opportunity. It would be bizarre to allow individual stakeholders to destroy this commitment as their dying act. After the fifty-thousand-dollar exemption, we would impose a payback obligation. If we use an interest rate of 2 percent to reflect the real rate of productivity growth in the economy, an eighty-year-old would then owe about $250,000 in 1997 dollars.[20]

Here we come to a fundamental design question. We could simply require that all estates pay back the stake before we allow any other bequests. Or we could design a more complicated payback schedule to take account of the legitimate role of nonprofit charities in American life. At present, these charities compete for bequests with children and other loved ones. For most people, the new system would cap bequests to family members at fifty thousand dollars. Above this level, they will confront a new choice. On the one hand, they will recognize a moral obligation to pay back the stake that gave them such an important start in life. On the other hand, they will feel the pull of other moral claims, including those exercised by churches, educational institutions, and other worthy organizations. How should tax law structure this choice?

We propose a balance: for every dollar that the citizen pays into the stakeholding fund, she may give a dollar to charity. This dollar-for-dollar ratio is not sacrosanct. The appropriate ratio would depend on many factors—most notably, the condition of the stakeholding fund. If the fund were flush and capable of paying out adequate stakes to the next generation, we would be more generous. If not, the question would be much more difficult: to what extent should we allow elderly Americans to give to charities and turn to other taxes to make up the shortfall in the stakeholding fund?

We leave this question to the day that it arises. For now, it is enough to consider how allowing charities into the picture reshapes the estate and gift tax. At present, donors can make large gifts to charity without paying any tax.[21] All the charities need to do is to convince them to ignore the competing pleas of family members. Our revised tax system modifies this choice, whether made during life or exercised at death. Family demands are capped at fifty thousand dollars. Thereafter, gifts or bequests to charities must compete with the stakeholder's moral responsibility to the next generation of citizens, and any charitable transfer must be matched dollar for dollar with a payment to the stakeholding fund.

To minimize bureaucratic hassles, we would provide an annual exemption allowing each taxpayer to make small charitable gifts totaling up to two thousand dollars. After that, the dollar-for-dollar ratio would apply. Similarly, within the family, each parent would be allowed to give each child up to one thousand dollars a year in holiday and birthday presents and the like. Present law already recognizes this escape hatch but makes it absurdly large, allowing each parent a ten-thousand-dollar annual exemption for each child. Savvy tax lawyers advise their wealthy clients to take full advantage of this loophole in order to pass large sums tax-free to their children. This would be intolerable in a stakeholding society, where the rich, no less than the poor, are assured their eighty thousand dollars. The rich have birthdays like the rest of us, but one thousand dollars a year should be more than enough to allow moms and dads to show familial affection. Anything more should be subject to significant taxation under the trusteeship principle.[22]

Under our basic structure, then, each taxpayer will have an annual exemption of two thousand dollars for gifts to charity and one thousand dollars for gifts to each child, and a lifetime exemption of fifty thousand dollars in either gifts or bequests. After that, the next big chunk at death either goes entirely to the stakeholding fund or is shared with charities. The same rules apply to gifts made during life. This leaves us with just two problems: how to provide for surviving dependents, and what to do with the superrich—those who have something left after paying back the stake.

With regard to the first problem, the trusteeship principle limiting gifts to the next generation obviously does not apply to spouses.[23] Here the principle of intragenerational freedom commands respect. If one spouse has worked at home and reared the children in reliance on a promise of lifetime support from the other, this deal is entitled to full respect by a liberal state. In contrast to transfers to children, this transfer does not endanger initial equality in starting points. Nonetheless, a problem remains. We have presented stakeholding as a strictly individualistic affair. When Citizen Single dies, his estate would immediately go toward paying back the stake. Why should Citizen Married get a better deal?

We think that this question is unanswerable. The liberal state should be neutral in its treatment of married and unmarried, gay and straight. At the same time, it would be intolerable to evict surviving elderly partners from their homes in order to satisfy the next generation's demand for stakeholding revenue. The sensible solution is to defer collection until the second partner dies before claiming assets to fulfill the first partner's payback obligation, placing a lien on the property in the meantime. When the second partner dies, the estate is liable for paying back two stakes with interest, not just one.[24]

This leaves us in the economic stratosphere—with the tiny minority who can leave more.[25] For present purposes, we are happy to accept the existing rates of estate and gift taxation—ranging from 37 to 55 percent—on all bequests made after the payback obligation has been satisfied.[26] An adequate treatment of the superrich would take us far afield. The case for stakeholding does not depend on whether you think that the superrich serve as an essential engine of innovation or as a corrupting force in democratic life. Stakeholding is built on a broader foundation: the imperative need to redeem the liberal promise, made to each citizen, of genuine freedom to shape his or her life.

# 6

# Taxing Wealth

The previous chapter invited you to consider stakeholding in long-run equilibrium. As each generation dies, it repays its initial stake into the fund, and if there is an anticipated shortfall, it also pays a trusteeship tax during its lifetime. By replenishing the fund, each generation passes on stakeholding intact to the next, which seeks to fulfill its trusteeship obligations in turn, and so on until the end of the Republic.

But this long-run view will not get stakeholding off the ground. If we are ever to begin, a substantial sacrifice will be required from Americans who never receive a stake. This simple fact raises two questions. Is it fair to require such a sacrifice? Is it politically feasible?

We leave the second question to a later chapter,[1] focusing here on fairness. We hope to persuade you that rich Americans should recognize a fundamental obligation to share their wealth with the rising generation. We begin with our arguments for wealth-sharing, seeking to integrate basic principles into a contextual understanding of the crucial facts. We then proceed to a concrete proposal for an annual wealth tax.

We challenge the self-serving view that taxes on the upper classes can't raise large revenues. To the contrary, an annual wealth tax of 2 percent should suffice to fund stakeholding completely. This is true even with an eighty-thousand-dollar exemption for every American, which would exempt the bottom 59 percent of households from *any* tax.[2] This single statistic emphasizes the dramatic inequality of the existing situation. The wealth of America is distributed so unequally that stakeholding can be financed by a tax that hits only the top 41 percent, with the top 20 percent contributing 93 percent of the total revenue.[3]

Like any other method of public finance, the wealth tax has its share of difficulties and complexities. These are very real, but there is no reason that they could not be mastered—as long as Americans found the political will to act decisively.

## The Wealth Gap

The basic facts on wealth distribution are stunning. In terms of net worth, a conventional measure of wealth, the richest 1 percent of Americans owned 38.5 percent of wealth in 1995.[4] Even a broader measure of wealth, which includes all pension and Social Security entitlements, reveals that the richest 1 percent of the population owned 21.2 percent of total wealth in 1989.[5] By any measure, the current concentration is extreme. Contrary to Americans' egalitarian self-perceptions, wealth is more concentrated in the hands of the superrich in the United States than it is in England or France—a sharp turnaround from 1900, when Americans could still contrast their traditions of economic democracy with the royalist legacies of Europe.[6]

And the trend is moving in the wrong direction. From the 1930s to the late 1970s, the share of American wealth held by the top 1 percent declined, from more than 40 percent to about 13 percent. But since then the trend has reversed.[7] Although average wealth grew between 1983 and 1995, only the top 5 percent experienced an increase in net worth.[8] Wealth declined in every other group, with the bottom 40 percent experiencing the sharpest drop.[9] Social science methods are never certain, but even conservative critics acknowledge an increase in wealth concentration since the 1970s to its present stratospheric levels.[10]

## Sharing the Wealth

For some of our readers, these numbers will speak louder than words: something *must* be wrong with a society in which the top 1 percent manages to get its hands on more than one-fifth of the wealth.

We respect this intuition but do not share it. To the contrary: if our country ever came close to achieving genuinely equal opportunity, we would take a very different view of the wealth gap. Putting to one side the continuing need for special assistance to those with serious physical or mental disabilities, we would then find ourselves switching sides in this great debate. If each American received a first-rate education and began adult life with a roughly equal stake, it should be up to him or her to decide what to do next. Subject to fulfilling his trusteeship obligations to the next generation, he should be free to make his own decisions on the right mix of work and leisure, spending and saving. If it *then* turned out that the top 1 percent gained 20 percent of the wealth, we would accept the legitimacy of the resulting gap. It is up to each of us to determine, on his own responsibility, the highest and best use of his initial resources.[11] If starting points were fair and some of us decided to work, innovate, and accumulate while others spent more on leisure and consumption, we would not challenge the ensuing distribution of wealth merely because the innovative savers had accumulated much more than the leisurely consumers. To the contrary, the ensuing distribution would simply be testimony to the diversity of ideals that motivate free men and women in a just society.

Our case for a wealth tax, then, is necessarily more complex than a simple appeal to the facts detailing disproportionate ownership. It is based on an additional and, to our mind, inarguable point: nothing like genuine equality of opportunity exists in America. As we have seen, privileged children begin life with overwhelming advantages—inherited wealth, social connections, and an educational head start—which we will call the unequal opportunity surplus.[12] To a certain extent, this surplus can be measured in dollars and cents. Even among the youngest wage earners between the ages of 19 and 30, there is roughly a ten-thousand-dollar difference in average annual earnings when we compare men who grew up in the most affluent 20 percent of households with those who grew up in the poorest 20 percent.[13] If the extra earnings were set aside each year in a modest savings account earning a real rate of interest of just 2 percent per year, the account would have a balance of more than $600,000 (in 1997 dollars) by the end of a forty-year career.[14]

But, of course, the value of early privilege should also be cashed out in more ineffable terms: the general sense of efficacy resulting from a childhood sheltered from the frustrations of material deprivation, the enhanced self-confidence born of years of deferential service in the marketplace, and the basic trust that your parents (and their checkbooks) will act as the ultimate barrier between you and your follies.

Even wealthy citizens who emerge from humbler backgrounds cannot rightfully claim that their wealth is fairly earned. These people may think of themselves as modern-day Horatio Algers, but they too have enjoyed an unequal opportunity surplus. At the very least, they would have encountered much stronger competition had their fellow citizens *not* been disadvantaged by the existing system. How can they tell how they would have fared in a truly fair race?

There is simply no way to know what would have happened. And certainly there is no practical way for the government to distinguish between justly and unjustly earned wealth and make that distinction the basis for taxation. Only one thing is clear: rich Americans cannot pretend that their gains are entirely the result of a fair system of equal opportunity. Just because it is hard to measure their advantage in individual cases does not make that advantage any less real. Given this fact, it strikes us as entirely appropriate to ask those who have accumulated the most to share the most.

To be sure, a progressive income tax also helps reduce the unequal opportunity surplus. But we have deliberately chosen a new wealth tax for reasons both principled and pragmatic. On the principled side, the opportunities that wealth confers are simply different from those that high income brings. The possession of wealth today buys personal security and a host of opportunities: to move in higher social circles, to bequeath assets to children, and to gain an effective voice in politics. High income can help, but the rich who spend all they make will forego the peace of mind and real power that accumulation alone can confer. Under conditions of unequal opportunity, the distinct advantages of wealth—as well as those of income—may fairly be taxed. On the pragmatic side, the income tax and estate taxes today are riddled with loopholes that benefit the wealthy.[15] An annual wealth tax ensures that the rich contribute a bit more to the workings of justice.

The case for the wealth tax is particularly compelling now, for the current generation has gained its wealth at an especially lucky moment in the history of the Republic. Because wealth is correlated with age, Americans over the age of fifty or sixty will bear the brunt of our tax.[16] But it is precisely these people who have participated most fully in the great postwar economic boom. The wealthy man or woman who is sixty in the year 2000 was born in 1940—just in time to avoid the agonies of the Great Depression and World War II, but just in time to reap the harvest. Having graduated from college around 1960, the typical up-and-comer was in a perfect position to take advantage of the rich array of opportunities made possible by America's rise to world power. The best universities, the most advanced companies, the biggest pool of capital—all of these were available for Americans who seized the moment. Admittedly, nobody could have become wealthy without one or another combination of effort, insight, and luck. But it would be blind for any sixty-year-old to ignore the role played by the simple fact that he was an American in an American age—and that he thereby gained enormous advantages created at great sacrifice by his parents' generation. Given the existing balance of generational advantage, it is especially appropriate to ask this group of elderly Americans to sacrifice to sustain the Republic's political and economic equilibrium.

Nobody can say for sure whether the recent wave of inequality will continue unabated for another quarter century. While explanations vary, most emphasize technological changes that have increased the relative productivity of skilled workers. Other important structural factors include the shift from manufacturing to service industries, the declining strength of unions, and increasing job mobility and global competition.[17] It seems unlikely that these trends will disappear any time soon; they may well accelerate in the increasingly globalized information economy of the future. All in all, the warning signs are serious enough to warrant serious measures like stakeholding to stop the cycle of inequality before it spins out of control. The question is whether wealthy Americans, who have profited so much from the American century, should recognize a special responsibility to respond to the clear and present dangers of deep economic division that lie ahead.

To put the same point within a different temporal frame: we are calling upon older Americans to remember that they themselves were the beneficiaries of similar acts of statesmanship by earlier generations. During the New Deal and Great Society, Americans recognized the elderly as a group that was particularly threatened by the inegalitarian operation of market forces. By responding with Social Security and Medicare, our predecessors ensured a decent life for millions of elderly Americans today. Without these programs, the distribution of wealth today would be even more unequal than it already is.[18] Is it not time, then, for the elder generation to reciprocate when the market threatens to undermine the promise of economic opportunity for millions of younger Americans?

This commitment should not come at the expense of retirees who depend on their monthly Social Security checks. We do not question the basic legitimacy of government pensions; to the contrary, the next part of this book defends them against fashionable libertarian critiques and tries to put them on a firmer basis for the future. So we reject the idea of funding stakeholding by raiding Social Security revenues. We simply urge prosperous older Americans to recognize the moral claim of younger Americans who will otherwise suffer lives of quiet despair.

Or not-so-quiet despair. After all, the prison population has soared over the past quarter century. In 1975 about one hundred of every 100,000 Americans were in the nation's prisons; now that number is about four hundred—and more than six hundred when the short-term jail population is included.[19] Young men, and increasingly women, are the prime candidates for prison—men and women who might find it within themselves to take a different path in a stakeholding society.[20] If inequality increases during the next century, are we really prepared to lock up more and more young Americans who react with rage at a system that has never delivered on its promises? If those with the greatest stake in the system do not take heed, who is supposed to?

It is time for the wealthy to accept stakeholding as part of the social compact.

## The Wealth Tax as a Trusteeship Tax

We emphasize, however, that our case for the wealth tax is based on the continuing existence of pervasive and substantial unequal opportunity surpluses. Ideally, we should be aiming for a society that simply eliminated these gross disparities and therefore no longer thought it appropriate to tax wealth. But as long as these disparities persist, we cannot ignore them in deciding how to fund stakeholding.

To be sure, the wealth tax will sometimes impose an illiberal burden. It will weigh more heavily on frugal savers than on their high-living counterparts, imposing a greater obligation on the Ants than on the Grasshoppers, as it were.[21] But there are very few taxes that do not have some distortionary features. Although wealth is an imperfect proxy for inequality of opportunity, it is still a good one, and the combination of a wealth tax and stakeholding can strike directly at the source of unequal opportunity in the next generation.

During the first half century of its operation, the tax will also serve to guarantee the trusteeship obligations of the first generation of stakeholders, operating as a "backstop" to the payback obligation. The annual collection of a wealth tax ensures that rich citizens cannot defeat their payback obligation by accumulating wealth and power over a lifetime but then dissipating it quickly just before death. As we suggested in the last chapter, the balance of argument may shift away from wealth taxation if stakeholding succeeds in catalyzing a new round of opportunity-equalizing reforms. In the year 2050 or 3000, a more equal America may decide that wealth taxation has served its purpose. In that far-off world, citizens may rightly decide to rely entirely on other forms of public finance. But for the present, we turn to considering how wealth taxation might actually operate in the real world of unequal opportunity.

## Designing the Wealth Tax

Although the wealth tax is unfamiliar to Americans, it has been a long-standing feature of European systems. No fewer than twelve countries in the Organisation for Economic Cooperation and Development (OECD) tax wealth annually, although only Denmark and Sweden have imposed rates as high as those we recommend and our proposed tax base is broader than the European standard.[22] We turn to consider some key issues involved in defining and administering the tax.

But before we begin, perhaps a bit of perspective is in order. Politicians too often talk as if "tax simplification" were the Holy Grail, and lawyers especially delight in pointing out every legal wrinkle. But "simplicity" is too often a smokescreen for schemes that shift tax burdens to the lower classes.[23] *Of course* it is more complicated to tax the rich, because they have the resources to exploit every possible loophole (and create even more). But we should not give up on the effort to use taxation to achieve social justice.

It is undeniable that a wealth tax will impose some extra administrative costs, particularly at first, as the system gets up to speed. This is a legitimate source of concern, and we will be on the lookout for ways to streamline administration. But it is important to recognize that these costs are incurred in the pursuit of a larger goal—equal opportunity for all.

### Setting the Rate

As in all matters of taxation, there is an inevitable arbitrariness involved in fixing precise rates. Given the indeterminacy, it seems fair to turn the question around and ask, What does it take to fund a stakeholding system that will provide each American with a "substantial" starting point in life, one that does not make a mockery of the promise of equal opportunity? If eighty thousand dollars is in the right ballpark, it makes sense to work backward from this judgment to its wealth-tax implications. The 2 percent figure falls out of this calculus.[24]

There is nothing special about eighty thousand dollars and 2 percent.[25] The key point is moral: it ill behooves the beneficiaries of the current distribution to entertain us with hypothetical cases "proving" that they would have done just as well in a truly fair competition. We call upon them instead to look at the facts of injustice and recognize that they have a special responsibility to take steps to end them. After all, our basic proposal only represents a step in the right direction. Even if stakeholding were adopted, we would be far from an America in which all children began adult life with first-rate educations and roughly equal resources, regardless of their parents' success or failure in the marketplace.

### The Base of Taxation

To fund the stake at a reasonable tax rate requires a comprehensive definition of wealth. We propose to tax individuals' wealth in whatever form it is held including not only stocks, bonds, and bank accounts but also houses and cars, family firms, and pensions.[26] To ensure that only the assets' net value is taxed, taxpayers could subtract the amount of any outstanding debt.[27] And we would allow each individual to claim an exemption. It is simply not worth the hassle to tax small wealth holdings—this, by itself, would justify an exemption of the first forty thousand dollars or so. But we would go further and exempt eighty thousand dollars, thereby allowing stakeholders to keep their initial stake without paying any wealth tax.[28]

This exemption level is generous. In 1995, only 41 percent of households would have had to pay any tax after taking the appropriate exemptions.[29] In that year, the median household owned property worth $73,600.[30] Stakeholding will change these figures over time, but the tax will continue to fall heavily on the richest stratum of society. In 1995, the median net wealth of the top 1 percent of households was $4.6 million, and the typical household in that group would pay an annual tax of about $90,000.[31] In the same year, the median net wealth of the top 20 percent of American households was about $555,000, implying an annual tax of about $8,300.[32] By the time we get to the second-wealthiest quintile, the median tax burden goes down to $1,100.[33]

Given this steep falloff, there is only one reason to consider further exemptions: to deprive opponents of cheap political arguments. They will predictably point to elderly couples who have paid off their mort-

gages and ask how the old folks will raise the money to pay Uncle
Sam. We believe that, as a practical matter, the private market would
quickly adapt, with banks offering elderly homeowners limited "reverse mortgages" that would provide the cash they needed to pay their
annual wealth tax. (Indeed, this product is already on the market.)

But perhaps you think that a tax that might require some elderly
people to mortgage their homes is unduly harsh. One way to reduce
this burden would be to allow cash-poor retirees to comply by giving
the government a first lien on their houses, exercisable upon their
deaths. The unpaid wealth tax would accrue in the meantime at a market rate of interest, just like any outstanding tax debt. This plan would
allow the elderly to continue living in their homes and let the government collect their tax, with interest, before others can share in their
estates. We prefer to save the enforcement costs associated with this
plan, but offer it as an example of the kind of accommodation that
might be made.

We are even less impressed with other predictable objections.
Family farmers and other small business owners invariably claim special hardship because so much of their wealth is illiquid. But if they
somehow manage to obtain bank loans for inventories and expansion,
they can also raise money to pay their public obligations. After all, we
are talking about some of the most successful people in America.[34]

As long as we keep the base broad, a 2 percent rate should get us to
our revenue target, using conservative assumptions that provide a realistic cushion for tax evasion.[35] If a shortfall nevertheless arises, we
would support additional progressivity. Undoubtedly, Steve Forbes
and other children of great wealth should pay at a higher rate than a
hardworking dentist from the inner city who has managed to put away
a quarter of a million dollars. And if we need more of Forbes's money
for full funding, we would be prepared to bear the added administrative complexities that a progressive rate structure would entail.

## The Tax Treatment of Families

We must also take account of the realities of family life. One likely problem is that family members will shift wealth among themselves to take maximum advantage of each individual's eighty-thousand-dollar exemption. Parents and grandparents in particular may decide to shift wealth to young children, much as they used to do under the income tax. The gift-tax regime outlined in Chapter 4 should discourage this. But we propose as an additional measure that the eighty-thousand-dollar exemption be denied to minor children.[36] Because they will be getting their eighty-thousand-dollar stakes upon maturity, it would be wrong to allow their parents to manipulate their tax status to undermine the financing of the program.

The married or cohabiting couple poses another wealth-shifting problem. Recall that our proposal would impose the wealth tax on individuals, not couples. Taxing partners as individuals does give them some flexibility in minimizing taxes, for they can thereby split their wealth in order to take advantage of each partner's full exemption. This is not a big issue in today's U.S. income tax, as married couples generally file joint returns.[37] But it is a familiar problem in other countries that require individual filing, and there is a short list of potential solutions, from respecting formal title to property to simply dividing each couple's total wealth equally between them.[38] We think it best to respect individuals' legal title; if spouses are willing to hold their wealth in common, they should be entitled to corresponding tax treatment.

## Problems of Administration

The wealth tax raises two basic problems—evasion and valuation. They are linked. The wealth tax gives taxpayers an incentive to hide assets when they can and undervalue them when they can't. With readily marketable assets—many stocks, bonds, and bank accounts—the temptation will be to stash the assets in secret accounts in Switzerland and other countries.[39] But we have much the same problem with the income tax today, and efforts to catch tax cheats range from familiar information-reporting requirements by banks and brokerages to esoteric information-sharing agreements with foreign countries. A wealth tax would make these efforts even more important—and more fiscally productive.

A more distinctive challenge is posed by wealth that is not readily marketable—about two-thirds of the total.[40] By far the biggest items are homes and privately held businesses.[41] As far as real estate is concerned, European precedents suggest a range of options, from piggybacking on state and local property tax valuations to various formulary methods.[42] In dealing with closely held businesses, the Europeans tend to adopt a pragmatic approach, taxing the value of the assets used in the business without estimating goodwill and other intangibles.[43]

And our wealth tax poses more novel challenges as well. Many European countries allow unlimited exemptions for homes, household furnishings, and pension rights.[44] That rule loses revenue and also invites people to avoid the wealth tax by "investing" large sums in houses and the like. We have included these items in the tax base, subject to the eighty-thousand-dollar exemption, which already eliminates 59 percent of taxpayers.[45] For the remainder, home equity will usually be the biggest item and can be dealt with under the usual rules for real estate. Pension rights will be easier to assess: the cash value of most pensions is readily determined, though some will also pose problems.[46] Valuing household furnishings, art, jewelry, and the like will be more difficult, but some creativity may once again come in handy. Taxpayers with valuable assets of these types usually insure them, and it may help keep taxpayers honest if the declared tax value of the items must match their insurance value.

No regime will be perfect, and the transition poses particular challenges. A significant fraction of America's assets will undoubtedly escape, and our calculations have been conservative on that score. The 2 percent wealth tax will be sufficient to fund stakeholding even if the authorities can reach only 79 percent of total taxable wealth.[47] This revenue cushion provides room for refinement of procedures over time as the IRS capitalizes on potential synergies with the administration of the income tax.[48]

## Coordinating the Wealth Tax and the Income Tax

Our initiative will also help fill some of the yawning gaps in the income tax, which is full of breaks for many kinds of capital income, including municipal bond interest, capital gains, income on pension savings, and the economic return to homeowners.[49] As a result, effective income tax rates vary significantly depending on the type of investment and how long it is held.[50] In contrast, the wealth tax would be broad-based to ensure that all wealth-holders would contribute to the stakeholding fund.

But the gaps in the income tax pose a serious issue for the wealth tax: is it fair to impose the full wealth tax on types of capital that are already subject to disproportionately high rates of income tax?

Although a wealth tax is not economically identical to an income tax, both fall on capital investments.[51] And in some cases, the combined rate could be high, particularly once state and local taxes are taken into account.[52] Consider a New York City resident who invests in a one-thousand-dollar taxable bond that yields 5 percent. The combination of federal income tax, state and local income tax, and the wealth tax would add up to a total tax of forty-three dollars, or 86 percent of the fifty dollars that she earns each year.[53] In the case of very low-yielding assets, the combined tax rate could exceed 100 percent of the income that the asset produces.

The central problem is that the wealth tax could compound the law's existing preferences for some kinds of investments over others.[54] As long as we persist in exempting income from owner-occupied housing while taxing income from corporate bonds at almost 40 percent, a wealth tax that places an equal burden on both assets maintains the income tax's relative imbalances.

One response would be to leave the solution to the drafters of the income tax. The root of the problem lies there, and income-tax law has in fact adopted measures to limit the most egregious preferences.[55] But we prefer an integrated approach that reduces the wealth tax for assets already subject to significant income taxation.[56] In effect, the taxpayer would pay an amount equal to the higher of the income tax or the wealth tax.[57] For lower-yielding assets, the taxpayer's total tax would be the wealth tax. For higher-yielding assets, it would be the income tax.[58] Such a hybrid system would narrow, but not eliminate, the "tax gap" between taxable and tax-preferred assets that now prevails.[59]

How much would this kind of integration cost? Although we do not have precise figures, we estimate the cost at roughly $55 billion per year.[60] As our Appendix explains, our wealth tax raises sufficient revenues to fund this additional cost.

### Foreigners

In a global economy, an increasing proportion of Americans' wealth will be held abroad, and the same is true for foreigners' wealth held in the United States. As far as American residents are concerned, we see no problem in taxing all their wealth, wherever it is located, much as we do under the current income tax.[61] Obviously, the same approach should not be followed with foreigners. As long as they keep their wealth outside the United States, we have no legitimate claim.

If, however, they want to take advantage of the American market, they should pay the tax and remain on a parity with U.S. investors. American tax law has only imperfectly followed this principle in the past. If a foreign company builds a plant in the United States, it is taxed as if it were an American venture. If a foreigner buys stock in a U.S. firm, he pays U.S. tax on dividends but not capital gains. And if he buys a bond, he escapes tax-free.[62] This patchwork reflects political pressure more than principle.

But for purposes of program design, we adopt the conventional approach.[63] Nonresident foreigners would be subject to a U.S. wealth tax only on U.S. real estate, U.S. corporate equities, and directly held business assets that are physically located in the United States.[64] The revenue impact is not trivial. Today, foreigners own nearly $900 billion of net U.S. assets in these categories—which would raise roughly $18 billion annually in wealth-tax revenue.[65]

It is true, of course, that foreigners will not gain the benefit of stakeholding, just as they do not now have the right to vote, to cross the U.S. border freely, or to claim other benefits of citizenship. But this should not be decisive. One of America's great attractions as an investment venue is its political stability, but this prospect is at risk without the ongoing effort to realize our nation's fundamental commitment to equality of opportunity. Foreigners should not be allowed to take advantage of our vaunted stability without paying their fair share of the price. More generally, the United States is something more than the richest free market in the world. It is a sovereign state devoted to the pursuit of justice. While we are emphatically in favor of opening our markets to the world, we reject the notion that any trader has the right to insulate himself from the efforts of the political community to anchor the market in its larger vision of legitimate order.[66]

Perhaps we should take note of a final problem. Won't some super-rich Americans respond to the wealth tax by renouncing their citizenship? If so, they should be barred from the country for life. If they wish to renounce America, let them do so. But they should really mean it.[67]

## Rewriting the Economic Constitution

Most of the taxes that we pay to the federal government flow into a vast fund of general revenue. This fund in turn provides our elected representatives with the resources they need to shift priorities over time—from defense to environmental protection, from welfare to job-training, and so on. We favor this kind of fiscal flexibility. Indeed, it would be downright undemocratic to take these inevitably contestable and constantly evolving matters of budgetary priority out of the hands of elected politicians. What else is Congress for?

But this presumption in favor of fiscal flexibility creates special difficulties at this stage in our argument. After all, we are not simply arguing for a new wealth tax. We want its massive new revenues explicitly dedicated to the special purpose of stakeholding. Why, then, do we propose to override our own presumption in favor of flexibility and make it especially difficult for Congress to raid the stakeholding fund for other worthy objectives?

We have precedents for our strategy. Social Security taxes are famously dedicated to old-age pensions, and gasoline taxes go into a trust fund earmarked for highways and mass transportation. But these are recognized exceptions to the general rule, and they have often been criticized. (Indeed, we will soon be questioning the particular kind of linkage that the Social Security system creates.) If we are to justify a new exception, we had better establish that stakeholding really does present an exceptional case.

Begin, then, with stakeholding's distinctively long-term perspective. Unlike many experiments in democratic lawmaking, here it would make no sense to enact the program in 2010 and then repeal it a couple of years later. Such a reversal would retroactively destroy the meaning of the initiative. When the first generation of stakeholders comes forward to make their claims in, say, the year 2011, they will do so as proud citizens inaugurating a new national commitment to social justice in America; a quick repeal would transform them into lucky winners of a national lottery. Stakeholding is an enduring social compact between young and old, between this generation and the next and the next. In short, it is a commitment of constitutional magnitude.

And one that can be readily expressed within the existing language of constitutional law. When the Founders sat down to write our enduring compact, the existence of slavery paralyzed their efforts to define American citizenship. Instead of endorsing white supremacy or directly challenging black slavery, the Founders utterly refused to define the sort of person who qualified as a citizen. Only after the Civil War were Americans in a position to define the concept in an explicit and affirmative fashion. The Fourteenth Amendment grants national citizenship to all "persons born or naturalized in the United States," and it protects their newly established "privileges" and "immunities" against impairment. The amendment did not take the next step, however, and enumerate the content of these privileges and immunities at greater length, leaving to subsequent generations the permanent challenge of making sense of its open-ended language. Some have been so intimidated by this task that they would have us ignore it entirely;[68] many have trivialized the privileges of citizenship by reducing them to a small number of relatively unimportant rights.[69] But neither approach captures the grandeur of the Framers' vision as revealed by the historical record.[70] While the amendment's Framers were confident about the fundamental principles of freedom and equality that they were adding to the text, they wisely left it to future generations to give concrete content to the privileges of citizenship as economic and social conditions changed over time.[71]

This is the point of stakeholding. By giving new meaning to the economic privileges of citizenship, it seeks to revitalize traditional constitutional commitments within the context of twenty-first-century realities. This aspiration in turn allows us to explain why we refuse to accept the presumption in favor of fiscal flexibility that normally accompanies tax policy. Quite simply, Congress should *not* be given great flexibility when it comes to protecting the fundamental privileges of citizens of the United States. Once a stakeholding fund is established, only specially exigent circumstances would serve as a politically acceptable reason for raiding the dedicated revenues. And this is as it should be.

This structural requirement diminishes the institutional gap that now separates the privileges of economic citizenship from privileges of other kinds. For example, when Congress passes a law repressing free speech, a citizen can readily go to court and ask it to strike down the statute. We would not go this far in protecting each citizen's right to a stake—because economic rights depend more on the vagaries of economic conditions, we would not put courts in the position of reviewing the legitimacy of future congressional modifications. But given the stake's likely centrality to the vitality of economic citizenship in the twenty-first century, we think it entirely appropriate to place a special burden of fiscal justification on future Congresses, lest they too lightly conclude that stakeholding is a luxury Americans can no longer afford.

Especially when the stake's tie to the wealth tax will graphically illustrate the nature of the problem that we collectively confront at the present moment. We are writing at a time when there is almost no public recognition of the deep injustices that the prevailing inequality of wealth threatens to perpetuate in the America of the twenty-first century. Under these conditions of heedless neglect, it is not enough to think about raising revenue technocratically. It is vital to use the funding mechanism to mobilize public support and convey that something *can* be done to respond to the market forces that are driving us apart.

The link between wealth taxation and stakeholding fulfills this need. The simple fact that a 2 percent wealth tax can fund such an immense improvement in the lives of ordinary Americans makes it plain how concentrated wealth has already become. It poses the issue fairly and squarely: are Americans still capable of using the democratic tools at their disposal to regain some modicum of equality of opportunity?

# 7

# The Limits of Growth—and Other Objections

We can now put our short-run and long-run perspectives together into an integrated proposal. Stakeholding comes onto the scene tied to an annual wealth tax of 2 percent, paid by all Americans whose individual wealth exceeds eighty thousand dollars at tax time. This form of financing continues unchanged for forty years or so until the first generation of stakeholders begins to die in large numbers. As financially successful stakeholders discharge their payback obligations at death, the wealth tax declines substantially—possibly, but not necessarily, reaching zero as the program matures into a second full generation. On the other hand, if trusteeship taxes are needed to sustain the program further, our successors should be invited to reconsider the form that these taxes take. Should subsequent generations continue to rely on a wealth tax? Or, if society has sufficiently advanced toward *genuine* equality of opportunity, would an income or consumption tax be more appropriate?

In developing this proposal, we have anticipated and confronted many objections, especially those likely to be raised by the libertarian camp. It is time to shift gears and confront more utilitarian critiques—those focusing on our initiative's impact on future growth rates. Do the new taxes and paybacks impose unacceptable burdens on economic growth?

We take this problem much more seriously than we do objections challenging the constitutional basis of our proposal. It will be news to most readers that there is any ground at all for constitutional doubt. But it is better to err on the side of caution and to briefly address potential legal concerns.

## Liberal Trusteeship Reconsidered

We cannot begin to grapple with the growth objection without placing it within a moral framework. Many politicians talk as if "growing the economy" were the answer to all the nation's problems. In contrast to someone beset with this growth fetish, the garden-variety utilitarian seems downright thoughtful. As we have already suggested, he does recognize that it may be counterproductive to require a relatively poor generation to scrimp and save in order to allow greater consumption by some future generation of richer Americans.[1] We share this skepticism. But we refuse to measure our obligations to the future in terms of aggregate welfare.

Our touchstone, instead, is the principle of liberal trusteeship.[2] Priority in time does not imply priority of right. Future citizens are our moral equals. When embarking on important decisions affecting their fate, we should test their legitimacy by imagining ourselves in dialogue with representative Americans of the future. By holding ourselves accountable in dialogue, we can build the foundations of a liberal community that endures over time. The challenge is to explain to our descendants how our basic decisions are compatible with their claims to equal citizenship.

This commitment to dialogic accountability generates a double-edged response to the problem of growth. On the one hand, it morally requires us to leave to Americans of the next generation at least the same endowment of resources, per person, that we have today. On the other hand, it does *not* require us to leave them more resources than we have had. We can, of course, choose to make a gift of growth. But we have no trusteeship obligation to do so.

To see why, imagine yourself in political dialogue with a representative citizen from the year 2060. Suppose that stakeholding had been adopted in the year 2010, along with the taxes and paybacks that make it possible. Suppose further that this package has had a modest negative impact on the economy: while the stakeholder society has continued to grow at a significant rate, it would have grown more rapidly had Americans remained content with the old inequalities. As a consequence, citizens of the year 2060 are not, on average, as rich as they might have been otherwise. But they remain a lot richer than we are today. Despite their greater per capita wealth, a hypothetical representative from 2060 insists that the taxes and paybacks required by stakeholding have done her generation an injustice: "You people of the year 2010 could have provided us with a bigger growth dividend had you not adopted this silly stakeholding idea," she asserts. "What gave you the right to deprive me of the extra resources?

This is not, we think, a very tough question. It suffices for us to respond: "We do not deny that, as fellow citizens, you are at least as good as we are. But you aren't any better for having been born later. You have no right, then, to insist on a larger share than the one we got. Because you remain better off than we were, we deny that our stakeholding decision has violated your claims to equal citizenship."[3]

To bring the implications of this conversation down to earth, we need to invoke a few empirical assumptions—but ones that seem plausible to adopt in setting real-world policy. Realistically, our generation runs the risk of failing to fulfill its trusteeship obligation in only two ways. First, we might blunder into a massive war. Second, we might ruin the planet through heedless exploitation of the environment. These risks shouldn't be minimized, but there is little that our funding proposals could do to control them. The best way to fulfill our trusteeship obligations is by adopting sane military and environmental policies, not by depriving millions of Americans of real equality of opportunity. As a consequence, we adopt a stance of technological optimism in addressing the growth objection. We assume that, barring military or environmental catastrophe, technological progress will generate real and steady improvement in living standards throughout the twenty-first century.

This assumption allows us to turn the tables on critics who condemn our wealth tax as antigrowth. The next section shows that these claims not only lack a convincing empirical basis but also fail to appreciate how different parts of our initiative interact with one another. But even if growth rates were to decline a bit, this fact would hardly be enough to condemn our initiative on trusteeship grounds. As long as the economy continues to grow, Americans at midcentury will still be far richer than we are today.[4] At worst, stakeholding will deprive them of some portion of the gift of growth that we will be giving them anyway.

But we deny that Americans of today have any obligation to make such a gift. In contrast, we *do* have a compelling moral obligation to do justice to fellow citizens rising to maturity in the next decade. Many of these men and women are among the poorest citizens who will ever exist in the future of the Republic. It would be wrong to deny them their fundamental right of equal opportunity merely to make rich Americans of the future even richer. We should not be giving gifts before we do our duty—and, as Americans, our duty is to do our part in sustaining the nation's fundamental ideals.

## Consider the Consequences

The utilitarian has not quite run out of objections. "Let's put aside the claims of the future. Won't *our* generation be worse off if stakeholding slows the economy? Thanks to the power of compound interest, even a reduction in the growth rate of, say, 0.5 percent per year adds up over thirty or forty years to a very hefty sum. Are you quite sure that young stakeholders would accept this long-run diminution in total welfare?"[5]

But even this more modest objection begs a big question. The problem is its focus on the welfare of society as a whole. The typical utilitarian is more than happy to reduce the resources available to the worst-off, provided that the utility gained by the better-off is even bigger.

We disagree. We focus instead on the position of the tens of millions of Americans who have been deprived of fair equality of opportunity. *Their* right to a stake should not be sacrificed simply to increase the growth dividend of those who began life in a privileged position.

This basic moral point has decisive practical significance. Even though the economy has grown mightily over the past quarter century, this great increase has not "trickled down" to every citizen. The growth dividend has instead been appropriated almost entirely by the top 20 percent, with the lion's share going to the very top.[6] Prospects look even worse in the future. There is every reason to believe that vast sections of the population will be increasingly left out.[7] Given this clear and present danger, it is simply wrong to deny Americans stakes merely to improve yet further the fortunes of those who make it to the top.

We do not deny that growth is good. Nor do we deny that an expanding pie does help ease social tensions and may inspire a more generous response from the upper classes (though this certainly hasn't happened recently). But because the growth dividend has not been widely shared, it is inadequate for efficiency-minded critics to talk vaguely about stakeholding's potential impact on aggregate growth rates. Instead, they should focus on ordinary Americans, not the elite, and explain why stakeholding will be counterproductive for this large group once its long-term impact on growth is taken into account.

But such a showing is not remotely plausible—at least if we keep within the parameters of serious economic argument and substantial economic data. Indeed, it is even possible that our initiative will encourage work, increase savings, and enhance growth. We do not pretend to certainty in this assessment; nor should our critics. Despite innovative work by many economists, we still know remarkably little about the effects of taxation on economic activity. Statistical models, methods, and data are often imperfect and incomplete, and results vary widely.[8] The research has produced no consensus on whether taxes reduce work and savings, and if so, by how much.

Before probing these mysteries further, let us begin with some certainties. The stake will serve as an unceasing engine of economic activity, as generations of young adults put their new resources to work in education and entrepreneurship. The program will also provide nest eggs for them to tap into during hard times, thereby encouraging citizen-stakeholders to take judicious business risks that they would otherwise have to avoid. Of course, lots of people will make mistakes. Many new ventures will fail, and some investments in specialized education will not pan out. But the ongoing empowerment of the most energetic Americans is sure to pay off over time in millions of innovations large and small, with a positive effect on economic and social life.

This pervasive "entrepreneurial effect" must be weighed against the more familiar "income effect": because many people will have more money, some may take advantage of the fact that they don't need to work as hard to support themselves and will therefore simply work less.[9] The likely magnitude of this factor is highly uncertain. For one thing, the stake provides a one-time grant, not a guaranteed lifetime income, and it is paid at a time when people are making choices about the course of their entire lives. Within this context, we doubt that many people will buy annuities so that they can reliably reduce their work hours.[10] Undoubtedly, there will be some who myopically exaggerate their "riches" and forgo useful education, training, and other productive investments in their future. While the newspapers will predictably linger over the plight of the no-goods who blow their stake in, say, a single night at Las Vegas, many more people will use it to get a start in an economically productive life. We should also be skeptical of standard economic notions of "work." If a woman spends extra time at home with her children, it is question-begging to suppose that she has dropped out of "productive activity." Taking the matter as a whole, we believe that the gains to education, entrepreneurship, and strong, stable families will far outweigh the foolishness that stakeholding makes possible.

Turning to taxes, we have a more complicated story. Despite endless political rhetoric about the "economic damage" caused by "high taxes," serious empirical work tells a more cautious tale. European experience provides one example. It is fashionable to claim that "big European welfare states" have been economically discredited.[11] But as recent work by Geoffrey Garrett suggests, the causes of slow European economic growth are complex and may mask a positive association between growth and generous welfare provision.[12]

In any event, we are in a very different position in the United States. Even after the adoption of stakeholding, the total tax burden as a percentage of gross domestic product would remain well below the average for OECD countries.[13] While international tax-rate comparisons are always tricky, this simple statistic should allay concerns that stakeholding would propel the United States into the tax stratosphere. And, once again, the destination of the tax revenue matters quite a bit. Stakeholding is an investment in youthful energy, not a cradle-to-grave safety net, and the program should help fend off, rather than promote, European-style interventions in the labor markets.

Turning to the home front, recent research suggests that people are less responsive to tax rules than was supposed by an earlier generation of economists.[14] Consider one widely studied issue: how responsive are savings to changes in tax rates? Early estimates suggested that savings were relatively elastic, but more recent studies conclude that savings are hardly responsive at all.[15] The emerging consensus regards savings as relatively inelastic.

The responsiveness of labor supply to taxation is also relevant. Although our wealth tax is imposed on capital, not wages, labor decisions may be influenced by workers' savings plans. A person who is inclined to be a saver may work less if he knows that his accumulation will be diminished by a wealth tax—or he may work harder to ensure that he continues to save enough to meet his goals. How does the tradeoff work out in reality?

Studies consistently suggest that the labor supply of working-age men is rather insensitive to changes in the net wage.[16] But there is more controversy about the labor supply of married women, single mothers, and teenagers.[17] Speaking broadly, the data are at least tentatively on our side: the modern trend is toward a certain skepticism about the effect of taxes on work and savings decisions.[18]

The wealth tax will undoubtedly add to the cost of doing business for foreign investors. But this is hardly the only cost relevant to their decisions. At present the country manages to compete very well despite its wage rates, environmental regulations, and so on.[19] Not only does its enormous wealth and talent serve as a magnet, but so does its political stability. Because stakeholding will vastly enhance this last attraction, it is very hard to guess what or how large the marginal impact of the wealth tax would be.

Over the longer term, wealth-tax rates will decline, as the first generation of stakeholders begin to die and repay their eighty-thousand-dollar stakes, with interest, to the fund. This mandatory payback generates a new set of incentive problems: won't it discourage work and savings by donors, particularly if the desire to leave bequests is an important motive for saving?[20]

Even if these anxieties prove to have empirical substance, they will not be on a scale that raises large normative problems. As we have suggested, Americans of the year 2060 are likely to be far richer, per capita, than those living today—and are almost certain to remain so even if the payback requirement reduces the growth rate a bit. As a matter of public morality, it is far more important to provide the next generation with a fair system of stakeholding than to tolerate increasing inequality in the name of greater growth.

What is more, economists continue to disagree about the crucial empirical issues, including the effect of the estate tax on donors' work, savings, and consumption; the importance of bequest motives for saving; and the significance of inherited wealth in the total capital stock.[21] To take just one example: even if strong dynastic ambitions drive people to accumulate large estates for their heirs—a simplistic picture of intergenerational relationships—the higher tax could encourage them to save more, not less, in order to realize this goal.

The payback requirement should also be understood as part of an intergenerational compact: those who started out in life with help from the liberal community have an obligation to pay it back if they succeed. Although skeptics will undoubtedly grumble, we do not believe that most Americans will look upon the payback as just another tax to be evaded if possible. Many may even come to look with pride on contributing their fair share to a polity in which inheritance is a universal right of citizenship rather than an accident of family ties and fortunes. No econometric model can account for the effects of such moral incentives.

## Is It Constitutional?

This is America, and undoubtedly some brave soul will take stakeholding into court, raising the cry of unconstitutionality. But we do not think that the prospect of a lawsuit should scare anybody—if stakeholding wins political support, the courts will readily recognize its legitimacy.[22]

The Founding Fathers' campaign for a new constitution was motivated in large part by the fiscal anemia of the old government, which was operating under the Articles of Confederation. Under the Articles, the Continental Congress could "requisition" the states for revenue, but it was powerless when these demands were ignored. The Founders proposed to put things right and were not content with half-measures. They began their enumeration of congressional powers with the broad grant "to lay and collect Taxes, Duties, Imposts, and Excises." Over the course of the next two centuries, the courts consistently upheld this power against taxpayers' efforts to whittle it down.

With one great exception. In 1895, at a time of economic depression and rising class war, the Supreme Court struck down an income tax by a vote of five to four in *Pollock v. Farmers' Loan and Trust Company*. The verdict did grievous institutional damage to the Court. It also led to a successful generation-long campaign to reverse the decision, which culminated in the Sixteenth Amendment in 1913. Even *Pollock* did not challenge the plenary power of Congress to impose those taxes that it believed furthered the cause of distributive justice. Instead, it struck down the income tax by distorting the meaning of a narrow constitutional provision that had been a part of the Founders' original compromise with slavery in 1787.

At that time, North and South struggled over slavery's implications for taxation and representation. In an obscene reversal of roles, each side took the other's moral position for bargaining purposes. The North wanted to maximize its political power by taking the South at its word: if slaves were property, they should no more be counted for purposes of representation in the House than cows or bank accounts were. The South protested that blacks were humans, too, and should count no less than white women or children for purposes of reckoning the number of House seats that the slave states received. The result was the notorious "three-fifths compromise." The southerners would get to count three-fifths of their slaves to enhance their representation in the House, but only at the cost of using the same ratio when it came to raising revenue—in the language of the time, representation and taxation would be linked by the "federal formula." To seal the bargain, Section 9 of Article 1 forbade any "Capitation, or other direct, Tax" to be levied "unless in proportion" to the federal formula that treated black slaves as if each were three-fifths of a human being.

Against all precedents, the *Pollock* majority ripped this clause out of its originating context and declared that an income tax amounted to a "direct" tax that required apportionment by the federal formula. To be sure, the formula had been changed as a result of the Civil War—blacks now counted as full citizens. Nevertheless, the decision led to bizarre results. Suppose that two states had equal populations but unequal wealth, State X containing a single millionaire, State Y containing a thousand. If income-tax liability were apportioned by population, both states would have to come up with the same amount of money. This, in turn, would require the single millionaire from State X to pay at a vastly higher rate than did the thousand millionaires from State Y.

Given this absurdity, courts consistently construed the "direct tax" clause very narrowly during the nation's first century, self-consciously treating it as an anomaly generated by the slavery compromise. *Pollock*, in contrast, transformed this relic of slavery into an engine of class war. In the words of the great dissent by Justice John Marshall Harlan, the decision "cannot be regarded otherwise than as a disaster to the country. . . . It so interprets constitutional provisions, originally designed to protect the slave property against oppressive taxation, as to give privileges and immunities never contemplated by the founders of the government."[23] In view of twentieth-century Americans' popular rejection of the decision, in the form of passage of the Sixteenth Amendment, we cannot imagine any future court walking down this road again.

It is quite true that in recent years the Supreme Court of Chief Justice William H. Rehnquist has begun to challenge modern constitutional ideas that give the federal government virtually plenary legislative powers. For example, the Court has struck down a federal statute banning guns in and around public schools, finding that this local matter was not embraced under Congress's constitutional power to regulate "commerce."[24] But in building a five-to-four majority for this conclusion, Chief Justice Rehnquist was careful to write an opinion that effectively conceded the national government's powers to regulate the economy. As far as taxing and spending are concerned, the Court has been even more cautious. There is every reason, then, to suppose that the Court will respond to our taxation initiatives as courts have traditionally responded through the centuries—by upholding the federal government's power to use the tools of taxation to further the majority's vision of social justice.

## The Next Step

We are under no illusions about this opening volley in the debate over stakeholding. While we would be surprised if critiques from the constitutional experts get off the ground, we will frankly be disappointed if we do not hear a lot more from our other critics—libertarians, utilitarians, and others too numerous to mention. Silence would signify only that we have failed to place our proposal on the public agenda for serious debate.

This is, of course, a very real possibility. It is beyond the power of any single book to determine whether our children or our children's children look back to the turn of the twenty-first century as a time when Americans revitalized their traditional commitments to equal opportunity for all. The best that we can do is to pose the question and make the case for a positive answer—if not to stakeholding, then to some better idea.

But it is not too soon to sound a more hopeful note. If the debate over stakeholding does take off, it can invigorate a much broader discussion over the direction of progressive reform. We have already seen, for example, how our basic proposal opens up new vistas in areas of public policy ranging from the criminal law to higher education. The next part of this book proposes to expand the range of potential reform yet further.

# Part 2

## Expanding the Stake

# 8

# From Worker to Citizen

Stakeholding challenges the basic priorities of the welfare state. Traditionally, the main concern has been with the provision of safety nets, most notably to the elderly. Our focus has been on the provision of equal opportunity, most notably to young adults. This new emphasis raises new concerns. Does our emphasis on younger Americans suggest a shift in the traditional treatment of the elderly? Does our stress on opportunities require a revised understanding of safety nets?

Our short answer is yes. Some safety nets ought to survive in the stakeholder society, but they should be reshaped in ways that better express America's evolving commitments to equal freedom for all. To suggest the needed reorientation, we focus on the system of retirement pensions bequeathed to us by Franklin Roosevelt. Although the New Deal system represents a great social achievement, it falls far short of the standards of justice made possible through an expanded version of stakeholding.

We will be contesting two New Deal decisions. The first keyed pensions to Americans' histories as workers rather than their status as citizens. This rule has had an especially devastating impact on women whose principal contributions occurred at home and in the community. Unless they qualify as spouses of "real" workers, they continue to be excluded. And many of the women who have moved into the marketplace continue to be shortchanged.[1]

In a second decision, Roosevelt sold Social Security as an insurance policy, with payroll taxes serving as the "premiums."[2] This metaphor has helped sustain the program's political appeal, but it has embedded in Social Security a host of morally questionable class distinctions that split Americans apart when they turn to collect their pensions.

Stakeholding points the way to a fairer system by liberating Social Security from the workplace. In contrast to the New Deal, which emphasized worker citizenship, our proposal would guarantee each American a citizen's pension, one that does not depend on her history as a wageworker. Under the reformed system, each American will be free to choose a mix of market and nonmarket work without endangering her basic economic security in old age. Nor will her pension depend on her marital choices or the economic fortunes of her partners.[3] It will assure her basic dignity in old age regardless of her decision to stay in the home and volunteer in the community rather than work for pay. The change from Social Security to citizens' pensions will not have quite the same revolutionary consequences for wageworkers. But it will vastly increase the fairness of the system for them, too—or so we will argue.

The experience of other countries establishes the practicality of citizens' pensions. Although they are unfamiliar to Americans, they play prominent roles in Canada, Denmark, Finland, New Zealand, Iceland, Norway, and other countries.[4] Admittedly, such a large change in American practice could take place only gradually, for the present generation has relied on the present system while planning for their own retirement. But for illustrative purposes, we will be speaking as if our citizen's pension program guaranteed each American $670 a month, or $8,040 a year, at the age of sixty-seven—the amount that is compatible with present levels of tax payments into the Social Security fund.[5]

Our initiative will not only deepen and broaden each citizen's claim to a dignified retirement. It will also open up a much-needed debate on how we finance public pensions now. As long as payroll taxes are treated as premiums for an insurance policy, they are tied into the sacred guarantee of Social Security for the elderly. Despite the growing tax burden, ordinary workers believe that they must pay into the trust fund if they hope to get anything back during their times of need.

But once retirement is secured to each citizen independently of the workplace, payroll taxes will no longer seem an inextricable part of the social insurance bargain. Rather than seeming like premiums, payroll taxes will begin to look like *taxes*—and regressive ones, at that. For the first time since the 1930s, the public will be prepared for a serious search for a better funding system.

There are many options here, but Chapter 9 presents a novel proposal that seeks to further our underlying commitment to genuine equal opportunity. As always, we do not wish to present our readers with an all-or-nothing reform. If our plan for financing citizens' pensions is found wanting, more traditional financing alternatives would work, too.

## Why Social Insurance?

To begin, let's be clear about the kinds of safety nets we are and are not talking about. A liberal state should take a different stance with respect to economic protections for adults than it does with respect to those for children. Adults are entitled to a stake, but thereafter they should generally be held responsible, within certain principled limitations described below, for their own well-being. Children are an entirely different matter. Because they haven't reached maturity, a liberal state has much greater obligations to them, including the responsibility to provide special care if they are disabled or in need of medical attention. Protections for children must also consider the parents or guardians who care for them. But these are subjects for another book. We do not suppose that they can be handled within the stakeholding framework.

We deal here only with the extent to which the liberal state may justly require *adults* to insure for their own future support. To set the stage, imagine that a hopeful Joan Doe, age twenty-one, arrives at the Stakeholding Office to claim the first installment of her eighty thousand dollars. Much to her chagrin, there is a final catch: she has to endure a discussion of the rich variety of social safety nets that the welfare state provides throughout life and especially in old age. To her surprise, these latter-day benefits are worth quite a substantial sum.[6] As this fact sinks in, Joan asks: "Why can't I simply cash out all these benefits? I'd much rather have a bigger stake now and take care of myself later." What to make of Joan's demand? Can a liberal state legitimately require its citizens to wait for these payments until they encounter a special need later on in life?

No, says the libertarian. Perhaps he would seek to assure himself that Joan has soberly considered her options. He might even require a compulsory interview with a team of smiling representatives from private insurance companies. But in the end, it is up to Joan to make her choices and live with them. Fifty years onward, Joan may bitterly denounce the shortsighted and unfeeling decisions of her youthful self, but the libertarian will remain unmoved. Her plight is her own doing, and she is free to throw herself on the charity market for relief.

This unhappy scene can only confirm the utilitarian's worst suspicions about his dogmatic opponent. This is what happens when one focuses myopically on freedom of choice and fails to construct a social policy that maximizes Joan's happiness over her entire lifetime. After all, the young Joan's myopia is entirely predictable. When she is twenty-one years old, she cannot reasonably be expected to sympathize with or even fully comprehend the pain and suffering of old age. Yet, whatever the young Joan might think, that little old lady she sees on the street will be her one day. Rather than deferring to the youthful Joan, policy-makers should study the plight of the elderly, as they exist today, and then design a sensible benefit package that will protect the next generation as it ages. This package will soberly and impartially weigh the welfare gains of the old against the costs of insurance suffered by the younger generation of taxpayers. Once this difficult balance has been struck by the political process, the youthful Joan has no right to complain. She will be grateful when the time comes to collect her benefits.

We are approaching a familiar impasse: individual freedom versus collective welfare. Is there a way out? Or should we simply grit our teeth and take sides in this classic debate, ignoring the pull of the competing arguments?

## A Third Way

Our effort to define a third way begins with the libertarian's focus on the individual. The concrete decisions made by young adults are much more morally significant than the utilitarian recognizes. When we choose marriage partners and careers, we are *constituting* our very identities in ways that we cannot subsequently eradicate. It seems odd, then, to discount altogether the moral significance of Joan's early decisions as to the proper shape of her life. If she thinks that it makes more sense to sink her capital into a small business now rather than to save it for old age, surely this decision is entitled to some independent weight. Once again, the utilitarian's single-minded concern for maximizing welfare stands in the way of an appropriate respect for individual freedom.

But at the same time, we challenge a fundamental assumption of the libertarian position, which makes the youthful Joan the absolute tyrant over her future. For us, she is best viewed as a trustee for her future self and is not entitled to discount the predictable objections that she will raise at a later point. Against the forward-looking Joan of twenty-one, we place the backward-looking Joan of seventy-five: how certain can we be that she will bitterly regret her youthful choices?

Obviously, a lot of guesswork will be required to generate sensitive answers. But this is no reason to reject the enterprise, as the trustee-ship failures of the youthful Joan may be too blatant to ignore. From the liberal perspective, these failures in *intrapersonal* trusteeship provide the moral foundation for mandatory insurance.

## Two Forms of Myopia

As she enters her stakeholder interview, Joan will suffer from two kinds of shortsightedness. The first involves a failure of sympathetic understanding. Perhaps a twenty-one-year-old has a good grasp of the way her attitudes will evolve through the age of thirty. Perhaps she has a rough image of herself at the age of forty. But things get fuzzy after that. Can she really imagine how she will feel at the age of fifty if she is "downsized" by her firm and cannot find a market for the skills that she has spent her lifetime developing? Can she really appreciate the indignities of old age?

Of course not. We should distinguish a range of relevant temporal horizons.[7] When dealing with the near term, we tend to the libertarian extreme: it is up to Joan, and not the state, to decide how much insurance she needs. We would make exceptions only for insurance that covers dire calamities beyond the normal range of experience. Nobody really has the capacity to comprehend sympathetically the plight of the paraplegic victim of an auto accident. If Joan refuses to insure against the consequences of such events, we would be prepared to doubt her capacities as a good trustee. But we would second-guess Joan's judgments very cautiously and sparingly.

As we move forward in the life cycle, we are more skeptical of the youthful Joan's exercise of her powers of trusteeship. When it comes to her interests as a seventy-five-year-old, we must compare her guesses about her uncertain future with the real lives of today's elderly. There is a tradeoff here. On the one hand, Joan might have a better sense of the idiosyncratic ways in which she may differ from the average seventy-five-year-old. On the other hand, social scientists will have a more informed sense of the standard set of complaints and disabilities suffered by the old.

We can generalize this point to the life cycle as a whole. Within earlier time horizons, Joan's sense of her particularities makes her the more reliable trustee. But because the structure of her life experience will inevitably change, perhaps dramatically, over the years, her present guesses become increasingly unreliable with each decade's remove, and collective experience becomes a superior guide for later time horizons. The switch may come at different times for different decisions. Joan's guesses about her needs for health insurance may be better than her guesses about her future demands for retraining. In the design of a nonnegotiable package of minimum insurance, a lot of this nuance will be lost in the bureaucratic search for broadly applicable standards. The important point is that a liberal state can retain a focus on the individual without adopting the indefensible libertarian notion that the youthful decision-maker is always the best judge of her future interests.

We have introduced the problem of myopia by emphasizing its psychological dimension—young people may not meaningfully appreciate the different life circumstances that they will encounter as they age. But there is a second form that deserves distinct treatment. It would remain if psychological failure did not exist. Even if Joan could vividly picture her future condition as a seventy-five-year-old, she may deliberately discount these interests in favor of those appearing at an early stage in the life cycle: "I *know* that I will be miserable at seventy-five, but it's more important to cash out some of my insurance so that I have a shot at running my own business. Overall, this is the best life for me."

Is this myopia, or a sober recognition of life's limitations? It begs a big question to treat "moral myopia" as if it were analogous to the psychological variety. As liberals, we do not believe it is the state's job to second-guess Joan on the best shape of her life. Of course, when Joan does reach seventy-five, she might bitterly reject her younger self's tradeoffs. But it is also possible that she will take great pride in her past decisions: "Even though I might not have much today, I'm glad I was my own boss during all of my working years." We reject, then, the claim that this second form of myopia is necessarily bad. Liberal citizens have the right to shape their lives in a variety of ways over time, and liberal policy-makers should take this right into account.

This point complicates, but does not undermine, our case for compulsory social insurance based on the first form of myopia. Practically speaking, youthful adults haven't the foggiest idea of the problems they will encounter fifty years down the line. This justifies us in rejecting Joan's demand at the stakeholding interview for the cash value of all her future social insurance benefits. Instead, we should craft her compulsory insurance package in light of her predictable myopia regarding her own life cycle. While the state should not force Joan to insure against most short-term risks, it should be willing to impose a more substantial package insuring against predictable problems arising in her remote future. Even here a certain caution is justified. The more money we put into the insurance package, the less flexibility we are affording youthful Joans in shaping the overall pattern of their lives.

### Moral Hazard and Adverse Selection

Although we have given pride of place to the principle of intrapersonal trusteeship, it would be a mistake to slight more familiar rationales for compulsory insurance. These seek to define contexts in which the private insurance industry cannot be relied upon to deliver adequate protection. One important market failure is defined by the theory of "moral hazard," which points to the disconcerting way in which private insurance may sometimes encourage the very behavior that the insured would otherwise reject.

To develop this point in the context of retirement pensions, consider the status of a means-tested pension in the stakeholder society. Thus far, our argument seems to endorse means-testing: given the youthful Joan's psychological myopia, the state should not allow her to cash in all of her retirement insurance. Instead, it should hold some money back so as to provide her with a citizen's pension of $670 a month at age sixty-seven if she ends up completely destitute. But if she wants more than this, she will have to buy private insurance, either out of her stake or out of subsequent earnings.

All this seems sensible until the "moral hazard" factor enters. The problem is that the means test itself may cause Joan to behave differently. Assume, for example, that Joan is willing to save enough during her working years to supplement her state pension and enjoy a secure retirement at $1,300 a month. But once the citizen's pension of $670 is means-tested, she may begin to think strategically—and act myopically. Should she forget about saving, spend all her money during her working life, and rely on the $670 provided by the state?

This is not her first-best choice—she would prefer to have $1,300 a month instead. But because she would lose all claim to the means-tested pension if she saved for this larger sum, her original life plan is now less attractive. The fundamental problem is that the government cannot readily detect Joan's strategic behavior. At age sixty-seven, Joan will have no assets and no income—and will demand her pension on the same basis as impoverished people who were never in a position to save for retirement.

The moral hazard problem will raise the overall cost of means-tested pensions. But more fundamentally, it imposes another burden on Joan—one measured not in dollars and cents but in individual freedom. The means test increases the same myopic behavior that it is intended to relieve. The relatively prudent Joan will begin to act as her more shortsighted peers do, reshaping her life plan in second-best ways that she would otherwise reject.

This is a serious problem for liberals. Can we ameliorate it through program design? The obvious answer is to abolish the means test. By telling Joan that she will receive $670, regardless of her other assets, we eliminate the moral hazard problem because she no longer must impoverish herself to get her state pension.

But only at the cost of creating another problem. In order to eliminate the means test, we will have to impose higher taxes or reduce Joan's initial stake. In short, we must strike a balance between two kinds of burdens on Joan's life-shaping capacities. With the means test, Joan will have more resources for her younger years but will have a strong incentive to dissipate them. Without the means test, she will have fewer initial resources but more freedom to shape her later years.

There is no mechanical way of resolving such tradeoffs. Speaking for ourselves, we resolve them against the means test. Experience with means-testing demonstrates that the moral hazard problem can be severe. In Australia, for example, means testing had a devastating impact on citizens' planning for their later years. As many as 75 percent of the elderly received the means-tested old-age pension, and most spent down their assets to obtain the full benefit.[8] Even more troubling is the stigma that means-testing has traditionally carried in our culture. This response is altogether inappropriate given the underlying reason for the program, which is not to provide welfare for charity cases but to ameliorate the predictable myopias that almost all of us experience when young.

A second form of market failure—adverse selection—is also important. The problem is generated by another asymmetry of information: Joan knows more about her present plans than anybody else does, and she may exploit this advantage in dealing with private insurance companies. This point is particularly relevant in the assessment of near-term risks. On moral grounds, we have urged extraordinary caution in the provision of near-term guarantees. But once adverse selection is taken into account, a somewhat more expansive approach may be justified.

Consider the case of unemployment insurance. Private companies will have great trouble determining whether Joan is about to launch herself into a career as an actress or as an accountant. Worse yet, if Joan can convince the company to sell her the low-cost unemployment insurance it reserves for would-be accountants, this may encourage her to try acting.

As a consequence, most private insurance companies will steer clear of these kinds of policies. At best, they will offer unemployment insurance at very high rates, encouraging only the worst risks to sign up, which in turn will lead to higher rates and lower coverages, in a destabilizing cycle.

Given this grim alternative, mandatory unemployment insurance looks more attractive. Granted, it diminishes the resources available to stakeholders, and it cannot solve the moral hazard problem. But there is a compensation in enhanced life-planning capacity. It may be the only feasible way of providing unemployment insurance for the many Joans who would want to buy it if it were available on the free market.

These market failures provide a second liberal rationale for mandatory social insurance. Similar problems of adverse selection plague private markets for disability and health insurance, providing a potential empirical argument—though not necessarily a definitive case—for mandatory provision.[9] Once again, there is no simple algorithm for weighing the enhanced freedom of some against the diminished freedom of others. However we design these programs, there will be some Joans who could have done better.

We should keep in mind the moral distinction between the two justifications for social insurance programs—market failures and trusteeship failure. Programs that respond to life-cycle myopia should be universal rights of citizenship, financed by broad-based taxes—just as stakeholding and citizens' pensions are. But market-correcting programs may legitimately have a narrower compass, in both their coverage and the taxes that finance them. By definition, market-correcting programs are simply substitutes for insurance that significant numbers of private citizens would like to buy, and so their terms can be tailored accordingly. Unemployment insurance, for example, might provide coverage only for unemployed wageworkers (and not homemakers).[10] In that case it ought to be funded by a payroll tax on covered workers—with premiums matching coverage—and not by a broader-based income tax.

### The Liberal Case for Old-Age Pensions

Working out the practical implications of these two principles is a long, complex, and contestable business. The responsible management of each important risk—unemployment, disability, illness, accident, entrenched poverty—requires separate and sustained analysis. Each proposed solution has consequences for the control of other risks. Rather than losing ourselves in this forest of complexity, we focus on the single issue of retirement pensions. Not only has Social Security, as "old-age insurance," served as the cornerstone of the New Deal legacy, but our liberal principles suggest that it thoroughly deserves this central position. As we have seen, it is naive to suppose, with the libertarian, that the young stakeholder is an adequate trustee for the basic interests of her seventy-five-year-old self.

At the same time, our principles suggest a more tightfisted approach than that offered by standard utilitarianism. The level of old-age pensions should not be determined on the basis of some freewheeling comparison of the pleasures of youth against the pains of old age. It should be set with a deep appreciation of each American's right to be different. These differences extend to disagreements about the shape of life as a whole and which periods of life are most important. For some, it will be crucial to arrange their affairs to assure a very comfortable old age; for others, it will make sense to stint on retirement and invest more heavily in earlier stages in life. The aim of liberal policy is not to second-guess these choices by supposing that everybody "ought" to save a lot for retirement if they are to maximize their happiness over their lifetimes. Its mission is more modest but more fundamental. It is to protect elderly citizens against the worst consequences of their earlier psychological myopia. The watchword is not utility maximization but the assurance of dignified existence in old age.

"Dignity" sounds nice, but what precisely does it mean? Old people will predictably need a minimum level of resources in order to avoid a constant stream of stigmatizing social encounters. Of course, determining this minimum will be an endlessly contestable matter, for it depends more on social meaning than biological necessity. The kinds of clothing, food, transportation, and shelter that lead to endless and profound embarrassment in one society might be perfectly compatible with a dignified, if spartan, existence in another. This line cannot be drawn technocratically. Its proper definition, we shall argue, should be at the center of ongoing democratic debate. But for now, it will suffice to advance our basic standard: although younger stakeholders should be given broad freedom to shift resources from one life stage to another, they should not be allowed to put this dignity-stripping minimum at risk. Despite the youthful Joan's bright plans for her next twenty years, the liberal state should intervene when there is a serious risk that Joan herself will bitterly condemn her own foolishness when she reaches old age.

## Rethinking Social Security

How does our proposed citizen's pension compare with existing arrangements?

There are many important divergences, but all have their root in a single difference. While the New Dealers took the ideal of economic citizenship quite seriously, they did not use it as the basic criterion organizing their emerging Social Security system. Under the New Deal regime, it is not enough to be a citizen to qualify for a retirement pension. You must also be a worker in the cash economy and must work long enough to make a substantial contribution to the pension fund through your payment of Social Security taxes. Only then can you and your spouse qualify for a retirement pension.

By linking payroll taxes to pensions, the New Dealers created a powerful rhetoric of economic entitlement. As far as the ordinary American is concerned, Social Security pensions are not public handouts because workers have earned them by paying their payroll taxes. This simple intuition is based on something that we will call the private insurance analogy, because it supposes that each worker is paying for his own retirement pension as if he were paying premiums into a private pension plan.

We do not deny the rhetorical power of this analogy. To the contrary, its public appeal was demonstrated recently when President Bill Clinton simultaneously led an attack on "welfare as we know it" while posing as the champion of Social Security. Progressives should think long and hard before abandoning Roosevelt's evocative symbol, given

its proven power to resist libertarian critique in the rough-and-tumble of political combat. Nonetheless, we believe that stakeholding provides an organizing metaphor that will prove equally robust against political attack—and at the same time provide a fairer basis for dignified retirement in the future.

It is true, of course, that in our brave new world, Americans will no longer believe that they have earned their pensions by paying "premiums" in the form of payroll taxes. But the stakeholding analogy has the power to create the same sense of fundamental entitlement that the insurance analogy creates today. Henceforth each American will receive his vested right to a retirement pension at the same moment when he receives his cash stake. Just as he will expect the state to keep its hands off "his" eighty thousand dollars, he will respond with similar outrage to any threat against "his" basic pension rights. By bundling vested pension rights into the cash transaction, expanded stakeholding will stand as a vivid symbol for the proposition that Americans *do* have a right to a dignified retirement. But rather than rooting this right in the insurance analogy, our new metaphor makes it part of a vibrant sense of American citizenship in a stakeholding society.

More than symbols are involved. After a half century's experience with the insurance analogy, we are in a position to see that it fuels a cascading series of morally questionable distinctions. At present, progressives are so impressed by the rhetorical advantages of the insurance analogy that they blind themselves to its darker side. We hope that a systematic contrast with stakeholding will shine some light.

### What's Wrong with the Insurance Analogy

For starters, the insurance analogy is false. The payroll taxes paid by individual workers are not actually a market price for the benefits they get. Although the patterns of redistribution are complex, high earners generally get a lower return on their contributions than low earners.[11] There is also a generational redistribution at work: Americans who retired during the first fifty years of the program have received much more than they "bought," and future generations will receive less.[12]

All this is, by and large, OK with us. Saying that high earners have a lower "rate of return" is just another way of expressing the progressive redistribution that Social Security accomplishes. There is also a reasonable case to be made for pay-as-you-go financing, which essentially makes Social Security a current expense of government.[13] Although Congress has been too eager in recent decades to buy elderly votes with fiscally unsustainable benefit increases, reasonable reforms can put the system back on a sound footing.[14]

The larger problem is that voters do not realize that the insurance analogy is myth from top to bottom. Taxpayers have been taught from an early age to think of "their" contributions as buying "their" pension payments. As a result, critics from the right can invoke the insurance analogy in support of "privatization" and other reforms that would gut the progressive redistribution achieved by the current system. If Social Security is just like private insurance, why shouldn't rich and poor alike get their money's worth?[15]

In contrast, expanded stakeholding places the right to a dignified old age on a different moral foundation. Rather than accepting libertarians' efforts to present Social Security as if it were a defective form of private insurance, we challenge the basic premise behind the analogy. We reject the libertarian view that each American's fate in old age ought to be exclusively a function of insurance decisions made at earlier stages of life. Instead of authorizing this tyranny of the younger self, a liberal state legitimately seeks to correct the predictable psychological myopias involved in these private insurance decisions.

In short, it is a mistake to base the case for public pensions on *any* analogy with the private pensions that Americans obtain through the insurance market. A stakeholding society guarantees a dignified old age precisely because a decent minimum will *not* be invariably achieved in an insurance marketplace controlled by myopic youngsters. Instead of allowing elderly Americans to reap the bitter harvest of their myopia, it is far better to intervene on behalf of these later selves beforehand and protect their fundamental interest in avoiding an old age of want and shame.

### Holes in the Safety Net

Because this interest is universal, it should be protected universally—and it should not depend upon the contingencies of each citizen's connection with the labor market. This does not happen under the New Deal system, which consigns large numbers of Americans to second-class citizenship. The overwhelming majority are women, who often spend many years out of the paid workforce or in low-paid part-time work while they raise their children. The insurance model provides them with little or no independent Social Security coverage. In 1996, for example, 65 percent of elderly female Social Security recipients received benefits based at least in part on their husbands' work histories.[16] To be sure, wives' and widows' benefits are a major source of economic security for elderly women.[17] But the insurance analogy ties their economic fate to their husbands'—provided they have them.

Even during the New Deal, the original designers were wrong to ignore the problem of family instability. But in an era of high divorce and declining marriage rates, the economic security of many women hangs on a complex and arbitrary set of rules.[18] An elderly wife with no earnings history can claim a "spousal benefit" based on her husband's work history.[19] But a divorcée can claim the same benefit only if her marriage lasted at least ten years. Otherwise, she is treated as if she had never been married and will receive a pension only if she has a long-term work history.[20] And because women's wages remain a fraction of men's, these pensions are often very low.[21]

All this would change in a stakeholding society. Instead of claiming derivatively through their husbands, all women will stake their own claims to a citizen's pension. Many may have worked in their families and communities without receiving much in the way of market wages. But this does not make their contributions to society any less fundamental.° Converting Social Security into citizens' pensions would grant equal respect to every American, without privileging some life plans over others.

### The Arbitrariness of "Wage Replacement"

The insurance analogy also authorizes gross forms of class discrimination among the elderly. Because different workers earn different wages, they pay different amounts of payroll tax each month. As long as these taxes are considered premiums, it seems "natural" that workers who pay more into the fund should take more out in retirement. And this is precisely what happens under the existing system. In 1996,

---

° Although citizens' pensions entitle every man and woman to an individual benefit, they would change the relative position of married and single retirees, leaving some widows worse off than under the current system. Today, a married couple often receives 150 percent of the retired worker's basic pension, while a widow succeeds to 100 percent. In our system, the couple receives 200 percent of the basic citizen's pension, and the widow receives 100 percent. For example, the widow of an average earner who retired in 1996 at age sixty-five would receive at least his benefit of $886 per month. Under our program, both he and she would receive $670 per month during life. After his death, she would continue to receive her own benefit, but nothing more. The citizen's pension is also less than what the average elderly widow received in 1996 ($711 per month), although this average conceals the wide disparities discussed in the text, whereas our reform establishes a uniform floor. See Social Security Administration (1997), table 5.A16.

Is the treatment of the widow under citizens' pensions harsh? We think not. During her husband's life and after his death, she receives the same pension as any other citizen, man or woman, single or married. If there is any harshness here, it is in the size of the pension; but if $670 is too low, then it should be raised for all, and not just for widows.

The underlying issue here is life insurance. If the couple did not buy insurance for the surviving spouse, why should the government provide it? Intrapersonal trusteeship is not at issue. Unless there are pervasive market failures that would prevent the life insurance market from working appropriately, it should be up to each citizen-stakeholder to determine her and her family's needs for life insurance.

for example, high earners typically collected around $1,250 per month at age sixty-five, while low earners collected an average of $537.[22] And many of the elderly received even less than that.[23]

A shift to a uniform citizen's pension of $670 a month, or $8,040 a year, would provide a dramatic increase to pensioners at the bottom and a perceptible lift to a broader group. Thirty-nine percent of elderly Social Security recipients—nearly 11 million in all—received less than $650 a month in 1996.[24] Fifty-six percent of all elderly women, and 41 percent of widows, would receive more than they did in 1996.[25] It is true that some women, especially wives and widows of high-earning men, would receive less than they do today. And some married couples would see their benefits fall. But benefits would be just as large or larger for about 51 percent of retired couples who now collect Social Security.[26]

These contrasts frame a basic moral question: why should a Wall Street lawyer—or his wife—get so much more *out of Social Security* than a factory worker does?[27]

The italics are crucial. We do not deny each citizen the right to enhance his public pension by buying private annuities. To the contrary, private pension planning is a fundamental tool enabling each citizen to shape the overall contours of his life. But it is one thing to say that everybody should be free to invest as heavily as he wants in a comfortable retirement, quite another to say that the public treasury owes skilled workers and their spouses more than it owes unskilled workers.

Defenders of the status quo will be quick to point out that Social Security's benefits are distributed progressively—the higher-paid receive a smaller return on their contributions than their lower-paid age-mates do. But once we abandon the insurance analogy, this kind of progressivity is no longer enough. Measured by the yardstick of a universal, flat-rate citizen's pension, the insurance analogy is authorizing everybody in the solid middle class and above to double-dip into the pension funds.

This is precisely backward if, as we have argued, the point of public pensions is to provide a minimally dignified old age for all. While we oppose means-testing,[28] we certainly do not see why the public treasury should be more generous to those who are least likely to be living on the edge.

Perhaps there was greater justification for such largesse when the system was established during the 1930s. At that time, the private market had not yet developed the plethora of pension options available today. Many members of the middle class might have encountered substantial transaction costs in buying extra annuities from private insurance companies. Given this market failure, it might have made sense for the government to step in and give richer workers the opportunity to obtain higher pensions. After all, the more you earn, the more likely it is that you will want to save for a comfortable retirement. And if private companies weren't ready to step in to provide you with what you want, shouldn't the government step in to fill the gap?

Whatever the validity of this market-failure rationale in the 1930s, it is a nonstarter today.[29] And yet standard discussions of Social Security regularly miss this point. The buzzword among experts is "wage replacement"—the notion that a public pension system should replace a certain percentage of a worker's wages before his retirement.[30] Defenders of Social Security argue that wage replacement helps cushion workers against the "shock" of retirement, when their accustomed living standard might otherwise drop dramatically.[31]

This is a worthy objective. But in a world of well-developed private markets, an individual worker should be allowed to decide for himself how much of his wages he wants his private pension to replace. As long as the state has provided a minimum that assures against dignity-stripping poverty, each citizen should be given freedom to make basic life-shaping choices on his own responsibility; if he decides to save less in middle age in order to pursue other life objectives, the government has no right to second-guess this choice.

## The Incentive Question

How will the adoption of citizens' pensions affect the economy?

By breaking the link to employment, citizens' pensions reduce the lifetime payoff to market work for many workers. If they currently think their wage includes extra Social Security benefits in old age, some will work less under our system.[32] But for other workers, our system will be an outright boon. Many wives pay Social Security payroll taxes for decades only to find that they receive no more than the standard spousal pension available to those who have never worked for wages in their lives.[33] The new system improves the situation for this large group, making work more attractive. Because women's work effort tends to be more responsive to tax changes, this effect will help cancel out any work reduction for men.

All in all, there is nothing in the economics of the proposal for citizens' pensions that provides a reason for agonizing reappraisal.[34] If anything, the elimination of heavy existing penalties on women's work is a large plus, which will help offset any potential disincentive effect caused by breaking the link to employment for male workers.

## The Dark Side

But there is a dark side. While stakeholding will abolish a complex set of discriminations based on family structure and economic class, it will create something new in its place. Suddenly citizenship will become important in defining pension rights, potentially leaving a new group out in the cold. At present, noncitizens qualify for Social Security pensions if they have put in their time in an American workplace. What should their status be under the new system?

We would include them. Although noncitizens would not qualify for the cash portion of the stake, those who spend a substantial period of time in America should be allowed to take advantage of the minimum established for pension rights. The length of the required period of residence is a matter for good-faith judgment. But the basic principle seems clear enough: by contributing substantially to America for a substantial part of their lives, these people have earned a reciprocating gesture in their old age.

This is, of course, a value judgment, and one that might not be endorsed by the majority when the political process plays itself out. Suppose Congress shortchanges the noncitizens or cuts them out entirely. What then?

This would be a serious blight on our initiative. Nonetheless, we do not think that it would be as invidious as the set of family and class distinctions authorized by the existing program.

## Asking the Right Question

We have not yet reached the end of our indictment of the insurance analogy that currently shapes Social Security. Apart from its substantive deficiencies, it grievously damages the quality of our deliberative process. As we have seen, the effort to define a public pension requires a collective engagement with a seemingly simple, but actually quite perplexing, question: how big a cash pension is big enough, if the goal is to provide retirees with a dignified old age in our society?[35]

A thoughtful answer requires a collective confrontation with incommensurables. A dignified old age is not merely a matter of eating enough calories and staying out of the cold. It is a question of receiving enough income to live in a way that avoids ongoing social embarrassment and affront. But how much is enough? To make matters harder, it is quite possible to be too generous—the higher the minimum deemed necessary for a dignified old age, the less life-shaping freedom is allowed the young. How, then, to make the tough choices?

By an appeal to the democratic process. A technocratic solution seems impossible, as does an answer achieved by reason alone. All one can properly say is that defining this minimum requires an informed and sympathetic understanding of the plight of the elderly, a sober recognition of the counterbalancing importance of saving most resources for more youthful projects, and a great deal of democratic debate.

To be sure, each generation of stakeholders has a right to know, well in advance, the dollar amount of their citizens' pensions, for only then will they be in a position to determine how much more they may want to save for retirement. But over time, it is reasonable to expect that the minimum will shift as the democratic debate proceeds.

The worst thing about the existing system is its distortion of the crucial terms of this debate. The insurance metaphor tells the middle and working classes that they have *earned* their benefits. Under the influence of this image, public debate has focused, not on the question of minimum entitlement, but on whether workers are getting their money's worth in exchange for the "premiums" that they have paid in the form of payroll taxes.

Of course, facts have a way of creeping into the conversation—in this case, the fact that Social Security utterly fails to provide an adequate pension to millions of elderly Americans.[36] Unsurprisingly, these gaps have proven socially unacceptable, leading to the gradual creation of a patchwork of second-class protections. These allow destitute retirees to claim minimal relief from the public treasury.[37] Theoretically, a focus on a fair minimum should be central in the design of this lower rung of our two-tier system. But because this tier is occupied by the most powerless people, the debate has an overwhelmingly paternalistic tone: "normal" people don't need to worry about a minimum; this is a problem only for the "failures" in life.

Consider how the entire question would be reframed under our initiative. Every five years or so, the stakeholding office should be required to prepare a report outlining a series of pension options to Congress. For purposes of illustration, assume that our expanded stakeholding system began with a citizen's pension of $670 a month, to begin at age sixty-seven, which is the sum implied by redistributing existing Social Security revenues along the universalistic lines we have been advocating.[38] Once this baseline has been established, the stakeholding office should be required to compute high and low options. For example, instead of remaining content with the baseline of an eighty-thousand-dollar stake and $670 a month in old age, should Congress change the mix of stakeholding rights so that the next generation would receive a ninety-thousand-dollar stake and a smaller old-age pension of $670 *minus x* dollars a month? Or should it cut the cash stake to seventy thousand dollars and increase the pension component to $670 *plus x* dollars a month?

These questions turn the definition of the minimum amount needed for a decent life into a problem for everybody, not just the "failures" in life. As a consequence, the painful inadequacy of existing definitions of minimal entitlement would become immediately apparent. At present, the standard starting point for public discussion is the official "poverty line." Despite its prominence, it is based on mechanical adjustments to an arbitrary benchmark.

It is downright embarrassing to reflect on the origins of this statistic. In the mid-1960s, Social Security Administration economist Mollie Orshansky cobbled together a rough poverty measure based on just two facts: the cost of a basic subsistence diet (the "economy food plan"), and the percentage of the average American family's budget spent on food in 1955 (one-third). Putting these together, Orshansky calculated a basic subsistence budget, equal to the cost of the economy food plan times three. She then counted as "poor" any family with a cash income less than this basic budget. Since then, the only attempt to add sophistication to this crucial benchmark has been a periodic adjustment for inflation.[39]

Contrast this malign neglect with the constant debate over the benchmarks central to Social Security and Medicare. Politicians have not been able to evade the necessity of addressing controversial issues, despite their legendary status as political hot potatoes. Do cost-of-living adjustments adequately reflect changed conditions? Are Medicare Part B premiums fair to different groups of beneficiaries? And on and on.

It is only the legacy of the New Deal that accounts for this two-tiered debate. Within the stakeholding framework, all classes will share a common interest in defining the floor for social insurance. A higher citizen's pension means a lower stake for everybody, and vice versa. Everybody will be confronting the same problem: how to trade off *ex post* insurance against *ex ante* stakes?

Not everyone will give the same answer,[40] but one thing is clear. The poverty line as currently constructed would be completely unacceptable to all. To be fair, Orshansky did describe her calculations as "quasi-scientific," and she never intended them to be used as the exclusive benchmark for public debate.[41] Most fundamentally, "poverty" is not merely a matter of "economical food plans" or other measures of "preference satisfaction." The relevant inquiry is better framed in social and psychological terms. Will the typical American be able to hold her head up high when she retires? Will every appearance in public be an occasion for embarrassment? The challenge is to provide graphic information about the resources required for different forms of life in old age, and thereby enable informed discussion and ultimately democratic decision. While American researchers have begun fieldwork that will allow public policy to move beyond Orshansky-style measures,[42] we are calling for something more than a few isolated efforts. In a stakeholding society, there would be a real interest in funding ongoing research that sought to link different life patterns in retirement with different pension levels.

Suppose, after listening to a broad base of testimony, Congress votes for the package of a stake of eighty thousand dollars and a monthly pension of $670. In casting their ballots, our representatives would be doing something more than choosing some numbers. They would be linking equal opportunity, market freedom, and dignity into an organized set of public values. Not only would the vote for eighty thousand dollars express a deep commitment to the ideal of equal opportunity; by giving each stakeholder full sovereignty over the money, Congress would be affirming the fundamental value of market freedom. Not only would the vote for the $670 pension express a deep commitment to the ideal of a dignified old age; it would make it plain that our public commitment to market freedom has its limits. This integrated affirmation of equal opportunity, market freedom, and human dignity would occur, moreover, within a larger framework that links an enhanced conception of economic rights to a renascent understanding of the importance of citizenship.

Equal opportunity, market freedom, human dignity, individual rights, economic citizenship: that's a lot for a couple of numbers to say.

# 9

# Taxing Privilege

Now suppose that America has expanded stakeholding to include old-age pensions. Citizenship, not the workplace, has become the centerpiece of a universal right to a dignified old age.

This large step forward will serve as a catalytic reform, pushing yet another big question onto the public agenda. Having lifted retirement benefits out of the workplace, one of the great pillars of the existing system of public finance suddenly loses its function. We are speaking of the payroll tax, whose status would immediately become a bone of contention.

Most Americans don't realize that this tax has revolutionized public finance in the past generation. In 1960, payroll taxes contributed only 15.9 percent of federal revenue; now they contribute 35.6 percent, as rates have more than doubled.[1] During the same period, the share raised by the income tax has declined from 67 percent to 56 percent.[2]

Our fastest-growing tax is one of our most regressive.[3] Even in these days of Republican ascendancy, the income tax takes more from the marginal dollar of rich people than from that of poorer people. But the payroll tax ostentatiously gives the rich an exemption. Poor workers pay tax on every dollar, but the richest workers pay at a vastly reduced rate once their wages go beyond $65,400.[4] Below this point, all workers pay a flat 7.65 percent, and employers kick in an equal share. It is generally recognized, moreover, that this "employer's share" is passed on to workers as well.[5] In sum, the tax reduces the pay of ordinary Americans by more than 15 percent but reduces the pay of a professional manager making $200,000 a year by only 6.95 percent.[6]

Payroll taxes are now more onerous than the income tax for most ordinary Americans. A two-earner family with two children must earn more than $80,000 before its income tax exceeds its payroll tax of $12,357.[7] Why, then, have protesters and politicians chosen to hurl their abuse at other targets: property taxes on the local level, taxes on income and capital gains, and even on estates, on the national?

It is too easy, although not entirely wrong, to see this as a triumph of public relations by the rich. After all, not only do they pay reduced rates for high wages, but the payroll tax entirely exempts their capital income. What could be better than to divert populist protesters in other directions?

And yet it would be a mistake to underestimate the importance of our old enemy: the insurance analogy. As long as payroll taxes are treated as premiums, they are inextricably joined in the public mind to the fate of Social Security. This means that any effort to cut or restructure payroll taxes is readily framed as an assault on cherished principles of social solidarity. Ordinary workers understandably refuse to rebel at payroll taxes, which promise their only guarantee of security in old age.

But once stakeholding removes old-age pensions from the workplace, it will become painfully clear that the payroll tax has served as a primary vehicle by which the rich have shifted their fiscal burden onto the middle and lower classes over the past generation.[8] Of course, *some* tax is required to continue to fund the social insurance system.

But once the insurance analogy has been exploded, we must return to first principles and ask how this sum might best be raised.

An obvious choice would be the income tax, but we prefer to think more broadly. Is it wise to jack up income-tax rates whenever progressives need more money? Or are there other, no less progressive, ways of proceeding?

We have already pursued a diversifying strategy by promoting a wealth tax, rather than an income tax, as the primary source of revenue for our basic stakeholding proposal. We follow a similar approach here, broadening the traditional mix to include something we will call the privilege tax.

Our case for the tax begins with some sobering reflections on the ultimate limits of stakeholding. Even if our initiative were fully realized, America would have a lot more work to do before achieving a rough approximation of equality of opportunity.

To some extent, the problem is rooted in the dynamics of a free society. After all, free choice in the marriage market hardly guarantees family stability—and children will often bear the brunt of the ensuing breakdowns. Even if all families were loving and stable, different parents would gain vastly different rewards in the marketplace and offer their children very different arrays of educational and social opportunities.

This much may be the inevitable consequence of life in a free society, but the current social response to inequality of fortune is not. When a child is shunted into a series of foster homes and fifth-rate schools, this is not the inexorable consequence of freedom but the avoidable failure of public institutions. It is here, of course, where stakeholding's limitations become plain: while our program for young adults will have constructive long-term consequences on child rearing,[9] the major role in equalizing opportunity at earlier stages of life must be discharged by other programs, ranging from Head Start through foster care and primary and secondary education. As long as we have not achieved breakthroughs on these fronts, stakeholding will not be enough to inaugurate a regime of fair and roughly equal opportunity.

We have not let these points distract us from making our proposals. Only fools look for panaceas—no single initiative will suffice to achieve an ideal as complex and demanding as *genuine* equality of opportunity. For this book at least, we cannot take on the larger task of addressing the problem of inequality during early childhood. Instead, we limit ourselves to a single and pessimistic question, which supposes that America continues to allow many of its children to grow up without first-rate educations and other essential support systems and that, as a consequence, young adults will continue to emerge from disparate backgrounds with vastly unequal advantages. The mere fact that they each receive eighty thousand dollars is hardly enough to afford them genuinely equal opportunity. Can tax law take any further steps to ameliorate, if not to eliminate, the consequences of these gnawing initial injustices?

If this is the question, our new privilege tax is the answer. We propose to fund our program of citizens' pensions by requiring each American to pay a tax based on the degree of privilege that she enjoyed during childhood. Our measures of unequal privilege will inevitably be crude, and this is one of the reasons that the privilege tax will be relatively modest. But it will have a progressive feature. A child born to unusual privilege will pay a higher tax than one born into severe disadvantage.[10]

Our privilege tax reflects the liberal life cycle. Until citizens reach the stakeholding age, at twenty-one, they pay no privilege tax. But payment is due every year from age twenty-one to age sixty-seven—until they qualify for their citizens' pensions.[11]

Everybody should pay something. It is a privilege to be an American citizen, as millions of would-be immigrants attest. Even those in the lowest privilege class will make a modest annual payment of, say,

$380.[12] Adults coming from the most privileged backgrounds will pay a multiple of this, say, $3,800 a year. If the average American pays a privilege tax of $2,090 a year, this will completely replace those payroll taxes presently funding retirement benefits. If the privilege tax catches on, we would go further. A tax of $6,300 on the most privileged, $3,465 on the average American, and $630 on the least privileged would allow us to eliminate *all* payroll taxes for Social Security and Medicare—payments that cost the average worker $3,935 per year in 1996 (Table 1).[13]

Politically speaking, it is hard to assess the long-run future of the progressive privilege tax. The idea is so novel that it may take a while to sink in. While everyone realizes the reality of unequal opportunity, it may seem discriminatory to take this fact into account in setting taxes. But any tax falls more heavily on some than on others, and the unique strength of the privilege tax is that its burden falls squarely on the recipients of unjust privilege. Empirical work also suggests that the privilege tax will be progressive in the more familiar sense—measured either by income or by educational achievement.[14]

Table 1.  Three Options for the Privilege Tax

| Option | | Tax liability ($) |
|---|---|---|
| 1. Replace current payroll taxes that fund | High | 3,800 |
| Social Security benefits to those over age 65 | Middle | 2.090 |
| | Low | 380 |
| 2. Replace payroll taxes needed to fund current | High | 4,500 |
| Social Security benefits on an actuarially | Middle | 2,475 |
| sound basis, without benefits reduction | Low | 450 |
| 3. Replace current payroll taxes that fund | High | 6,300 |
| Social Security and Medicare | Middle | 3,465 |
| | Low | 630 |

Source: 1996 data. See detailed discussion of methods and data in the Appendix.

In any event, people will have plenty of time to get used to the idea. Our initiative will emerge with full force only after a generation-long transitional period. When all is said and done, the privilege tax lacks the immediate political appeal of other elements in our program. It remains a *tax*, and who can get very excited about replacing one tax with another?

Nonetheless, there is a surprising amount to be said on its behalf.

## Privilege in America

Americans don't like to talk about class. But the facts speak for themselves. Millions of Americans get a head start simply because they are born into privileged circumstances. Many others are disadvantaged during childhood and stay that way for life.

The statistics are strikingly consistent. Children who grow up in poor households are more likely to become teen mothers, to drop out of high school, to accumulate fewer years of education, and to perform worse on cognitive tests.[15] Children whose parents did not complete high school are much more likely to become dropouts themselves.[16] The adult children of the poor are more likely to be unemployed as young adults and more likely to be on welfare.[17] Although there is significant controversy over the role of money in causing these divergent outcomes, the correlation is strong and widely acknowledged.[18]

When we turn to the high side of the social scale, the link between money and prospects is obvious. SAT scores are strongly correlated with parental income.[19] High-income students can more easily afford special coaching, remedial help, and private schools.[20] And because they are more likely to attend prestigious private colleges, they have better odds of being admitted to graduate and professional schools.[21] All these advantages are particularly valuable at a time when the economic returns to higher education are high and rising.[22]

We are, of course, dealing with averages, and many deviate from the typical profile of economic attainment. We can all think of successful people from humble backgrounds, and privileged people who fail to make good use of their advantages. But class background still matters, especially for the 75 percent of Americans who do not graduate from college.[23] For example, a son whose father's income was in the bottom quarter of the income distribution has only a 39 percent chance of earning more than the median income himself. But a son whose father's income was in the top 5 percent has a 76 percent chance of earning more than the median and a 42 percent chance of being in the top 20 percent.[24] Over all, even the youngest men from the richest fifth of America's families earn significantly more ($26,168 per year) than those from the poorest fifth ($16,772 per year).[25]

None of this, we repeat, is really controversial. Liberals and conservatives disagree only about the causes of these yawning disparities. The present debate focuses on the causal role of low income in generating bad outcomes for children. In the classic view, poverty itself is an important cause of failure. Revisionists argue that the personalities and cultural deficiencies of parents cause both their low incomes and harmful child-rearing practices. In this view, parental income is merely correlated with the child's later performance, but the causes go deeper.[26]

This is an important debate for anybody trying to design a responsible program that seeks to confront the root causes of unequal opportunity. But this is not, alas, our present concern. Rather than attempting to root out inequality, we are merely asking how tax law might seek to ameliorate some of its morally indefensible consequences. It would be far better if Americans had both the knowledge and the political will required to launch a deep-cutting initiative. But at the very least, we believe that tax law should take into account the overwhelming data documenting a significant correlation between childhood privilege and adult advantage.

To be sure, we would not see "perfect" economic mobility even in a stakeholding society that went beyond the guarantee of eighty thousand dollars to secure each child a first-class education and a stable home environment while he was growing up. Once all Americans had been assured a level playing field, inequalities would still result from differences in inherited cognitive abilities (though recent studies find that "no more than 10 to 15 percent" of income differentials are associated with such factors).[27] But it would be cruel, as well as intellectually suspect, to attribute the existing correlation between class background and economic success principally to the workings of individual choice and inherited talent.[28]

## The Case for a Privilege Tax

In assessing a higher privilege tax on the children of the rich, we do not need to inquire too deeply into the causes of their enhanced self-esteem, social connections, and economic opportunities. It is enough that they have them, that other citizens don't, and that these differences are attributed not to random misfortunes but to the systematic distribution of advantage from the earliest days of childhood.

Of course, it is conceptually possible to tax all these advantages away, leaving the scions of privilege to rue the day that they were born on Park Avenue. But our proposed schedule falls far short of this. Granted, a taxpayer in our top bracket will pay about $1,700 a year more than most Americans. But few would say that this cancels out the enormous social advantages of speaking fluent and standard English, going to an elite private high school or to a prosperous high school in the suburbs, and being surrounded with eager guides to the skills of social advancement and the mysteries of college selection. Taxing privilege instead of payrolls is simply a way of bringing the principle of equal opportunity in touch with the facts of American life.

To put the point another way, contrast the situation of two successful American families, each with two professional parents earning $100,000 a year as lawyers. One couple reaches the yuppie heights after negotiating the challenges of a privileged childhood in America's suburbs, moving on to Harvard, and then marrying each other while they were students at Columbia Law School. The other two come out of the slums of America's big cities, work their way through state universities and law schools, and then scramble their way to success. As far as income and payroll taxes are concerned, each family's $200,000 is treated equally. But is this really right? Wouldn't replacing the payroll tax with a privilege tax add a useful dimension of fairness?

These questions seem especially worth asking in the present context, where we are trying to find a suitable funding source for retirement pensions. As we have seen, the liberal case for these pensions depends on each young adult's obligation to see his current circumstances as belonging to only one phase in a larger life cycle and to take the interests of his future self into account. But if we push this life-cycle point further, it leads to a distinctive argument for privilege taxation.

A simple chart can illustrate our point. Contrast the lifelong situations of three representative American citizens who enjoy very different levels of privilege during childhood (Table 2). The plus signs, zeros, and minus signs represent differential privilege while growing up. This, in turn, is capped by the egalitarian gesture of stakeholding—

Table 2. Privilege and the Liberal Life Cycle

| Privilege level | Stage 1: childhood | Stage 2: ages 21–24 | Stage 3: maturity | Stage 4: old age |
|---|---|---|---|---|
| High | + | $80,000 + ? | ? | $670 per month + ? |
| Standard | 0 | $80,000 + ? | ? | $670 per month + ? |
| Low | – | $80,000 + ? | ? | $670 per month + ? |

marked by the entry for eighty thousand dollars in all three columns. Then come the question marks signifying the manifold ways in which free men and women combine their early backgrounds with their stakes to live a bewildering multiplicity of lives, yielding very different results. After this long period of freedom, a fixed and equal quantity enters once again into each citizen's profile. Under expanded stake-holding, each citizen receives a minimum pension for his or her old age, here denoted by $670 per month, although each is free to increase it by any amount he or she chooses, here denoted by question marks representing private pension savings during earlier stages of life.

Within this framework, we are proposing to link the first and last phases of a citizen's life. Because the government will have to raise the money for citizens' pensions from somebody, isn't it fair to ask the most privileged to put more money into the kitty?

America would be a much better place if the government had effectively intervened to provide a first-class learning environment to all children, regardless of the wealth of their parents. If all three representative citizens in our table had begun adult life from roughly equal points, we would be the first to reject the privilege tax. But we will be far, far away from this ideal condition for a long time to come. And in the meantime, it is only fair to tax those who have profited from unequal opportunity.

So far, we have been talking the language of justice. But a second range of arguments becomes available once we shift our terms to questions of efficiency and tax neutrality. As any economist will tell you, the payroll tax imposes a "deadweight" loss on our economy. Because workers fork over 15 percent of hourly wages to the social insurance fund, they can't take into account their full marginal contribution to the production process.[29] If, for example, a worker generates $10 an hour, he gets to take home only $8.50 after the payroll tax has done its work. This in turn distorts each person's decision about how much and how hard to work.

Different people respond to lower effective wages in different ways. Some may work fewer hours, retire early, or remain unemployed. Others may work harder to achieve their aims in life. But our objection to the payroll tax does not stand or fall on predictions about its overall impact.[30] Regardless of how each worker responds, there is a larger principle of political legitimacy at stake: the state offends liberal commitments to neutrality among ways of life when it singles out wages for specially detrimental tax treatment, penalizing work relative to other life choices.[31]

The privilege tax lifts these distortionary burdens. Each taxpayer's payment will now be keyed to the level of his privilege as a youngster and will not affect marginal incentives at the workplace. Generally speaking, workers will take home more of the marginal revenue that they produce and hence will more efficiently make the inevitable tradeoffs between work and other aspects of life. A deadweight loss will be removed from this inevitably difficult decision.

Some efficiency-minded critics may respond skeptically to this basic point. Although they may concede that our new tax removes a distortion from the choices made by the younger generation, they may argue that the tax simply displaces the burden onto their parents. Once high-income parents realize that their economic success comes at the cost of imposing a heavier privilege tax on their children, they may respond by working and saving less.

This is possible, but not very likely. Under our proposal, parents will have to sacrifice nine or more years of high income during their children's early years in order to reduce their adult children's future tax bracket.[32] Within this structure, even very altruistic parents would be silly to cut back on their family's present income to create tax benefits for their children in the remote future.[33]

In short, the privilege tax looks like the sort of neutral tax that economists dream about. As we shall see, the rigidity of the tax—its persistent focus on the enduring consequences of early childhood advantages—has vices as well as virtues. Indeed, it will sometimes seem unfair to impose the tax on adults who have utterly failed to make income-producing use of their early childhood advantages. For this reason, we will support the creation of an "escape hatch" from high-privilege tax brackets under special conditions. But as long as we make it tough to use the escape hatch, our efficiency and neutrality arguments will remain largely intact.

All things considered, there seems a lot going for our basic idea. After all, in matters of taxation, it isn't too often that justice and efficiency point in the same direction.

## Designing a Privilege Tax

How might privilege taxation actually work in practice?

The most obvious problems involve the measure of "privilege." There are plenty of rich kids who have miserable childhoods; many poor children grow up with admirable discipline provided by loving families. Don't these complexities preclude any attempt at determining a fair basis for the privilege tax?

No, but they do motivate a two-pronged approach. The first prong is based on the well-documented truth that wealth generally has its privileges. The second prong is more finely tuned to the particularities of individual cases. Under a suitable showing of hardship, high-privilege taxpayers should be given an opportunity to escape into a lower bracket. There is nothing particularly original about this two-part structure—the law uses it to manage innumerable problems in all areas of life. Nonetheless, each part deserves extended discussion.

### Defining Privilege

We propose to measure privilege by looking at one, and only one, feature of each child's environment: the amount of money that his parents earn while he is growing up. Not only is money the most measurable unit of social power, but it also correlates with enduring advantage. Perhaps poor parents provide their children with poor opportunities because they have absorbed deep "cultural pathologies" that disable them from adult achievement. But it is not necessary for the tax authorities to probe into such contestable realms of cultural critique. It is enough for them to know that poor children, for whatever reason, systematically underperform on a wide range of economic and social skills that are useful in a vast array of life patterns.[34] Although other factors—like parental education—may be even more strongly correlated with a child's relative disadvantage, there is no readily administrable way to measure them.[35]

The same points hold when we seek to assess superprivilege. Tax authorities need not consider whether the advantages of growing up with rich parents are caused by the superior role models that they provide, by the first-rate education that their money buys, by direct transfers of cash, or by social connections. It is enough that parental income is roughly correlated with all of these things.

This said, the crucial first step in calculating a privilege tax is well within the existing bureaucratic capacities of the Internal Revenue Service—at least for the children of the 150 million Americans who file income-tax forms each year.[36] Since 1987, parents have had to report their children's Social Security numbers in order to claim the tax exemption for dependents.[37] This should be enough to establish a sound basis for a two-bracket privilege-tax system. Stakeholders coming from high-income families will be assigned to a higher tax bracket than the bulk of Americans. Our own calculations indicate that the top bracket will include about 20 percent of American taxpayers—representing adults who spent nine or more years of their childhood in the very highest income group.[38]

Tougher problems arise in implementing a lower bracket for disadvantaged taxpayers. About 20 percent of the total population spends seven or more years of their childhood in the lowest-income group.[39]

The question is how to identify them. Many have never filed income-tax returns, many have never been on welfare, and in any event, current welfare records are a mess.[40]

The solution is to cast a broad informational net. Taxpayers should be invited to proffer several kinds of proof. Evidence of a prolonged stay in foster care or a long-term spell on public assistance should serve as reliable indicators. More difficulty enters when the taxpayer seeks to infer disadvantage from a negative. For example, the Social Security Administration has extremely good records of earnings and payroll-tax payments that stretch over decades. It should be quite easy, then, to prove that one's parents reported low or nonexistent earnings. But what if they earned lots of money off the books?

Happily, the system will have plenty of time to grapple with these difficulties. A complete transition from the payroll tax to the privilege tax will take a full generation. For the first decade or two, the privilege tax, if used at all, would be of quite modest dimensions and could be readily handled by a two-bracket system—dividing the top 20 percent from the remaining 80 percent.[41] By the time privilege taxes become substantial, we should have a better informational base for a three-bracket system.

### Policy Questions

Once the basis of privilege has been defined, a series of policy decisions will be required to assign each taxpayer to an appropriate bracket. Computers would be used to calculate parental income during each of a taxpayer's first eighteen years of childhood. The highest—or lowest—seven to nine years would determine whether the taxpayer would be in the high, medium, or low bracket.[42] The use of a longer period, and not a single-year snapshot, will generate a better indicator of overall advantage and reduce incentives for tax gamesmanship.

We also think that a certain sophistication is called for in designing an appropriate rate schedule. Instead of hitting twenty-one-year-olds with the full privilege tax, the rate should increase gradually until it reaches full strength at, say, age thirty-five, by which time most people will have settled into their solid earning years.[43] At this point, we would leave the rate unchanged until the taxpayer qualified for a citizen's pension, at which point the tax would drop to zero. Of course, we have no stake in the precise schedule. Should a twenty-one-year-old pay 40 or 60 percent of the privilege tax paid by a thirty-five-year-old? Should payments begin to decline when the taxpayer reaches fifty-five?

We take a similar approach to other key policy questions. Most obviously, how should a child in a five-child family earning $200,000 be compared to an only child with the same family income?[44] What about children of divorced and remarried parents?[45] How can we ensure that high-earning parents do not report artificially low incomes through the use of nontaxable fringe benefits, deferred compensation, tax-exempt bonds, and the like?[46]

While we explore a range of options in the endnotes, it makes no sense to search for a single "right" answer. As in many other areas of tax law, the best we can do is to design a sensible compromise. These exercises in drawing lines should not divert us from the big picture: we all know that a significant percentage of children do indeed enjoy systematic privilege, and we should not allow quibbles on the margins to obscure this central fact. The ruling categories of tax law have never captured the nuances of life. The question is whether these new tax brackets will create a system that is a lot fairer than the regressive payroll-tax categories they will displace.

## Escape Hatches

The rough-and-ready character of the privilege brackets suggest the wisdom of allowing "hardship cases" to take advantage of an escape hatch. Because high parental income is only statistically correlated with enduring economic and social advantage, taxpayers should be allowed to establish that they are exceptions to the general rule. An overriding aim should be to avoid bureaucratic intrusion into highly personal and contestable matters. The IRS should obviously not be interested in the subtle emotional abuses visited upon a taxpayer by her rich parents. It should focus only on the taxpayer's revealed economic behavior. If a superprivileged person fails to make much income year after year, this is the best evidence that the statistical correlation does not accurately reflect the facts of her upbringing. A similar escape hatch should be available for a person in the average privilege bracket whose consistently low earnings suggest that she too may be suffering from hidden disadvantage. But in either case, a person should be able to move down a notch (or two) on the privilege scale only by showing very significant economic hardship.[47]

We should also design the escape hatch to prevent predictable abuses. Law and medical students, for example, go through long periods of low pay as a preliminary to a lifetime of high earnings. It would discredit the system if John D. Rockefeller IX could escape his high-privilege bracket by demonstrating low income during his years at Oxford and the Yale Law School. University students, then, should not be allowed to use their years of "poverty" as evidence that their upbringing was less privileged than it seems.[48]

A second problem arises when a taxpayer's reported income fails to convey her effective command over resources. Given our individualistic bent, we envision each citizen filing her own privilege-tax return. But this will lead to trouble whenever a taxpayer can reliably depend on others for support in ways that do not show up on her tax return. Consider the married couple whose income is earned almost entirely by one spouse. Because the IRS does not require the nonearning spouse to report half the family income as her own, she will mistakenly appear to be poor and potentially eligible for a tax-bracket downgrade.[49] But the answer here is better bookkeeping: for purposes of the escape hatch, each spouse should report half the couple's total income. Income will also be a poor measure of economic status in a few cases because wealth is invested in low-earning or tax-exempt assets. But the new wealth tax will provide a useful alternative measure of tax-paying capacity.[50]

As a third safeguard, we would make the income (and wealth) threshold for tax relief quite significant. Simply because a child of privilege chooses to become an elementary-school teacher rather than a businessman, he should not be allowed to escape paying his fair share. After all, many fellow citizens were never given the effective opportunity to make such choices. It is only if a privileged person consistently earns less than, say, 175 percent of the poverty threshold that the IRS should take his claim seriously.[51] And the income threshold for moving into the lowest privilege bracket should be even stricter, requiring a below-poverty-level income for an even longer period.

Opinions will differ as to the best place to draw the line. Some may even conclude that the bureaucratic complexity involved in creating escape hatches outweighs the potential for individualized justice—especially once the risks of bureaucratic arbitrariness and corruption are entered into the scales.

We do not agree.

### Problems of Enforcement

With the escape hatch put aside, a final question of administration arises: how can we ensure that people pay their privilege taxes? And what should be the penalty for nonpayment?

For most people, enforcement will simply piggyback on the income- and wealth-tax systems. When you file your income- or wealth-tax return, you will have to declare and pay your privilege tax too. Wage withholding during the year could be increased to reflect tax-payers' privilege-tax brackets. And tax evaders would be subject to the usual penalties: seizure of assets and income. Because the amount of the privilege tax will be fixed and known in advance, the IRS's only enforcement task would be to find individuals and, if they don't comply, their assets.

But things will be harder at the bottom. Because poor people are exempt from income taxes, it may be tough to find them if they fail to pay their privilege tax. Without the payroll tax, the IRS could no longer use these computerized records as a cross-check—although we might want to maintain them for just this purpose. And welfare records, kept by the states, may be inadequate to the task.

Finally, there is the enforcement problem posed by people who keep their activities off the books. Although this is a real problem under the existing income-tax system, it will be harder to evade the privilege tax. To see why, consider that only people who entirely avoid the notice of the IRS can hope to escape privilege taxation. In contrast, people can cut their income taxes by working partly off the books. Instead of underreporting sales a bit here and taking an exaggerated deduction there, as income-tax evaders do, privilege-tax evaders must make the leap into clearly fraudulent, intentional tax evasion and must stay well out of sight if they're not to get caught. This will not trouble the hardiest tax evaders, but it will be more difficult and risky for middle- and upper-class doctors, lawyers, and businesspeople.

Undoubtedly, some people will manage to escape making payments for years before they are detected. What should we do when they are finally caught? Suppose that a disadvantaged person has scraped through life, working off and on at odd jobs, never paying her minimal privilege tax. At age sixty-seven, she turns up at the stakeholding office, expecting to collect a citizen's pension. It would be useless to confiscate her assets, since she has none, other than the promised pension. Should we turn her away?

There is no easy answer. Giving her a full pension would reward scofflaws. But denying her everything seems draconian: it would leave a disproportionate number of the least-advantaged citizens out in the cold at the end of life as well as at the beginning. The answer lies somewhere in the middle: penalizing evaders without completely denying them pensions.

## Class Warfare?

Suppose we have convinced you that privilege taxation is well within the administrative capacities of the computer-assisted governments of the twenty-first century. This hardly suffices to respond to the questions of principle that may be raised against it. Most obviously, doesn't the tax signal the rise of explicit class warfare?

No more than our present taxes do. The progressive income tax is expressly justified on the ground that the rich should pay more. Even more conspicuous is the payroll tax, which is explicitly and egregiously pro-rich. In urging its elimination, we are not the ones who are introducing class into the debate. We are simply trying to put on a sounder footing the question of what different classes owe to one another.

At present, our tax categories reflect an older, Marxist understanding of the class struggle. The capital-gains tax burdens "capitalists," and the payroll tax burdens "the working class." In contrast, the privilege tax proceeds from the fundamental concerns of liberal individualism. It is not one's relationship to the means of production that should shape tax status but the extent to which liberal society has honored its promise of equal opportunity.

It is no disgrace for tax law to recognize the unfulfilled character of this promise. To the contrary: our sense of political community is in greater danger if America refuses to confront its failures and pretends that utopia has arrived. One of the greatest advantages of the privilege tax is its continuing reminder of the imperative need to build a world of genuine equality of opportunity, a world where a privilege tax would no longer be necessary.

But this is not our America. We live in a place where the reality of privilege is hidden by the mythology of classlessness. And in such a world, privilege taxation is simply a way of bringing truth to the everyday life of dollars and cents.

## More Criticisms

As professors at Yale, we have been overexposed to one complaint about our proposal. Won't the children of the rich be deterred from devoting their lives to low-paying public service jobs by the need to pay an extra $1,700 year in privilege tax? Won't this reduction in the supply of Ivy Leaguers with noblesse oblige impoverish the public good in innumerable ways?[52]

We think that any shortfall will be smaller than our critics predict. Most public service jobs don't pay that badly. And there is nothing to stop a proud mom or dad from offering to pay all or part of the privilege tax for children bent on public service in schools or churches or politics. It is hard to believe that a prospective tax of $1,700 a year will deter many from lucrative careers in business or law. Keep in mind, too, that the privileged person is also getting an eighty-thousand-dollar stake. Converting the stake into an annuity of four thousand dollars per year would more than cover liability for the privilege tax. And the tax will also have the highly salutary effect of enabling less-privileged people to devote their time to public interest jobs without paying a commensurate payroll tax.[53]

Suppose, however, that we are wrong about this, and the new tax does substantially depress the flow of young idealists into the public service sector. Even in this scenario, basic economics suggests that the affected job sectors will respond to the diminished supply by increasing salaries to make up part or all of the difference. All in all, this objection is minor at best.

A second problem is more serious. It focuses on our proposal's likely impact on women. After all, a woman will have to pay her tax even if she spends all her time raising children. Won't the tax force her into the labor market or into further dependence on a wage-earning partner?

Yes, but we think that this objection is misplaced. For one thing, women will also have their eighty-thousand-dollar stakes to serve as a buffer. For another, the real problem is not the privilege tax but how our society presently pays for child-rearing. Although this book is not about the early years of life and we cannot fully argue the case, we support the basic idea of family allowances. Given the concerns of the liberal state with equal opportunity, it only makes sense to compensate caregivers for their crucial work at the moment of each youngster's greatest vulnerability.

If this were done, the liberal state should maintain tax neutrality between competing ideals of motherhood. Once a woman is provided with a child allowance, it should be up to her to decide whether to pay herself and stay at home or to pay someone else to care for her child while she worked. Similarly, she should not be told that she can escape the privilege tax by pursuing one option rather than another.

Granted, the United States does not presently have a European-style universal family allowance. But we resist eroding the simplicity and moral force of the privilege tax by creating exemptions keyed to other pervasive injustices. Given their number, the tax would soon be riddled with exceptions. Moreover, a privilege-tax exemption would have perverse consequences. A mother from a poor background would gain only $380, whereas one from the right side of the tracks would gain $3,800—for the same work. It is better to channel reform energies into more constructive paths.

## Getting from Here to There

We turn finally to the distinctive problems raised by the transition from the old system to the new. Americans count on their retirement pensions long before they receive their first check. As they chart their lives over time, their prospective claim on the government shapes all their other savings decisions—as well as the pension plans provided by (some of) their employers. By the time most people turn, say, fifty, they have already significantly relied on the prospect of receiving Social Security, and it would be unfair to change the rules after they have made most of their basic life-shaping decisions.

This means that there should be a long period of peaceful coexistence between the old and new systems. The first stakeholders will emerge from their interviews with eighty thousand dollars and a guaranteed citizen's pension, but those older than fifty will keep their Social Security entitlements. As for the generation in between, we have more room for policy discretion. To avoid unnecessary political upheaval, it is probably wise to retain the old system for everybody over twenty-four. This would protect the interests of those who have relied on the promise of Social Security in making life plans, while also permitting a clean integration of the basic proposal and its expanded version. But we wouldn't object if the virtues of the new system were so clear that the middle-aged began a campaign to join in.

As for taxes, the principal issue is the future of the payroll tax during the period when Social Security and citizens' pensions coexist. Under one approach, older workers who will retire under Social Security should continue to pay payroll taxes at the rates that would have applied had the program continued indefinitely. Doomsters to the contrary, the Social Security fund is in pretty good shape, requiring only incremental adjustments to ensure it stays that way.[54]

But what of the stakeholding generation? As long as the citizens' pension fund is maintained on a pay-as-you-go basis, there is no need to begin assessing a privilege tax until the first group of stakeholders is just about ready to retire—in about fifty-five years. At that point, the payroll tax would phase out as the Social Security system expires, and the privilege tax would be phased in, as more and more citizens claim a citizen's pension.[55]

Citizens' pensions and the privilege tax mark a first effort to expand stakeholding beyond our basic proposal. If our initiative catches on, it can provide a framework for many more efforts to rethink other aspects of the existing welfare state. But for now it is more important to stand back from the trees and take a final look at the forest.

# Part 3

# Defending the Stake

# 10

# Ideals

Two hundred years ago, Tom Paine surveyed the revolutionary world that he helped create and saw that something was missing: "A revolution in the state of civilization is the necessary companion of revolutions in the system of government."[1] This could be accomplished, he was convinced, only through stakeholding. Every citizen, Paine insisted, had a right to a stake of fifteen pounds sterling "when arrived at the age of twenty-one years . . . and also the sum of ten Pounds per annum, during life, to every person now living of the age of fifty years, and to all others as they shall arrive at that age."[2] In a remarkable gesture for the year 1797, Paine provided that this expanded stake should go to every man *and* woman. Regardless of his or her claims on private wealth, each should be accorded an economic stake in the commonwealth.

Paine directed his essay to the revolutionary government of France, but he plainly intended it for a much broader audience: "Already the conviction that government, by representation, is the true system of government is spreading itself fast in the world. The reasonableness of

it can be seen by all. The justness of it makes itself felt even by its op-
posers. But when a system of civilization, growing out of that system of
government, shall be so organized, that not a man or woman born in
the republic, but shall inherit some means of beginning the world, and
see before them the certainty of escaping the miseries, that under
other governments accompany old age, the revolution of France will
have an advocate and an ally in the heart of all nations."[3]

Paine's thoughts on revenue-raising were a bit more primitive, but
once again there are striking parallels to our proposal. He urged the
creation of a "National Fund" from a special tax levied on all inheritances: "The subtraction will be made at a time that best admits it,
which is, at the moment that property is passing by the death of one
person to the possession of another. . . . The monopoly of natural inheritance, to which there never was a right, begins to cease. . . . A generous man would not wish it to continue, and a just man will rejoice to
see it abolished."[4] Unfortunately, Paine failed to recognize that his initiative could never be effective without being supplemented by a system of gift and wealth taxes. Nonetheless, the similarity between
Paine's National Fund and our payback requirement is clear enough,
despite the distance of two centuries.

Paine was the greatest but not the only visionary who has glimpsed
the promise of stakeholding over the years.[5] While we are encouraged
by these examples—Paine's essay *Common Sense* helped spark the
American Revolution—there is, as always, a darker side. After all,
Paine and the others utterly failed to catalyze a strong popular response for stakeholding. If they failed, why should we succeed?

## Two Mistakes About Redistribution

Perhaps because two centuries of experience have exposed the limits
of other solutions to the systematic injustices of the market economy.

Paine's brand of stakeholding was first overwhelmed in the nineteenth century by other, more utopian projects of social reform—most notably (but not exclusively) Marxism. In its familiar diagnosis, the real enemy was the capitalist system itself, and the only serious response was an all-out assault on private property. For Marxists, radical reformers like Paine appeared to be self-deluding "petit bourgeois intellectuals" who failed to confront the irreversibly oppressive character of capitalism. Rather than wasting time designing Band-Aids, serious reformers should join the revolutionary struggle for a brave new world.

Many thoughtful people resisted this temptation even during Marxism's heyday. Nonetheless, its massive attraction served to place progressive liberalism on the intellectual and political defensive. Even in the United States, New Deal Democrats did not look to radical liberals like Paine for inspiration and adopted workplace systems of social security as a result. But we think that the intellectual climate really is changing today.

Nationalization of industry is on nobody's agenda anymore. People are slowly recognizing that "capitalism" is a Marxist label concealing a wide range of systems built on the foundation of private property and competitive markets—some bitterly unjust, others striving for a world worthy of a free and equal citizenry. It is time to stop dreaming about the abolition of private property and get to work creating a commonwealth in which all citizens are property owners.

Nor should we be deflected by a second set of priorities—those focusing on the construction of safety nets. We refuse to look upon the modern welfare state as if it were simply doling out a secularized version of Christian charity. We are certainly in favor of charity, but its primary pursuit is best left to churches, unions, and community organizations. While we have carved out a constructive role for social insurance and citizens' pensions in the stakeholding society, we have followed Paine in linking these programs to the republican ideal of free and equal citizenship.

## The Political Case for Stakeholding

Tom Paine was not alone. In America at least, our leading Founders also acknowledged a deep relationship between property and citizenship. When James Madison viewed "the merits alone," it was clear to him that "the freeholders of the Country would be the safest depositories of Republican liberty" and that the propertyless should be excluded from suffrage.[6] Standing before the Constitutional Convention, he did not conceal his anxiety as he glimpsed a future day when the "great majority of the people will not only be without landed, but any other sort of, property."[7]

But in 1787, this grim prospect could be deferred to the remote future. The Founders treated the problem of propertylessness just as they dealt with the curse of slavery. They did not seek a definitive solution, leaving it to some later generation to confront the crisis when it became acute.

This seemed sensible enough. A vast frontier beckoned to generations of yeomen farmers. As long as the government could sell virgin land at low prices, the link between property and citizenship could be more or less preserved for the foreseeable future. As the nineteenth century progressed, this Jeffersonian vision of a republic of farmers became increasingly obsolete. By the time of the great Homestead Act of 1863, the statute's provision of free land on the frontier was already out of sync with the needs of the rising urban masses of the East. If the link between property and citizenship were to be sustained, provision of free land would no longer suffice. With the closing of the frontier, something like Tom Paine's vision of stakeholding was required to guarantee each citizen a property interest in America.

But by then Paine's voice had become a muffled memory. The mainstream of reform was flowing in other directions: Populists, Progressives, New Dealers, and the partisans of the Great Society sought to regain control over the market economy, but none moved in the direction of citizen stakeholding. Their overriding aim was not to broaden the property-owning base but to regulate property more intensely in the public interest. As we have emphasized, we do not seek to jettison the legacy of legislative achievement left by these great waves of twentieth-century reform.[8] But the time is ripe to reassert the enduring insights of an earlier age and reconstruct a direct linkage between property and citizenship along the inclusionary lines that Paine envisioned.

The political case for stakeholding begins with certain classical republican themes. We do not imagine that a stake of eighty thousand dollars will enable Americans to don their togas in the manner of the patricians of ancient Greece or Rome. The citizens of these classical republics had slaves do the work while they blabbed in the agora and fought on the battlefields. But we do believe that modern stakeholding will create a certain space for civic reflection in millions of lives now dominated by economic anxiety. Fewer Americans will be living on the economic edge; stakeholders will have more energy left to turn their attention to larger things, including the fate of the nation. Property will also breed sobriety, a resistance to the charismatic appeals of the demagogue, a willingness to consider the longer term. Broadening the property base enhances the stability and the quality of political life of the republic. These points were made by Aristotle in classical Athens and James Harrington in Commonwealth England.[9] They are no less true today.

But times do change, and there is something more to be said about the special circumstances of twenty-first century America. For classical writers of Greece and Rome, a solid republic was built not only on a broad economic base but also on a pervasive uniformity of moral values. Different republics might affirm different values, but none could survive without a repressive uniformity. Throughout the classical texts, there is enormous admiration for Sparta and its remorseless efforts to root out any hint of nonconformity. Yet these ancient aspirations for republican virtue seem absurdly totalitarian today. We cannot build political solidarity by forcing all Americans to worship together, let alone engage in the fierce military exercises at the core of classical republican life. Recognizing this, most modern-day communitarians display a disturbing vagueness in their impassioned calls for a reinvigoration of political community. In too many cases, there lurks in the background a Norman Rockwell picture of the 1950s, in which Americans have somehow returned to their traditional values of family, church, hard work, and sexual abstinence, without the old-time racism, sexism, and hierarchy that accompanied them.[10] But modern communitarians are curiously weak in explaining how this moral revival is to occur without trampling on the rights of millions who persist in living lives that break one or another traditional mold; are these people to be denounced as un-American?

Stakeholding, by contrast, builds a common sense of citizenship without the constant threat of moralistic repression. Each American will use his eighty thousand dollars in the way that makes the most sense to him. But each will tell a story that weaves his American citizenship into the fabric of his personal life: "Without the eighty thousand dollars, I never would have had the guts to try this, or avoid that." However different their life experiences and moral ideals, Americans will share something in common in the practice of citizen stakeholding—something that penetrates each life more deeply than existing rituals like voting or civic possessions like a passport.

By creating a public foundation for private life, stakeholding will also encourage a purer form of patriotism. It will not demand adhesion to one or another narrow version of the American creed. It will emerge instead out of simple gratitude to the nation for an expansive conception of economic citizenship that enables each citizen to enter adult life with a certain independence and resiliency against the recurring economic shocks of the competitive marketplace. As she reflects on her life, each stakeholder will be well aware of the very personal debt that she owes to her country, and most citizens will be silently on the lookout for opportunities to repay it. This accumulating fund of goodwill will sustain our political and social institutions during normal times and provide a precious resource for the unknowable crises that lie ahead.

When we turn from the stake to the means of financing it, the same republican themes emerge from our more particular proposals. Most discussions of tax policy take up the perspective of the central authority. How much does the government require? How can that amount be raised cheaply and fairly? These are important questions, but they are inadequate without a second perspective on the problem—that of the citizen. To be sure, nobody likes to pay taxes. But it makes a big difference how citizens understand the taxes that they are called upon to pay.

We have returned to this symbolic point repeatedly. In dedicating the wealth tax for the exclusive use of stakeholding, we are doing more than raising money. We are creating a new bond between haves and have-nots, between the old and the young. In paying the wealth tax, each citizen will be recognizing that he *does* have a concrete responsibility to assist his fellow Americans who are starting out in life in search of the American dream.

So, too, for the privilege tax. We favor it not only because it is fairer than the payroll tax but because it carries a better message. Every time a citizen pays her privilege tax, she will be acknowledging the extent to which America still fails to redeem the promise of equal opportunity—and the need for further measures in the years ahead.

The symbolic side of taxation is generally given short shrift in policy discussion. But it is a serious mistake to get caught up in the dollars and cents of revenue collection. Now that we have abolished the draft, taxation is the most onerous sacrifice that the nation demands of its citizens. The forms that taxation takes and the messages that it carries are fundamental in the ongoing dialogue that constitutes the polity.

Against the cynicism of the age, we are not embarrassed to announce our message: by the taxes they pay as well as the stakes they receive, Americans should be prepared to reaffirm their common commitment to economic citizenship as an enduring aspect of a revitalized political identity.

Stakeholding promises to revitalize our politics in a more immediate way. If we ever hope to move beyond the present politics of drift and scandal, political leaders will have to begin again to speak about serious issues in a language that is *directly* accessible to ordinary Americans. In contrast to the stream of technotalk coming out of think tanks inside the Beltway, stakeholding puts on the table a practical proposal that every American can understand.

Nobody we've met has the slightest problem grasping the idea of eighty thousand dollars—or the possibility of funding the program by requiring a payback and taxing wealth. Lots of people don't like our initiative, but at least they know what they are disagreeing with—and this kind of clarity is absolutely essential if we are to have a rebirth of democratic politics. Unless progressives come up with substantive projects that are transparent to the common understanding, the politics of scandal will have no real competitor in this country. The general public has no patience for a policy debate that speaks a technocratic language accessible only to people with advanced degrees. If Beltway babble is the alternative, ordinary Americans will turn with relief to news of the latest personal indiscretion by leading politicos. Only a program like stakeholding can focus the public mind on the prospects for real change. It raises, in a singularly straightforward and concrete way, one of the leading questions of our age: should Americans take a serious step to assure more equality of opportunity, or should we follow our present course of trickle-down economics?

We do not know how most citizens will answer this question. Like all serious political proposals, stakeholding will be divisive. For many of our friends, the pressing need to redeem the promise of equal opportunity is one of those self-evident truths that Jefferson talked about; for others, stakeholding only seems to be the latest in a long line of crackpot schemes that fail to improve upon the invisible hand.

There can be no hope of ending this great debate between progressives and conservatives. Nonetheless, the doubts of conservatives did not stop previous generations from embarking on great reforms that most Americans now take for granted. Why should they stop us now?

Our proposal will generate other lines of conflict. Most obviously, it will divide haves and have-nots. The fact that 59 percent of Americans will pay nothing in wealth taxes will force politicians to think twice before opposing stakeholding, but it is easy to predict emphatic opposition from many rich Americans. The initiative will also intensify the clash between generations that increasingly marks our politics. Because wealth is heavily correlated with age, successful men and women who are over sixty will bear the brunt of our new tax. While many may be persuaded by the justice of our proposal—and the prospect of their grandchildren gaining a solid start in life—it is only natural to expect much skepticism as well.

Stakeholding will look very different farther down the age distribution. Consider the situation of a married couple of forty blessed with two children of ten and twelve: will they vote to give their kids a stake of eighty thousand dollars apiece in a decade or so, or will they be deterred by the prospect of heavy wealth taxes as they grow older and richer?

This answer will be pretty easy for most forty-something parents, who will be paying absolutely no wealth tax because their total assets won't exceed the eighty-thousand-dollar exemption.[11] Many may hope that, in twenty more years, they will have accumulated a lot more. But if they are like most parents and care deeply about their children's future, they may be perfectly willing to exchange the uncertain prospect of higher taxes later for a rock-solid eighty-thousand-dollar stake accruing to each child in the nearer term.

The same is even truer for the vast majority of Americans in their twenties and thirties who either have very young children or are thinking about becoming parents. They may regret that stakeholding has come too late for them, but they will have every interest in seeing that their children gain this precious advantage when their time comes.

Obviously, the calculus will look much different for the substantial number of childless adults and for the relatively small group of younger and middle-aged Americans with large assets.[12] But we have never suggested that our proposal is to everybody's advantage. Nor do we suppose that everybody's position will be determined by a narrow economic calculus focusing on self and family. As in all political exercises, each voter will come to judgment after filtering self-interest through a sense of civic obligation and the substantive merits. Some will vote against stakeholding even though it might profit their kids mightily, simply because they think it's an awful idea. And vice versa.

Nevertheless, we have said enough to suggest that the political potential of stakeholding is considerable. Although the idea might be unfamiliar, it is not utopian. The first politician who seriously takes it up will find herself appealing to the very concrete interests of a massive majority of Americans. Of course, the fate of the initiative will depend on the political skill of the leadership that emerges on both sides of the debate. But it will also depend on how ordinary men and women answer a simple question: do Americans believe in equal opportunity any more?

Maybe not. Only time will tell. But it is far too early to dismiss stakeholding as a pipe dream that could not command the attention of ordinary people.

In making the political case for stakeholding, we envision a two-stage process. For the next generation, the initiative can inspire a serious politics of mass engagement, which would give renewed meaning to American citizenship in this time of drift. Over the longer run, the political success of stakeholding will generate an ongoing system of taxation and entitlement that revitalizes our social contract and serves as an enduring source of civic identity for our children and our children's children.

## The Individualist's Case for Stakeholding

One of the great banalities of our time sets "the individual" against "the community," as if the two were locked in inexorable combat: what's good for one is bad for the other. But stakeholding suggests the contrary, and at several levels.

Begin with the most obvious. In contrast to most public programs, this one does not restrict the rights of private property on behalf of some collective good. It is based on the opposite premise: property is so important to the free development of individual personality that everybody ought to have some. Without stakeholding, formal freedom easily degenerates into farce—as Anatole France once jested, the equal right to sleep under the bridges of Paris.

The most frequent response to France's famous quip is an ironic shrug rather than an embrace of the obvious solution—make every citizen a property owner. In proposing stakeholding, we do not mean to exaggerate the link between property and personhood. Having millions in the bank hardly guarantees a fruitful or secure life; personal growth requires an understanding of the limits of what money can buy.[13]

Nonetheless, a propertyless person lacks crucial resources needed for self-definition. He can never taste the joys and sorrows of real freedom—and the possibilities of learning from his own successes and mistakes. He is condemned to a life on the margin, where the smallest shocks can send him into a tailspin. He can never enjoy the luxury of asking himself what he really wants out of life, but is constantly responding to the exigent demands of the marketplace.

It will be easy for culture critics to sneer as Joe American uses his stake to agonize over the car he should buy or the clothes he should wear. But these mundane decisions are profoundly expressive of our ordinary identities and offer continual opportunities for personal re-definition and development. Their human importance should not be dismissed by fashionable talk about "commodification" as the root cause of alienation in modern life.

We do not deny that something important has been lost in the shift to the modern marketplace of mass production and consumer choice. There was a dignity in growing your own food and having long-lasting relationships with your neighbors. Indeed, some brave souls will un-doubtedly use their stakes to reestablish more authentic communal re-lationships or seek to live in greater harmony with nature. We respect these efforts, but refuse to privilege them: it is up to each American to decide on his own responsibility whether modern life is worth its moral costs. The glory of stakeholding lies not in any individual's par-ticular answer but in the new space it opens for each citizen to con-front such questions.

Stakeholding, in short, takes individualism seriously by enabling each of us to take himself seriously. The economic independence af-forded by eighty thousand dollars hardly provides insulation against all the hazards of life But it would be silly for mere mortals to aspire to so absolute an independence. It is even possible to have too much inde-pendence from the market, rather than too little. Imagine, for exam-ple, that America were magically placed in a position to add a couple of zeros to each stake, pushing the number from $80,000 to $8 million for every young adult: would it really be good to transform the average American into a spoiled brat living in New York on an overly large trust fund?

There is no danger of that. The question is not whether Americans will become spoiled brats, but whether they should enjoy the kind of relative economic independence that many children of the upper middle class take for granted today.

In making the case for stakeholding, we also wish to confront squarely another standard anxiety expressed by individualists. According to their familiar critique, an unacceptably collectivist idea of human nature haunts the standard arguments for economic redistribution. Perhaps, these individualists grudgingly concede, such grand egalitarian projects would be justified if each individual's talents were properly conceived of as collective assets of the community. But we should reject such collectivist imagery and, with it, the redistributive impulse. The community doesn't own your talents. You do. And it is profoundly mistaken for the community to suppose that it can redistribute the fruits of your talents in the way that best serves the collective welfare.[14]

In framing our own response, we do not deny that many standard arguments for redistribution proceed from the "talent-pooling" premise that critics have identified. But we have made every effort to distance ourselves from any such notion. To be perfectly clear, we do *not* view each citizen's talents as a form of community property. We understand them as emerging from an ongoing process of self-definition beginning at birth. As we mature, each of us explores our native abilities by assessing them in action, revising our assessments after initial rounds of experience, and developing our talents further in light of the opportunities that the world presents. By the time a citizen reaches adulthood, it is perfectly appropriate for her to view her talents as *constitutive* of her identity—and to protest when policy-makers treat her hard work in developing them as if they were merely community assets.[15]

But this point does not have the powerful anti-redistributionist implications so often attributed to it. To the contrary: it is precisely because each individual is profoundly constituted by her ongoing effort during childhood to define and develop her talents that she should be given an equal stake to develop them further as a young adult. Our case for redistribution, in short, is not based on the notion that the community owns each individual's abilities. It is based on the community's obligation to give each person equal respect by providing her with equal resources to develop her unique talents.

Here, as elsewhere, our vision of the stakeholding society invites you to transcend easy dichotomies between individualism and collectivism in order to glimpse a life that reinforces both aspects of our identities. When our children or grandchildren come forward to claim their stakes, they are doing it for themselves *and* for America; they are recognizing their common citizenship *and* gaining the effective freedom to take their own projects of self-definition seriously.

They are building a liberal community.

## The Dark Side

A pretty picture, but there is a dark side. On the collective level, our initiative indubitably draws a sharper line between "us" and "them"— between longtime resident Americans, who will enjoy the economic advantages of stakeholding, and everybody else. On the individual level, what will be the fate of those Americans—and there will be some—who blow their stakes and then turn to the community for further assistance? Having thrown away their eighty thousand dollars, these people may fare even worse under the new regime. Won't stakeholding, in short, inaugurate an ugly new era of chauvinism and harshness in America?

There are dangers here—but we think that they should not be paralyzing. On the collective level, the fear of chauvinism is in part a complaint about the very idea of the nation-state. Unless and until we move to a scheme of world federalism, the inhabitants of the earth will be sorted out into different countries. Whenever any one of these countries makes a step toward justice among its own citizens, this creates a greater disparity between it and other countries. If this increasing disparity were enough to condemn the initiative, no country should ever make any moves toward justice for fear of disparaging the rest of the world. But this can't be right.

Turning from morals to politics, we think that stakeholding is more likely to diminish xenophobia than encourage it. Unless some serious steps are taken to assure a broader distribution of the benefits of our globalizing economy, it is only a matter of time before we will see a powerful backlash from the majority who are left behind. In contrast, the sort of politics that will yield stakeholding may turn out to be quite benign for those who do not share directly in its advantages. When all is said and done, the fate of our initiative depends on a politics of inclusion—stakeholding will become a reality only if tens of millions of Americans can be persuaded to transcend their deep skepticism about government and work together for a common goal. When this has happened in the past—during Reconstruction, the New Deal, and the civil rights revolution—the politics of inclusion had sufficient momentum to embrace others far beyond its original concerns. This could happen once again: though resident aliens might not share in stakeholding, they might well gain from the larger concern with social justice that a more democratic and inclusionary politics reflects.

Only one thing seems clear: the possible danger of an ugly chauvinism is too speculative to serve as a decisive reason for rejecting stakeholding. To the contrary, we think it much more likely that the ultimate outcome will be benign. Given America's influence in the world, its success in moving forward with stakeholding may encourage other countries to make similar experiments. And wouldn't that be a good thing?

We can be less Panglossian when it comes to the problem posed by citizens who blow their stakes on a BMW and a wild fling in Las Vegas. These people will not encounter a very sympathetic audience when they plead for further assistance from their fellow citizens. Nor should they. Freedom and responsibility are deeply linked in a liberal state. If a person uses his freedom unwisely, he cannot expect to avoid accountability for his actions.

There may be extenuating circumstances. In many cases, but not in all, the stakeblowers will have come from disadvantaged childhoods and so may justly claim that they have still been deprived of their full measure of equality of opportunity. Nonetheless, we are not inclined to move too eagerly or too far down this path of extenuation. The best way to respond to these other injustices is to eradicate them, not to declare that their victims should be treated as something less than responsible adults.

But all adults make painful mistakes, and there certainly should be room for compassion in any good society. While churches and other institutions of civil society should play a leading part in helping people in trouble, the state should play a backup role—even though the level of assistance to stakeblowers will seem low in comparison, say, to the levels prevailing in European welfare states. It is a hard call, but one that must be made: it is more important to ensure that all Americans enjoy more equal freedom to shape their lives than to give more generous relief to those who fail the test of freedom.

We console ourselves with one bitter fact. America is so ungenerous in its welfare policies at present that it is hard to imagine it getting much stingier. Nonetheless, the plight of the stakeblower does emphasize the divide between our proposal and those emerging from the utilitarian philosophies that have inspired the welfare state over the past century. At the end of the day, there *is* a choice to be made, and we make it on behalf of the right of each and every individual to real freedom to shape his own life and take responsibility for his own fate.

# 11

# Alternatives

All this prepares the ground for a response to a criticism that we have frequently encountered: "Stakeholding sounds nice, but aren't there better and cheaper ways of fighting poverty?"

We will consider concrete alternatives shortly, but first we want to challenge the question. Stakeholding is not a poverty program. It is a citizenship program. It is not concerned simply with raising the bottom. It aims to realize our commitment as Americans to freedom and equality for all. Our initiative will succeed whenever a young man or woman from the suburbs gains the freedom to start a family or small business, as it will whenever a child of the inner city grows up knowing that there *is* a pot of gold at the end of the rainbow if he graduates from high school and keeps clear of crime.

Some will fail the test of freedom. But even failure will cut across class lines. Some spoiled brats from the suburbs will blow their stakes, while millions of poor kids from the center city will make the most of their one big chance. For all the frightened talk of an American "underclass," the number of seriously troubled young adults is relatively small, and we have taken steps to place their stakes in trust.[1] As a matter of principle, we reject the notion that the predictable failure of some should deprive all of the opportunity to give reality to the promise of freedom.

It is from this vantage that we turn to consider a broad range of alternatives to stakeholding. We begin with the existing agenda, from traditional tinkerings with the tax code to newer proposals to privatize Social Security. After this brief survey, we turn to more visionary proposals. Compared to the present mix of moral drift and symbolic politics, all of them seem quite promising. Each has advantages and disadvantages when compared to stakeholding. It is up to you to tote up the balance sheet and determine how we might best move beyond the status quo.

## The Existing Agenda

Republicans and Democrats worked together on taxes in the 1980s and 1990s, but their efforts at bipartisanship have had very different consequences. In 1986, Ronald Reagan and Dan Rostenkowski presided over a much-needed cleanup of the tax code.[2] More recently, and especially in 1997, President Bill Clinton and House Speaker Newt Gingrich have joined together to fill the code with symbolic gestures, proliferating loopholes, and scandalously generous handouts to the rich.[3]

### The Politics of Symbolism

Recent "tax reforms" consist of symbolic gestures whose principal recommendation is that they don't cost much.[4] Individual Retirement Accounts do little for the bottom half of the population, and exempting home sales from capital gains taxes is political pandering at its worst.[5] Even those tax breaks that cost more—like the tax credit of five hundred dollars per child—are mere Band-Aids.[6] It is ludicrous to suppose that five hundred dollars a year will improve parents' child care options or allow them to take time off from work to care for their kids. Worse yet, this gimmick cannot be used by the parents of 30 percent of America's children—these families don't earn enough to qualify for the credit.[7]

We are also skeptical of another emerging boomlet: enterprise zones, which use tax incentives to encourage businesses to reenter the inner city. Jack Kemp, a Republican, has been the most vocal cheerleader, but Democratic president Bill Clinton endorsed a cheap version of the initiative—with the grand name "empowerment zones"—as part of the tax package of 1993.

Inner cities are in bad shape, and we agree that there is a powerful case for well-coordinated government action.[8] Individual entrepreneurs are understandably reluctant to be the first to reenter a blighted zone, and a coordinated program of development might persuade firms that an area is ripe for recovery.

But this kind of coordination requires more than the handful of modest tax breaks that the program offers to firms that operate in empowerment zones.[9] While the federal tax breaks are too new for empirical evaluation, the experiences of states with similar programs has not been very positive.[10] The cost per job created has been extremely high, and the economic benefits to communities have been minimal. As symbolic politics goes, empowerment zones don't do too much harm. But it would be silly to take them seriously as an alternative to stakeholding or as a meaningful strategy to help the inner cities.

## Education
The 1997 tax law takes a small step toward making college more affordable for more families. Middle-class parents can now claim an array of new tax credits to help pay for their children's college tuition and can save for future college costs in tax-favored accounts.[11] These are nice gestures, but they are worth only fifteen hundred dollars a

year at most.[12] And the new rules are so complicated that most parents will need a tax accountant to figure them out. By comparison, stakeholding takes a giant step toward expanding access to higher education.[13]

Even with the most generous education subsidies imaginable, the majority of Americans will never earn four-year college diplomas—nor should they. Expanding opportunity is a good thing. But college is not for everyone, and it should not be the sole avenue for young men and women to gain the resources they need to shape their lives as free and equal citizens. Higher-education subsidies only serve to strengthen the current two-class system, divided between those with college degrees and those without. Stakeholding is different. To *all* Americans, and not just to the college-bound, it gives the economic independence that they need to gain training in ways that make sense for them and design their own path to a meaningful life.

### Welfare Reform

While the middle class is being treated to child tax credits and the upper classes are enjoying a sizable cut in taxes on capital gains and bequests, America is turning its back on the poor.[14] Recent welfare reforms impose strict new work requirements and a time limit on cash benefits.[15] The new approach promises to "end welfare as we know it," but it comes at the expense of millions of vulnerable people. When they can find jobs, most welfare recipients earn wages too low to support their families, even at the poverty level.[16] And barriers ranging from inadequate or no child care to limited transportation often make it difficult for them to get and keep a job.[17] Although the current economic boom is cushioning the transition to the new rules, the next business downturn will throw millions out of work.[18] Welfare time limits make for good sound bites, but they cannot alter the business cycle. The only certainty is that another generation of children will be denied their claims to equal opportunity.

As we have emphasized, stakeholding is not an alternative to welfare reform. A thoroughgoing antipoverty program would begin with the failures of early-childhood education and continue on through high school.[19] It would also address the market failures and misguided public policies that have left the inner-city and rural poor to suffer in geographic and economic isolation.[20]

There is no quick fix. Today's welfare reforms have opted for the cheap and punitive approach. A comprehensive antipoverty program would be more costly and more complicated.[21] Stakeholding can help, even at the bottom, by giving poor parents better options for themselves and their children. But it is not a panacea. Indeed, we would be advocating an even larger stakeholding program were it not for the need to hold resources in reserve in order to fund serious efforts to improve opportunities for those at the bottom. Americans could afford to fund a bigger stake.[22] But we have contented ourselves with an eighty-thousand-dollar target so that stakeholding might become the catalyst for further reforms in the name of genuine equality of opportunity.

### Social Security "Privatization"

Turning from the tax code and welfare reform to Social Security, we encounter the rage today for "privatization." This buzzword can mean many things, but all the permutations draw their strength from the insurance analogy. If payroll taxes are "premiums," shouldn't the account of each premium-payer reflect his own "contribution" to the fund?[23]

The most radical plans enable each individual to manage his "account"—making retirement benefits depend on investment skill and market luck. Worse yet, the new accounts could provide many women with even less than they now receive under Social Security.[24]

These plans push a bad metaphor to the point of moral bankruptcy. Even if you manage your retirement account poorly in your youth, you should not be stripped of a decent citizen's pension in old age. Without any serious moral discussion, privatizers are promoting programs that would render the elderly hostage to investment decisions made many decades previously. We have sought to expose this position as morally unacceptable.[25]

The challenge for Social Security reform lies in a very different direction. Rather than driving the insurance analogy to its logical absurdity, we should challenge its hold on the collective imagination. Your right to a dignified retirement should not depend on the money that you or your spouse earned at work. It should instead be understood as an inalienable right of American citizenship. We can and should come up with a much better solution than privatization to the problems left behind by Franklin Roosevelt's New Deal.

## The New Agenda

The current agenda for "reform" is grim and getting grimmer. The challenge is to look beyond this dark period and collect our intellectual forces for the time—and it will come—when the injustices of the status quo become intolerable. Stakeholding is our effort to keep this conversation going. We are glad to see that others are similarly inclined.

### National Service?

Like us, Mickey Kaus aims for a rebirth in civic commitment.[26] But he does not seek to rekindle the flame by giving new economic reality to America's promise of equal opportunity. His book *The End of Equality* treats increasing economic inequality as an inexorable feature of modern capitalism and urges progressives to resign themselves to the yawning gap between the rich and the poor. Rather than reasserting the moral importance of distributive justice, we should aim to make these grinding inequalities more tolerable. If Americans were constantly rubbing elbows with one another in a host of public settings, perhaps we could preserve our democratic heritage despite the striking differences in our economic resources. Kaus's goal, in short, is to revitalize democratic life in public spaces, not to redistribute private wealth.

But this is not so easy, as Kaus would be the first to admit. He provides a sober survey of the ways in which many of our public spaces have been hollowed out over the past half century. The decline and fall of the citizen army is paradigmatic. In his effort to recapture the sense of genuine citizenship won by those who fought in World War II, Kaus comes up with an obvious solution: why not reintroduce a universal draft for all young Americans?

Kaus recognizes, of course, that the modern military can use only a tiny fraction of the nation's 3 to 4 million eighteen-year-olds—10 percent or less under post–Cold War conditions.[27] But he responds by proposing to draft the other 90 percent to serve together for a year in a giant civilian corps dedicated to projects of national improvement. This massive operation would work to relieve a host of pressing problems, but for Kaus the overriding aim of the civilian corps would be "to mix the classes in a common endeavor."[28] For a year of their lives at least, all of America's children would encounter one another on relatively equal terms—just as they did when fighting the Germans and Japanese. And these democratic experiences would cement a common bond throughout life.

Kaus recognizes that his civilian corps would be "almost surely inefficient."[29] But this is too gentle a way of describing the incredible logistical problems involved in processing more than 3 million Americans each year, let alone mixing the classes together for constructive social work. While this task would be daunting in itself, three groups would make it overwhelming: politicians seeking to control the new bureaucracy for partisan advantage, labor unions struggling to protect their members against low-price competition, and parents using all their influence to obtain advantageous placements for their children.

This is a recipe for a corrupt and politicized boondoggle. Rather than recreating the civic spirit of the citizen armies of World War II, we would construct a parody of the failed community-action programs of the 1960s, writ large.[30]

Compulsory national service won't work. But even if it could, we would object in principle. Quite simply, we hate compulsion. A draft is appropriate when the nation is facing a life-and-death threat to its existence. But we dishonor our principles of liberty by forcing millions of unwilling eighteen-year-olds "to do their duty" despite their stubborn conviction that they are wasting their time.

The stakeholder society travels a different path to patriotism and public service: treat Americans fairly as economic citizens, and you will be surprised by how many will "pay back" their stakes by giving generously of themselves in the social and political realm. In contrast to the forced service of an army of unwilling draftees, these countless acts of voluntary citizenship would serve as a true marker that America has reconnected with its civic roots.

### Rewarding Work

In contrast to Mickey Kaus, Edmund Phelps is a kindred spirit.[31] Like us, he is a liberal who wants to rethink the foundations of the welfare state; like us, he rejects the classic libertarian phobia against redistribution; like us, he wishes to take advantage of the last generation of liberal philosophy—he explicitly draws on the work of John Rawls—as the inspiration for a practical program of reform; and like us, he is interested not in Band-Aids but in something that would make a real difference to tens of millions of Americans.

But Phelps's book *Rewarding Work* takes a direction different from stakeholding. His centerpiece is job creation at the bottom, not equal opportunity for all. In taking this step, he rightly rejects the device presently favored by politicians: raising the minimum wage.[32] While modest hikes might not be too harmful, the big increase needed to make a real difference—say, a raise of three dollars an hour—could have catastrophic consequences on the demand for low-skilled labor, throwing out of work the very people whom the policy is supposed to help.[33] We also join Phelps in questioning massive job programs in which government serves as the employer of last resort. In America at least, there is simply too great a danger that a jobs program would promote corruption and political patronage without in fact delivering meaningful work to those who need it. Such a fiasco would only serve to further discredit the claim that activist government can deliver on social justice.

Phelps has a better idea. He proposes to subsidize private employers for hiring low-skilled workers. If a firm were willing to pay a worker four dollars an hour, the government would kick in an extra three dollars. The subsidy schedule would phase out for higher wage rates: for example, for workers earning five dollars an hour, the grant would be only $2.30.[34] Phelps predicts that competition would lead employers to pass on the full subsidy to their workers.[35]

Under this program, a four-dollar-an-hour worker would take home seven dollars per hour. For full-time work, that amounts to a subsidy of six thousand dollars per year and a total wage of fourteen thousand dollars—just over the 1996 poverty line for a family of three.[36] Moreover, the higher wages—funded by the government subsidies, at no cost to the employer—would induce more low-wage workers to get jobs. All this would not come cheap. Phelps estimates that it would cost $125 billion a year, although he thinks that much or all of it would be offset by savings from other government welfare programs.[37]

We applaud Phelps's ambition. We hope that his book heralds a new round of liberal dialogue. We mean to continue this dialogue by considering the salient differences—both philosophical and practical—

that distinguish our alternative proposals. What accounts for the fact that our broadly similar projects yield different bottom lines?

Begin with our contrasting definitions of the basic problem. For us, it is inequality of opportunity. Phelps is more outcome-oriented. He is concerned with the fact that working-class wages are falling farther and farther behind middle-class salaries.[38] Given his focus, his proposal—to close the gap by subsidizing wages at the bottom—makes sense. For us, these outcomes are important as a signal of increasing inequality of opportunity for the working class. The challenge is to go to the source of these inequalities by providing resources through which each citizen may invest in his skills and otherwise enhance his opportunities.

A second disagreement involves the scope of liberal community. Phelps locates the sense of justice in the workplace. In his view, high-wage earners have a responsibility—which they already intuit—to their low-wage collaborators. They recognize that their own high salaries are due in part—albeit in ways that are difficult to measure—to their less well paid coworkers. And they understand that justice requires them to share these collaborative gains fairly. Phelps's government subsidy implements this workplace intuition.[39]

We invoke a different community. Our appeal is to our fellow citizens, not our fellow workers. This difference shapes the structure of our entire proposal: it is as Americans, not as workers, that stakeholders claim eighty thousand dollars, as Americans that they accept their citizens' pensions, and as Americans that they make their contributions through the wealth tax, the payback, and the privilege tax.

We could well imagine a world in which Phelps's choice made more sense. In such a world, people would primarily think of themselves not as citizens of a nation but as workers in an industry. When they wished to organize for social justice, their first instinct would be to join their fellow workers in a union, not agitate among their fellow citizens for economic reform. This was, indeed, precisely the aspiration of the Socialist International, the worldwide federation of socialist parties and labor unions that was shattered by political hostilities at the onset of World War I.

More important, this kind of appeal does not work with Americans, who are notoriously skeptical of worker solidarity. If—a big "if"—the next generation is to witness a reaffirmation of social justice in this country, it will be by an appeal to the conscience and enlightened self-interest of its citizens. It is high time to renew and deepen our nation's founding commitments to liberty and equality.

These principles motivate a third crucial difference between our program and Phelps's. We propose to devote $255 billion to providing *every* American with a taste of real freedom. Phelps proposes that the country spend $125 billion and aim most of it at the bottom 30 percent of the population.[40] Our program proceeds within the framework of liberal citizenship, equality, and freedom; Phelps's continues in the tradition of secularized charity to those at the bottom of the socioeconomic scale.

Which brings us to a fourth basic difference. Phelps places an overriding weight on the value of work. For us, the overriding value is freedom. The two values are intertwined: by raising wages from four dollars to seven dollars an hour, Phelps rightly thinks that low-wage workers are also getting more real freedom. Similarly, we hardly suppose that stakeholders will be indifferent to the value of work. But it will be up to each of them to decide how much, and what kind of, work to do. In making this choice, they will each have eighty thousand dollars in their pockets, and this fact may make them either more or less willing to accept low-wage jobs. But the final judgment will be their own.

This freedom will be especially precious to women. With their eighty-thousand-dollar stakes in hand, they will be in a much better position to balance the real rewards of market work against family commitments. As they choose how best to combine the demands of work and family life, they will confront wages that reflect the marginal product of their market work. If this is low, perhaps they are right to think that they should be spending more time with their children. While it is unfair to expect women alone to bear most of the dual burden of family duties and work, this is precisely the situation of most working mothers today. In the short term, stakeholding will enhance the power of women to make the most sensible accommodation to an unjust reality. In the longer term, it will not only convey a symbolic message of support for gender equality but will also give enterprising women the real resources they need to challenge traditional expectations and make their own way in the world.

In contrast, Phelps wants to reinforce men's connection to the workplace and women's economic reliance on men. For him, market work has intrinsic benefits that trump the value of freedom. While he slights the distinctive situation of women, he views the situation of low-skilled males, especially minorities, with alarm.[41] Phelps emphasizes the precipitous drop in participation in the labor market, the explosive growth in prison populations, and other signs of social disintegration among members of this group.[42] Within this context, work has therapeutic value, providing a lost generation with the structure and discipline that they need to gain a sense of their human dignity. By engineering a massive increase in the effective wage rate, Phelps hopes to lure these lost workers away from the competing attractions of crime and welfare. With higher wages, he claims, these men can once again take on the role of breadwinners, with benefits for their wives, their children, and their communities.[43]

Stakeholding also extends new hope to the disadvantaged—but without invoking outdated gender roles. From their early years, underprivileged children of all races will be looking forward to the stake as their key to upward mobility. The promise of a citizen's stake of eighty thousand dollars, moreover, is far more compelling than the difference between four dollars and seven dollars an hour.[44] Parents and teachers can be counted upon to stress to every child that he won't get his eighty thousand dollars unless he graduates from high school and that he will fritter it away unless he prepares himself for the hard work ahead. No less important, stakeholding allows the child to dream. While it can supplement low-wage work, it can also provide the resources for fueling bigger ambitions. Instead of subsidizing people to stay in low-skill jobs, stakeholding gives them the wherewithal to move up.

We do not deny that some stakeholders will eventually end up worse off under our initiative. They will waste their stake on frivolous joyrides and face the prospect of endless low-wage labor or a life of crime and dissolution. But given the powerful educational impact of the stake, these losers may turn out to be less numerous in a stakeholding society.

It is here that our philosophical differences with Phelps become most apparent. The case for stakeholding does not ultimately rest on its effects on employment, marriage, or crime. It rests on each American's claim to respect as a free and equal citizen. This claim carries with it an acceptance of personal responsibility—for failure no less than success. Although our plan would continue to provide some safety nets, these will be less generous than those offered by Phelps's plan, at least for those who can take up his offer of subsidized low-wage work.

A fifth difference is more practical. Despite Phelps's criticism of the old-fashioned welfare state, his initiative suffers from familiar bureaucratic pathologies. Employers will have powerful incentives to pad their payrolls, understate wage rates, and inflate hours worked. Every lie can earn them as much as three dollars an hour. Moreover, the wage subsidy will go to workers with very different needs and family incomes—teenage children of the middle class will be making seven dollars an hour flipping hamburgers at McDonald's. Indeed, only 22 percent of workers earning the minimum wage live in families with incomes under the poverty line.[45] Phelps's program is neither a truly universalist effort like stakeholding nor a narrowly targeted antipoverty effort.[46]

In contrast, stakeholding comes with minimal bureaucracy. Each citizen gets the same amount, and given the size of the payments, it will be worthwhile to set up an airtight system against fraud.

Finally, stakeholding provides a superior platform for engaging in a more thoroughgoing reform of the welfare state. While Phelps is critical of existing social insurance programs, his proposal does not provide an easy way of accommodating his critique. Indeed, his emphasis on the workplace may reinforce the existing system of social insurance based on payroll taxes.[47] In contrast, stakeholding builds a framework for a fundamental critique of the New Deal system and a demystification of insurance arrangements.

Don't get us wrong. Although we think we have a better idea, we would run to the polls to support any politician who hired Phelps as a principal policy adviser. Compared to the status quo, a large subsidy for low-wage workers would make America a more decent place. But we should set our sights higher.

### Basic Income

This brings us to a bold initiative that is even closer in spirit to stakeholding. Proposals for a basic income call for guaranteeing an unconditional cash payment each year to each adult. Everyone would get the basic income, regardless of their other income or wealth. Although details vary, the typical plan provides a substantial sum, but one far below a subsistence-level income.[48] For rough comparability with stakeholding, let's set the sum at four thousand dollars per year.

The basic income is not an entirely new idea.[49] In the United States, George McGovern proposed a one-thousand-dollar "demogrant" in the 1972 presidential election. Although McGovern's proposal encountered political skepticism, the basic income has lived on in the scholarly literature in economics and philosophy.[50] Most recently, the idea has begun to make a good deal of headway among progressive academics and politicians in Europe.[51]

We urge its serious consideration in the United States. Like stakeholding, the basic income puts the emphasis on freedom. With a basic income, everyone could count on at least four thousand dollars a year. This sum hardly opens up a life of leisure, but it would grant most Americans greater freedom to shape their lives. Some people would continue to work just as hard and use their extra money to buy something: a better car, a better house, or perhaps private or parochial school for their child. Others would use the extra money to buy time: to go to school, to take care of young children, or just to take a month off. And others might use the extra income to take a risk on changing jobs or moving to a new community.

This extra freedom would have the greatest value for those in the bottom half of the income distribution. Some people at the top would have to pay higher taxes that would more than offset their four-thousand-dollar basic income.[52] But even many of them might gain a real benefit over the course of their lives. Anyone who falls on hard times or decides to make a hard change in life—getting a divorce, leaving home, venturing to find a new job—could count on the annual payment. Only a very privileged few at the very top can confidently predict that they would never, under any circumstance, find comfort or real aid in a basic income.

Like stakeholding, the basic income grants this freedom and security without strings attached. It automatically supplements low wages without bureaucracy or complex wage subsidies. And with a basic income, more people can choose for themselves whether to work full-time or part-time, making their own tradeoffs between more money and more leisure.[53]

On the whole, we are even more positive about this plan than Phelps's important initiative. But it diverges from stakeholding in a way that we believe tips the balance in our direction.

The basic contrast is simple enough. Under stakeholding, each citizen receives a stake of eighty thousand dollars one time in her life, but under a basic-income program, she would receive four thousand dollars every year. Of course, any lump sum can be converted into an equivalent stream of annuity payments, and vice versa. But basic-income proposals typically do not allow recipients to "cash out" their stream of payments by pledging them to a bank in exchange for a big cash payment.

The question, then, is whether this restriction on each individual's freedom to plan the shape of her life is legitimate. Shouldn't we leave it up to each young adult to decide on her own whether it is better to buy a four-thousand-dollar annuity or to use her eighty thousand dollars in other ways that make more sense of her life prospects? We can think of two reasons for imposing such a severe restraint on personal liberty—but, in the end, find neither persuasive.

The first rationale invites us to think deeply about the very meaning of personal identity: is Joan at age twenty-one really the same person as Joan at forty? If not, this supports the case for basic income over stakeholding. If the forty-year-old Joan is really a completely different person, or so the argument goes, the older Joan would take cold comfort in the fact that *somebody else* called Joan received eighty thousand dollars long ago—especially if that somebody else had spent the money on activities that the forty-year-old found valueless. Rather, she would treat the stake received by Joan-at-twenty-one as morally equivalent to the eighty thousand dollars received by some other person—let's call him Jim. The fact that Jim and Joan-at-twenty-one received stakes only makes it less fair that Joan-at-forty isn't receiving any money.

For anyone who holds this discontinuous view of the self, the basic income looks much fairer: Joan-at-forty receives precisely the same four thousand dollars received by Joan-at-twenty-one and by Jim-at-fifty-five. All discontinuous selves are treated equally.

No conclusion, however, is better than its premises. Although we concede that the discontinuous view has a surprisingly large number of philosophical adherents in these postmodern times, we ourselves remained profoundly unconvinced.[54] We do not deny, of course, that life contains many surprising changes and that Joan at forty may be engaged in projects radically different from those that she thought sensible twenty years before. Nonetheless, when she tells the story of her life, she will not suppose that it began yesterday. She will recognize that the configuration of her present life is inextricably connected to the decisions made by Joan-at-twenty-one. While she may profoundly regret some of these decisions, she will recognize them as her own.

Each of us has only one life, despite the fact that our experiences, desires, and ideals change a lot over time. This life begins at birth and ends at death, and there is no evading the challenge of giving it meaning. Indeed, one of the big differences between children and grown-ups is the way in which they deal with this challenge. Children may imagine that their choices have no consequences for the meaning of their life as a whole, but adults know better. To be sure, nobody supposes that he can successfully micromanage his life or evade its many surprises. Nonetheless, there comes a point where each competent citizen should be deemed responsible for shaping the larger contours of his existence—for better or for worse. To treat him otherwise is to treat him as an eternal child.

This is the train of thought that leads us to prefer stakeholding over the basic income. Granted, we have embraced certain limitations on the young adult's right to take charge of his life. Although we are firmly committed to a continuous view of the self, we also agree that young adults may not always understand or empathize with their future circumstances, especially when there is a fifty- or seventy-five-year gap between them and their successor-selves. Given these predictable failures in empathetic understanding, even a liberal state may justly intervene on behalf of the elderly self, forbidding the youthful stakeholder to cash out the citizen's pension that guarantees him a dignified retirement. To this extent, we do prefer a basic income over stakeholding, for our citizen's pension is, in effect, a basic income under another name. But it is one thing to authorize a limited incursion on the right of adults to take responsibility for the shape of their lives, quite another to allow the state to deny that we are ever grown up enough to use a large chunk of resources to give our lives an enduring shape.

At this point, the first rationale for the basic income merges into a second, more frankly paternalistic line of thought. As far as the paternalist is concerned, the basic income is better because we are more likely to prevent people from "wasting" their stake if we pay it out in dribs and drabs over time. Even if people dissipate one year's payment, they cannot prespend next year's—and by then, we hope, they will act more wisely.

We have taken a few steps to accommodate these anxieties. We have denied high school dropouts control over their eighty thousand dollars; instead, they receive what amounts to a basic income of four thousand dollars' interest on their principal. And we recommend that the stake be paid in four installments, rather than all at once, to give people a chance to learn from their own and others' mistakes. Even if someone were to waste his first twenty thousand dollars, he would receive a second chance, and a third, and a fourth. The difference, of course, is that the basic income would give him a new chance every year.

At the same time, the small amounts dribbled out annually never really encourage the kind of sober reflection that stakeholding invites. It is just too easy to spend four thousand dollars a year on incidentals without ever confronting how the extra resources could help you re-shape the larger contours of your life. One year, the four thousand dollars may go for a slightly better car, the next year for a nicer vacation, but there will never be an occasion for more fundamental reappraisals and restructurings. If we judge from the anecdotal evidence, this has been the experience of Alaska's mini-basic-income program, which grants each citizen about one thousand dollars a year. Most Alaskans seem to be using their money on consumerist binges; the grants are just too small to encourage more fundamental reassessments.[55]

In contrast, eighty thousand dollars does provide the framework for a period of basic appraisal, and at an age when such questioning may make a real difference. You have a chance, once in your life, to step up to the plate. If you plan ahead and act sensibly, you may win big. But if you mess up, you live with the consequences. The basic income cushions failure; stakeholding is a launching pad for success.

But perhaps we could have it both ways. A number of leading commentators, ranging from James Tobin to Roberto Unger, have suggested a variation on stakeholding: give every young person a "human capital account," which she could draw on for certain prescribed purposes, among them higher education, vocational training, and medical expenses.[56] The rationale, of course, is freedom-within-boundaries. Give the young people the capital they need to lead productive lives, but make sure that they spend it responsibly.

This approach has undeniable appeal. And if these restrictions were the political price for enacting stakeholding, we would be willing to pay it. But as a matter of principle, we reject this notion of freedom-within-boundaries. Of course, the boundaries may be so wide that many will hardly notice them. The college-bound, for example, might fare almost as well under the restricted plan.[57] But a large middle group will be denied real freedom. For them, building "human capital" may not be the best life plan. Like Bill and Brenda, they may want to use the money to move out of a dangerous neighborhood.[58] Like

Mike and Mary Ann, they may put a premium on some seemingly friv-olous, but to them important, item like foreign travel or an unforget-table wedding. We believe that these young men and women should be no less free than their college-bound peers or the richer kids across town who are making similar decisions with their parents' money. We are repelled by programs that require kids from the wrong side of the tracks to justify their lives to a government bureaucrat.

## What Kind of America?

This returns us to the nub of the matter: the fate of the vast majority of ordinary Americans in our globalizing economy. These men and women are perfectly competent people, despite their lack of college degrees and the professional skills that earn big rewards today. As stakeholders in American society, they will confront the future with the confidence befitting a free people. The wrenching economic changes of the twenty-first century will not send them reeling with the first shock from the marketplace. They will have the resources to stand up to economic challenges with their heads held high and to make the best of the emerging opportunities. Some will succeed and others fail, but all will have had a real chance at the pursuit of happiness.

And even those who fail will know that they have not deprived their children of a fair opportunity to start again. They too will be citizens, with their own stake in the country.

But another America awaits. Unless we take the future into our hands, our country may travel yet farther down the road of social divi-sion. Despite the wave of political advertising that will greet the new millennium, the real world of the twenty-first century will harden into a brittle three-class structure: a lower class condemned to dead-end jobs and frequent unemployment, an upper class of professionals en-joying fabulous prosperity, and a vast middle class increasingly embit-tered by continuing economic stagnation. As the ideal of equal opportunity recedes and the rich retreat into their gated communities, America will become a very ugly place. How long will democracy itself survive under such grim conditions?

Our political thinking has not caught up with this emerging three-class reality. On the one hand, we heap large subsidies on the college-bound. On the other, we offer modest help to the underclass. But we have done remarkably little to enhance real opportunity for the vast middle class, who are by now understandably skeptical that government will ever do anything serious for ordinary people like themselves.

Stakeholding can break this impasse by adding a crucial term to America's social contract. At the same time, it marks a radical break with the elitist tradition of social engineering. Give ordinary citizens their stake in America, and let them inaugurate a new age of freedom.

The stakeholding society is no utopia. But it does provide a genuine alternative to social division and moral drift. Rather than entrusting our fate to the invisible hand, this generation of Americans has work to do if it is to be equal to our political ideals. Perhaps we will never completely realize the American dream of equal opportunity. But if we abandon that dream, we will surely lose our way.

# Appendix

# Funding the Stakeholder Society

This Appendix provides more detail on the expected effect of stakeholding on federal government revenues. These projections are necessarily approximate, but they provide enough solid information to show that our proposals are fiscally realistic.

## The Stake

If implemented today the stake would cost the United States about $255 billion per year.

We arrive at this conclusion via several steps. The first estimates the number of eligible stakeholders. The data are surprisingly imprecise, but in 1997 there were about 3.1 million twenty-one-year-old U.S. citizens.[1] One must then subtract the small number of citizens who will fail the residency test for stakeholding and the larger group who will forfeit their stakes due to criminal convictions.[2] At the same time, the base should be increased to include longtime resident aliens with a new and powerful incentive to naturalize. As a rough cut, we have treated these competing effects as a wash.

We assume, then, that approximately 3.1 million Americans would have come forward, at age twenty-one, to claim their stakes in 1997. Recall, however, that stakeholders who enroll in higher education can claim up to twenty thousand dollars per year as soon as they have graduated from high school (which is assumed to occur at age eighteen). This difference in timing affects the overall cost of the program. Because college-bound stakeholders will receive their eighty thousand dollars sooner, we want to maintain financial equivalence by paying interest to other stakeholders for the three more years that they must wait. In making this calculation, we use the same 2 percent real rate of interest employed to determine payback obligations.[3] Stakeholders in the non-college-bound group would collect $21,225 every year between the ages of twenty-one and twenty-four, for a nominal total of $84,900, which has a present value (at age twenty-one) of $82,435.[4]

Our cost estimates take these timing differences into account, using a couple of rough but reasonable assumptions. We assume, first, that 27 percent of all stakeholders will attend four-year colleges from the ages of eighteen to twenty-one,[5] and, second, that they will spend their entire stake on college tuition and related costs. (In 1996–1997, the average four-year institution cost $18,476 for tuition, room, and board).[6]

Within this framework, the cost of stakeholding in 1997 would have been $255 billion.[7] Annual costs will vary with demographic trends. We are now experiencing a "baby boomlet" in the United States— four-year-olds numbered 4 million in 1997. Paying stakes to those kids beginning in 2011 would cost about $320 billion.[8] But national wealth will also be higher then.[9]

Two statistics will help to put this flurry of numbers in perspective. The federal government's budget in 1998 was about $1.7 trillion.

Stakeholding would have raised the total to about $2 trillion, an increase of 15 percent.[10]

The cost of stakeholding is lower once we take into account collateral benefits. Chapter 3 describes how the program will replace a significant chunk of current federal and state spending on higher education, which now amounts to about $55 billion.[11] We estimate that stakeholding would cut this amount in half, to $28 billion, although this is a speculative calculation. If we had wished to engage in some creative accounting, we could have banked on these estimated savings in government spending and reduced our estimate of the total revenue cost of stakeholding from $255 billion to $227 billion. But we choose instead to view these savings as a rebate to the states, one that would help them offset the reduction in real property revenues that the introduction of a federal wealth tax could engender.[12]

Stakeholding could also reduce crime and welfare spending, and increase tax revenues, as newly trained young adults take better-paying jobs. We think that these effects would be substantial, but because they are also speculative, we have not included them in our calculations.

## The Wealth Tax

Estimating the revenue effects of a new tax is tricky, because one is never sure how the tax may change the behavior of taxpayers. We can measure total wealth today, but the new tax may lead people to hide assets or work and save less in order to avoid the tax. These effects are uncertain, and we have not attempted to model them directly.[13] Instead, we have constructed a static revenue estimate that includes a large revenue "cushion" for behavioral changes. We estimate that, under ideal compliance conditions, our 2 percent wealth tax would raise $378 billion each year.[14] Subtracting the roughly $55 billion that it would cost to coordinate the wealth tax with the income tax (explained below), the wealth tax raises $323 billion. The cost of stake-holding is much less—$255 billion. Thus, even if behavioral changes reduced wealth-tax revenue by as much as 21 percent, a 2 percent wealth tax would suffice to fund the stake. Although we do not antici-pate economic effects of this magnitude, we have chosen to err on the conservative side, and what follows describes our methodology and as-sumptions in more detail.

Our wealth-tax revenue estimates were constructed by Mark Wil-helm, formerly an assistant professor in the Department of Econom-ics at Pennsylvania State University and now at Indiana University–Purdue University at Indianapolis. He used data from the Federal Re-serve's 1995 Survey of Consumer Finances (SCF), the most recent and most comprehensive data on individual wealth available.[15] His rev-enue estimates assume that the wealth tax would be imposed on net wealth (assets minus liabilities) and that it would include an exemption of eighty thousand dollars per individual.[16]

Our methodology is conservative in several respects. First, the SCF generally does not include the value of consumer durables other than homes, cars, and other vehicles.[17] With few exceptions, the survey omits household effects, jewelry, antiques, and so on, as well as ordi-nary furnishings. In contrast, such items as these are included in the wealth-tax base.[18]

Second, we have chosen to value private pensions in a way that un-derstates their probable worth. Wilhelm's estimates use the "current legal value" of pension rights, meaning the value of defined-benefit or defined-contribution benefits to which a worker would be entitled if she left her job today.[19] The estimate thus ignores future benefit ac-cruals—even if the taxpayer intends to remain in her job. As we ex-plain in Chapter 6, we have not included Social Security pensions in the base for wealth taxation.[20] It would be hard to do so in any event, as their present value is highly sensitive to each recipient's future work history and marital status.

Third, we have apportioned wealth between members of married couples and long-term partners in a way that minimizes tax revenue. In our one departure from the static method, we have assumed that all couples will shift assets to maximize the advantage of their eighty-thousand-dollar exemptions.[21] Thus we have divided all wealth (other than pensions) equally between members of married and cohabiting couples.[22] This is a highly conservative move on our part, because it adopts as the benchmark the outer bound of possible behavioral response.

Fourth, the 1995 SCF data necessarily omit the extra financial wealth created by the stock market boom of the mid- and late 1990s. We have not attempted to estimate the additional revenue, but it may be substantial. For example, in June 1995, the Dow Jones Industrial Average hovered around 4,500; by June 1998, the index stood at nearly 9,000, for a gain of about 100 percent.[23] Although stock ownership among middle-class families has increased rapidly in recent years, it is still concentrated in the richest families, and so stock gains accrue disproportionately to wealthy taxpayers.[24]

A fifth conservative move was to omit from the estimate the revenue potentially derived from taxing U.S. wealth held by foreigners.[25] This omission reflects data limitations: the SCF includes only U.S. households. The Federal Reserve Board's Flow of Funds accounts provide one measure of foreign financial wealth in the United States, including government and private debt and equity holdings in U.S. companies as well as foreign direct investment. For the fourth quarter of 1997, foreign assets were $4.654 trillion, and liabilities were 2.267 trillion, for net assets of $2.387 trillion.[26]

The difficulty lies in determining how much of this wealth would be subject to U.S. tax and would exceed the exemption level (once imputed to individual foreign holders). As Chapter 6 suggests, the only categories of foreign-owned U.S. wealth that would be taxable are equity in a U.S. business or U.S. real estate. In 1997, foreigners' U.S. corporate equities and foreign direct investment were $881.7 billion and $837 billion, for a total of $1.719 trillion, or 37 percent of total foreign assets. Netting out a proportionate share of total foreign debt,[27] foreigners' taxable wealth was $882 billion, which would yield $17.64 billion in wealth-tax revenue.

This figure does not impute eighty-thousand-dollar exemptions to each ultimate individual owner. We model our approach on the current income-tax rules, which tax nonresident foreigners at a flat rate of 30 percent and deny them certain deductions received by U.S. taxpayers.[28] This approach also facilitates an entity-level collection mechanism for the wealth tax, which is crucial because foreign individuals cannot be expected to file wealth-tax returns.[29] Thus the $17.64 billion estimate is another rough but reasonable approximation.[30]

Taken together, these conservative moves increase the revenue cushion for stakeholding to quite generous proportions. These extra resources give us the option of including a final modification of the wealth tax that will cost a bit of revenue—coordinating the wealth tax with the income tax. Data are limited, so we provide a range of estimates. In 1994 (the most recent year for which data are available), individual taxpayers reported a total of $220 billion in net income from taxable interest, dividends, rents, and royalties.[31] Assuming that these items were taxed at an average effective rate of 20 to 30 percent,[32] the income tax paid was $44 to $66 billion. Taking the midpoint of the range, the annual cost of $55 billion would reduce the net (static) revenue raised by the wealth tax from $378 billion to $323 billion.

Wilhelm's estimates of the distribution of wealth and of the effects of the wealth tax appear in Table 3. (The figures in the table represent households, not individuals.) We recognize that stakeholding and the wealth tax may gradually change the allocation of wealth in society, which will in turn affect the revenue and distributional effects of the wealth tax. But a static distributional estimate is nevertheless useful—and a striking illustration of wealth concentration.

Table 3.  Distribution of Wealth and Wealth-Tax Liability, by Household

| Wealth class | Median wealth ($) | Median tax payment ($) | Ownership of total U.S. wealth (%) | Liability for total wealth tax (%) |
|---|---|---|---|---|
| Bottom quintile | 450 | 0 | −0.08 | 0 |
| Second quintile | 21,710 | 0 | 1.8 | 0 |
| Middle quintile | 73,600 | 0 | 5.7 | 0.3 |
| Fourth quintile | 172,990 | 1,110 | 14.0 | 6.9 |
| Top quintile | 554,820 | 8,344 | 78.6 | 92.9 |
| Top 1 percent | 4,611,750 | 90,140 | 29.0 | 38.9 |

Source: Wilhelm (1998), pp. 15–17, 19. Percentages do not add to 100 due to rounding.

## Payback of the Stake

Over time, stakeholders will begin to make substantial contributions to the fund by paying back their initial eighty thousand dollars with interest. But estimating the magnitude of this effect is extremely speculative because substantial sums won't be forthcoming for a half century.

Existing data are also woefully inadequate for our purposes. Internal Revenue Service estate tax records are radically incomplete for our purposes, because current law applies only to estates and bequests that exceed the exemption amount ($650,000 in 1999).[33] But the payback requirement will generally apply to all estates (or lifetime gifts) in excess of fifty thousand dollars.[34]

For what it's worth, the IRS reports that, in 1995, almost seventy thousand decedents left gross estates of $600,000 or more (the exemption level in that year).[35] Assuming that each taxpayer died owing a payback of $250,000, this group would have contributed more than $17 billion to the stakeholding fund, in addition to actual estate tax revenue in 1995 of $11.841 billion.[36] But these estate tax returns cover less than 4 percent of 1995 deaths,[37] and we have no way of estimating how much revenue would have been raised from the other 96 percent. Nevertheless, the wealth data presented in Table 3 suggest that the revenue yield would be substantial.[38] If just 10 percent of decedents paid back their stakes in full, the stakeholding fund would collect $48 billion each year.[39]

We also have limited data on annual inter vivos gifts. Although the SCF reports gifts made and received, the data are internally inconsistent and difficult to interpret; a recent study suggests that the plausible range of annual gifts ranges from $18.9 billion to $62.3 billion.[40] Without knowing the distribution of these gifts, we cannot estimate the payback revenue that they imply.

## Citizens' Pensions and the Privilege Tax

To calculate the value of our proposed citizens' pensions, we have used the existing outlays for Social Security pensions as our base. Our illustrative numbers assume that our initiative was immediately effective—even though, in our transition proposal, the first citizens' pensions would not be paid for another generation.[41] For consistency, we use 1996 data throughout, and we take no credit for the potential reductions in Supplemental Security Income (SSI) benefits.

This allows us to avoid the tricky project of projecting Social Security expenditures and demographic changes into the future. But we are not able to avoid entirely some problems of translation. The first centers on the retirement age. Now sixty-five, it is scheduled to rise to sixty-seven in 2027.[42] Citizens' pensions, if eventually adopted, would also be payable at age sixty-seven. But to make the present-day calculation as comparable as possible, we simulate citizens' pensions payable at age sixty-five. (This is a conservative move on our part, because the monthly citizens' pensions would be bigger if funds paid today to the sixty-five-and-older set were payable only to those sixty-seven and older.)

In 1996, the Social Security Administration paid total retirement and survivors' benefits of $273 billion to 32 million elderly Americans, for an average benefit of $718 per month.[43] In the same year, 34 million Americans were sixty-five and older.[44] A citizen's pension today could be set at a universal benefit of $8,040 per year, or $670 per month.[45]

Calculating the privilege tax raises another issue in translation. The simplest method—and most favorable to us—calculates the privilege tax needed to fund citizens' pensions on a purely pay-as-you-go basis. On that approach, we would have to raise only $273 billion. But this method doesn't take into account the portion of the current payroll tax that is now accumulating in the Social Security trust funds in order to build a surplus for the baby boomers retiring early next century.[46] To complicate matters further, actuarial projections show that current revenues are inadequate to meet Social Security obligations over the long run and that therefore benefits must be cut or taxes raised.[47]

Given these problems, we have presented three privilege-tax estimates. The first replaces those payroll taxes dedicated to old-age pensions. This comparison takes current law as the baseline, without attempting to achieve solvency in the Social Security trust fund. Today, payroll tax revenues devoted to the old-age and survivors' program (OASI) are 104 percent of benefits paid.[48] Accordingly, the first version of the privilege tax must raise $284 billion, or 104 percent of the $273 billion annual cost of citizens' pensions.[49]

Recall that the privilege tax will apply to residents who are older than twenty-one and younger than sixty-five (rising to sixty-seven in the next century) and that we expect about 20 percent of the population to fall in the highest bracket, 60 percent in the middle bracket, and 20 percent in the lowest bracket. In 1996, 151 million Americans were over twenty-one and under sixty-five.[50] Some will default on their payment obligations: we have arbitrarily assumed 10 percent, equally distributed among the brackets, leaving a taxpayer population of 136 million.[51] We have also assumed that the top-bracket group will pay an annual amount ten times the tax for the low-bracket group and that the middle group will pay the average privilege tax.[52] Using these parameters, we calculate an annual privilege tax of about $3,800 for the high-bracket group, $2,090 for the middle group, and $380 for the low-bracket group.[53]

The second simulation assumes that the retirement pension fund will be put on a fiscally sound footing *only* through raising taxes, although cutting benefits is also a possibility. Thus, this estimate sets an upper bound on the cost of funding citizens' pensions. The best projections suggest that an immediate 2.17 percentage-point increase in the payroll tax would ensure long-term solvency for Social Security as a whole.[54]

In 1996, taxable payroll was $3.05 trillion, so this increase would have yielded an additional $66 billion.[55] But we do not need to raise this entire sum, for 20 percent of it is paid to the nonelderly (that is, the disabled and survivors).[56] Thus, if imposed today in an actuarially sound system, the privilege tax should raise about $337 billion per year ($284 billion, calculated above, plus 80 percent of the $66 billion increase needed, or $53 billion).[57] Using this method, we calculate an annual privilege tax of $4,500 for the high-bracket group, $2,475 for the middle group, and $450 for the low-bracket group.[58]

Both of these methods rely on the privilege tax to replace only the portion of the 1996 payroll tax needed to fund citizens' pensions. They leave in place payroll taxes needed to fund disability and survivors' benefits for the under-sixty-five group as well as Medicare. Under our first method, this leaves in place payroll taxes of $189 billion.[59] Under our second, $202 billion.[60]

Our third calculation considers the level of the privilege tax needed to replace all Social Security *and* Medicare payroll tax revenues of $472 billion in 1996.[61] This book does not otherwise consider the distinctive problems of Medicare, but we provide these estimates merely to give the reader a sense of the extent to which privilege taxation may serve as a revenue raiser. (In making these calculations, however, we have not considered any tax increases that might be required in order to guarantee the actuarial soundness of Social Security or Medicare.) The resulting privilege tax would be $6,300 for the high bracket, $3,465 for the middle bracket, and $630 for the low bracket.[62]

# Notes

## Chapter 1: Your Stake in America

1. See McMurrer, Condon, and Sawhill (1997), pp. 8–9 (in past years, children were more likely to do better than their parents because of economic growth or changes in the occupational structure); for more detail, see Chaps. 2 and 9.
2. See Wolff (1998), pp. 136–137 (from 1983 to 1995, only the top 5 percent experienced an increase in net worth; in every other group, wealth declined, with the bottom 40 percent experiencing the sharpest decline); for more detail, see Chap. 6.
3. See Gottschalk (1997), pp. 21–40; Blank (1997), pp. 60–64.
4. Gottschalk (1997), p. 30 (between 1979 and 1994, real wages for college graduates increased by 5 percent, while real wages for high school graduates fell by 20 percent).
5. See U.S. Bureau of the Census (1997b), p. 470, table 725 (showing that in 1993, 1994, and 1995, the top 5 percent received 20.0 to 20.3 percent of total income); and Danziger and Gottschalk (1995), p. 42, table 3.1 (in 1947, the richest 5 percent of U.S. families received 17.5 percent of aggregate income; in 1989, 17.9 percent; in 1991, 17.1 percent).
6. U.S. Bureau of the Census (1997a), p. vi.
7. See, e.g., Okun (1975).
8. See Levy (1987), p. 17.
9. See Blank (1997), pp. 57–72.
10. See Wilson (1996), pp. 150–153; Blank (1997), pp. 66–67.

11. See Chap. 8.
12. See Smith (1997).
13. See Silver (1990), pp. 163–195. In contrast to stakeholding, Thatcher's program lacked evenhandedness and was justly criticized for it. Not only were poor people living in private housing excluded, but the value of the "Right to Buy" depended on the quality of each tenant's house. Moreover, despite the substantial discounts, many tenants found it difficult to come up with the money needed to exercise their option. As a consequence, Thatcher's program tended to leave the least advantaged as tenants in worsening accommodations. See Flynn (1990).
14. See Rapaczynski and Frydman (1994); Shafik (1995). Unfortunately, Klaus did not combine his support of voucher privatization with a regulatory regime—like the American Securities and Exchange Commission—that would have protected the interests of citizen-stakeholders from predictable abuse by insiders. This failure has led to increasing public dissatisfaction with Klaus, but it would be a mistake to allow it to cast a shadow upon his earlier successes as a policy innovator.
15. See Brown and Thomas (1994), p. 43. The popularity of the program is so great that some believe that it prevents the use of the funds for more important purposes. Compare Brown and Thomas (1994) with O'Brien and Olson (1990). While this may be correct in the Alaska case, we will argue that the value of stakeholding is sufficiently great to justify a priority over most other competing programs.
16. See Holmes and Sunstein (1998).
17. See Moon (1997), pp. 67–68; Kingson and Schulz (1997), pp. 51–52.

## Chapter 2: Citizen Stakeholding

1. This basic commitment is central to a great deal of philosophical work, though theorists differ on a host of important matters. See, e.g., Ackerman (1980); Okin (1989); Rawls (1971); Sen (1992); Van Parijs (1995); Dworkin (1981a, 1981b). For obvious reasons, we will be relying on the framework developed in the first of these volumes, though most of our concrete proposals are compatible with a much broader range of contemporary liberal theories.
2. Meade (1964), pp. 38–39.
3. The poverty rate for children in 1996 was lower than in 1959 (27.3 percent) but higher than in the late 1960s to mid-1970s, when it hovered around 15 percent. U.S. Bureau of the Census (1997a), pp. vii, C–5. Official poverty rates may understate the extent of material hardship among families with children. Mayer and Jencks (1989), pp. 99–100, 111.
4. Scarbrough (1993), pp. 64–67; U.S. Bureau of the Census (1997a), p. 24, table 5.
5. Id.; see also Danziger and Gottschalk (1995), pp. 74–76.
6. In 1960, only 31.9 percent of married women participated in the labor force; by 1992, 59.4 percent did. U.S. Department of Labor (1993), p. 40. By 1996, 70 percent of wives with children under age eighteen were in the workforce, as were 62.7 percent of wives with children under the age of six. U.S. Bureau of the Census (1997b), p. 404, table 632.

For the importance of women's earnings to their families' incomes, see Danziger and Gottschalk (1995), pp. 80–81 (from 1973 to 1991, mothers' rising earnings were especially important for children's standard of living).

7. Although methodologies and findings differ, most studies have not found that mothers' working outside the home has significant, long-term adverse effects on their children. See, e.g., J. R. Smith et al. (1997); Blau and Grossberg (1992); Haveman and Wolfe (1995).

8. NICHD Early Child Care Research Network (1997).

9. In 1980, 19 percent of families with children were headed by single mothers (22 percent by single parents); by 1996, 27 percent were headed by single mothers (and 32 percent by single parents). U.S. Bureau of the Census (1997b), p. 63, table 75.

10. Choy (1997), pp. 22–23.

11. Parrish et al. (1995), pp. 17, 30–32; McMurrer and Sawhill (1998), p. 64. Although the impact of dollars spent on educational quality is debated, data show that students at more affluent schools have greater access to programs for gifted students, diagnostic and prescriptive services, and extended day programs. Young et al. (1997), p. 9.

12. Mullins et al. (1994), pp. 42–45, 86–87, 142–143, 200–201, and 315–316.

13. See Sturm and Guinier (1996), pp. 988–992.

14. See id. for a discussion of coaching and its effects on SAT scores.

15. Cuccaro-Alamin (1997), pp. 34–36 (within ten years of high school graduation, 88.3 percent of students of high socioeconomic status [SES], 48 percent of low-SES students, and 69 percent of middle-SES students had enrolled in postsecondary education).

16. Id., p. 36.

17. For a review of theories and empirical evidence on the causal role of income, see Duncan and Brooks-Gunn (1997), pp. 601–605. Susan Mayer has recently argued that the causal role of income has been exaggerated and that other factors, including parental personality, educational background, and cultural practices, may explain both low income and bad outcomes for children. See Mayer (1997), pp. 8–15, 79–142. For more detail on this debate, see Chap. 9, p. 161.

18. See Ackerman (1980), especially chaps. 4 and 5.

19. See McMurrer and Sawhill (1998), p. 76 (summarizing recent studies finding that no more than 10 to 15 percent of differences in earnings or income is associated with differences in cognitive ability); Fischer et al. (1996), pp. 84–86 (concluding that parents' socioeconomic status is significantly more important than test scores in explaining differences in income).

20. For an excellent discussion of early-childhood education initiatives, see McMurrer and Sawhill (1998), pp. 88–89.

21. U.S. House of Representatives (1998), p. 1010, table 15-37 (number of children enrolled in 1996). As Head Start serves one-third of eligible low-income children (Glazer [1993], p. 291), full funding would cost about $10.8 billion per year.

Currently, Head Start spends about $4,600 per child. A more expensive program, like the Perry Preschool model, would cost $7,000 per child. McMurrer and Sawhill (1998), pp. 88–89. The total cost for 2.2 million children would be $15.75 billion.

22. See the Appendix.
23. For an especially sensitive treatment of the problem, see Hochschild (1984).
24. See Orfield and Eaton (1996).
25. See McMurrer and Sawhill (1998), p. 64.
26. Kelman and Lester (1997), pp. 71–82, 118–124, 138–152, 158–160.
27. Ackerman (1980), chap. 5.
28. U.S. Bureau of the Census (1997b), p. 160, table 245 (26.5 percent of adults ages twenty-five to thirty-four had a bachelor's degree or more).
29. See Chap. 1, n. 4, supra.
30. See Wolff (1998), pp. 144–145 (in 1995, households in the fortieth to sixtieth percentile had financial reserves sufficient to sustain only 1.2 months of current consumption or 1.8 months of near-poverty-level consumption; poorer households had even fewer financial reserves).
31. To qualify for benefits under the Federal-State Unemployment Compensation Program, an unemployed worker must meet several requirements. These vary across states, but in general the worker must have worked at least two calendar quarters during a recent one-year period, have earned a minimum amount during that period, have been fired or laid off or have quit for "good cause," and be currently available and willing to accept suitable work. U.S. House of Representatives (1998), pp. 327–339.
32. See Orfield and Eaton (1996).
33. We recognize that the revenue side of our proposal is more complex, but we propose to build on current U.S. tax law and administration and to draw on the experience of European countries. See Chaps. 5 and 6.
34. See Chaps. 5 and 7.
35. A good deal of evidence points to late adolescence as the crucial period for the successful forging of adult identity. See Marcia (1997), pp. 99–104.
36. For spending on public primary and secondary education in 1994, see U.S. Bureau of the Census (1997b), pp. 156, 447 (tables 237, 692) (total federal, state, and local spending on public primary and secondary education was $265.3 billion; GDP in 1994 was $6.9357 trillion).

      Also in 1994, total OASDI benefits were $332.58 billion. U.S. House of Representatives (1996), p. 17, table 1–7b; in the same year, Medicare cost the federal government (net of premiums paid) $144.747 billion. Id., p. 134, table 3–1. The total expenditure, $477.327 billion, is 6.9 percent of 1994 GDP of $6.9357 trillion.
37. GDP in 1996 was $7.5761 trillion. U.S. Bureau of the Census (1997b), p. 447, table 692.
38. See n. 28, supra.
39. See, e.g., Newman (1993), pp. 1–27 (describing the demoralizing effects of decreased opportunity on the current generation of working Americans).

40. The average life expectancy was 49.24 years in 1900 and 75.8 years in 1992. U.S. Department of Health and Human Services (1996). Life expectancy is projected to increase. A boy and girl born in 1995 can expect to live to 72.5 and 79.3, respectively. A boy and girl born in 2010 can expect to live to 74.1 and 80.6, respectively. U.S. Bureau of the Census (1997b), p. 88, table 117.

41. See Langbein (1988), p. 732.

42. Data on inter vivos gifts are sparse, but recent work suggests that the wealthy give away far less to their children during life than a rational tax-minimization strategy would suggest. Poterba (1997a), p. 26.

43. Langbein (1988), pp. 730–736.

44. Id., p. 746.

45. At a 5 percent (nominal) interest rate, an eighty-thousand-dollar stake would earn four thousand dollars per year. This is approximately the rate of total return on long-term government bonds. Ibbotson Associates (1997), p. 33.

46. See Chap. 3.

47. See Zelizer (1994), who perceptively describes the ways in which social context can encourage people to earmark different sums of money for very different purposes.

48. As Chap. 3 will explain, each stakeholder's account may have more or less than eighty thousand dollars in it by the time she reaches her early twenties. But for purposes of illustrating clearly how the stake might be disbursed, these details can be deferred for now.

49. Studies that measure the "underclass" confront two key issues. First, does the term describe individuals or neighborhoods? The neighborhood concept unconscionably lumps together very different people—poor and not poor, jobless and employed, criminal and law-abiding—simply because they live together. We reject this approach. Individuals should be evaluated on their own merits and not by the habits of their neighbors. Second, what exactly does the term "underclass" mean? For some, it simply means poor people; others say that the key criterion is joblessness. We reject both these criteria as far too broad: in an era of extreme inequality of opportunity, we refuse to treat the jobless poor as per se "irresponsible."

We focus instead on estimates that attempt to identify individuals with "multiple social problems," as evidenced by a *combination* of single parenthood, welfare receipt, dropping out of high school, and unemployment. These ways of identifying the underclass are by no means perfect but at least offer more subtlety and flexibility.

Mincy (1994) provides a useful summary. Among the more nuanced attempts, the upper bound is Reischauer's (1987) estimate that, in 1982, 8.1 million people lived in persistently poor families with a head of household who had little education and had worked less than three-fourths of the year. The lower bound is Ricketts and Sawhill's (1988) estimate that, in 1979, 1.1 million people were poor residents of neighborhoods with high numbers of single parents, high school dropouts, welfare recipients, and unemployed males. (Note that the figure in

Mincy describing Kasarda [1992] is a misprint; that study found 1.25 million individuals, not "5.3 million households.") Using figures on total population for 1979 and 1982 (U.S. Bureau of the Census [1997], p. 15, table 14), Reischauer's estimate represented 3.5 percent of the population; Ricketts and Sawhill's estimate represented less than .5 of 1 percent.

50. See Jencks (1992), p. 171; U.S. Department of Education (1997b), p. 17, table 8 (in 1996, 87 percent of twenty-five- to twenty-nine-year-olds had completed high school).

51. For a review and critique of "culture of poverty" claims, see Katz (1989), pp. 16–52.

52. Consider Edin and Lein (1997), chap. 3 (facing dismal job prospects and significant child care responsibilities, welfare mothers chose to stay on welfare, despite its indignities and hardships; most, though, planned to return to work eventually).

53. To be sure, different young adults have different resources and expectations, but it is hard to predict how individual self-interest will shape the tradeoff. Consider a typical blue-collar worker's calculus. While he has good reason to save his stake for a future rainy day, spending the stake *now* may mean buying a decent house for his family. At the other end of the economic spectrum, a young Wall Street lawyer might also lack clear priorities. She accurately supposes that her chances of destitution in later life are low, but she also may not need the eighty thousand dollars for a pressing current need—leaving her more likely, perhaps, to blow the money on a fancy car and Armani suits. There is, in short, no particular reason to suppose that stakeholding decisions will divide easily along class lines.

54. See, e.g., Glendon (1991); Sandel (1996).

## Chapter 3: The Stake in Context

1. There are no serious constitutional problems raised by denying stakes to noncitizens. See *Mathews v. Diaz,* 426 U.S. 67 (1976).

2. An identical problem is raised by citizens who are born abroad of American parents and who do not spend a significant period of their childhood in the United States. We would treat them exactly as we do native-born citizens.

3. U.S. Department of Justice (1996), pp. 136, 164 (in fiscal year 1996, 1,044,689 people were naturalized; 104,134 were under age twenty-five).

4. This rule will allow native-born citizens who lived out their earliest years in America to qualify, even if they then spent their last ten abroad. We do not think that this problem is big enough to worry about.

5. *Schneider v. Rusk,* 377 U.S. 163 (1964), is the leading case establishing a principle of equal treatment between native-born and naturalized citizens. A congressional provision had stripped naturalized Americans of their citizenship if they returned to their country of origin and took up long-term residence. A divided Court struck the provision down as discriminatory: "A native-born citizen is free to reside abroad indefinitely without suffering loss of citizenship. The discrimination aimed at naturalized citizens drastically limits their rights to live and work abroad in a way that other citizens may." Id. at 168–169. There is a big difference between the facts posed in *Schneider* and the present problem. Whereas the

plaintiff in that case was threatened with the total obliteration of the classic rights of citizenship, our present initiative leaves all these rights intact. We are simply imposing a residency requirement for an economic benefit that has never previously been associated with citizenship status.

Nonetheless, invidious discrimination among classes of citizens is rightly a source of constitutional concern even when it merely involves the distribution of economic benefits. Indeed, when individual American states discriminate against citizens of other American states by imposing residency requirements, the Court has often struck them down. *Zobel v. Alaska,* 457 U.S. 55 (1982), is the decision that most closely resembles our present problem. It involved Alaska's initial effort to establish a stakeholding program out of its North Slope oil income. In its original scheme, not all citizens of Alaska received the same annual payment from the state's fund of oil revenue. Instead, the dollar amount was keyed to the number of years of residence, so that newcomers received much less than old-timers did. The Court held that Alaska could not discriminate against newly arrived citizens from other states of the Union. Because these newcomers were American citizens, with the right to travel freely anywhere in the Union, Alaska violated the equal protection clause when it discriminated against them for exercising this right by setting up residence in Alaska.

But these concerns about federalism are not relevant to our present problem. We are not dealing with the efforts of one state to lock out Americans living in the other forty-nine. We are concerned with the power of Congress to extend a new economic benefit to all citizens as long as they live *somewhere* within the country. As far as we can tell, this issue has never been squarely considered by the Supreme Court. Cf. *Rogers v. Bellei,* 401 U.S. 815 (1971) (upholding a requirement, imposed on children of American parents who were born abroad, to reside for a sustained period in the United States during their years of early adulthood). Nonetheless, we are reasonably confident that the Court would uphold such a restriction, as long as it did not trench upon the classic rights of citizenship.

6. Special treatment should, of course, be given to children of American diplomats and soldiers on long-term assignment abroad.
7. Cuccaro-Alamin (1997), p. 34.
8. U.S. Bureau of the Census (1997b), table 245.
9. For purposes of our calculations, we assume that everyone graduates from high school at age eighteen.
10. Gladieux and Hauptman (1995), p. 3, table 2 ($132.297 billion in 1990–1991).
11. Id. (state and local governments pay $41.27 billion, including $39.058 billion of appropriations for public institutions).
12. Id. (showing $13.481 billion in 1990–1991); U.S. Department of Education (1998); U.S. Department of Education (1998) (fiscal year 1997 appropriations for Office of Postsecondary Education totalled $12.7 billion).
13. Cuccaro-Alamin (1997), p. 34 (in 1972, 42 percent of high school graduates were enrolled in college in the year after graduation; in 1995, the figure was 62 percent).

14. See pp. 26–27, supra.
15. U.S. Department of Education (1997a), table 2 (in 1994, 36.5 percent of low-income students had not enrolled in postsecondary education, compared to 20.7 percent of middle-income students and 6.9 percent of high-income students).

    The figures targeting enrollment in colleges only show an even greater bias in favor of upper-income students. See Clotfelter (1991), p. 40 (in 1988, 17.9 percent of students from families with incomes under ten thousand dollars were enrolled in college, compared to 58.7 percent of students from families with incomes of fifty thousand or more).
16. Cuccaro-Alamin (1997), pp. 38–39 (57 percent of students in the lowest quartile of socioeconomic status [SES], but only 10 percent of students in the highest SES quartile, delay enrollment in postsecondary education; those who delay are twice as likely to attain no degree). These correlations do not necessarily imply causation; enrollment delays reflect disparities in ability and educational opportunities as well as financial resources. Nonetheless, the orders of magnitude are so large as to justify grave concern.
17. U.S. Department of Education (1997a), table 2; U.S. Department of Education (1990), p. 44.
18. See Hout (1988); McMurrer, Condon, and Sawhill (1998).
19. Gladieux and Hauptman (1995), pp. 34–46.
20. U.S. Department of Education (1997a), table 7 (69.6 percent of students at public two-year colleges live at home, and 79.5 percent of them work an average of twenty-seven hours per week).
21. We have been unable to find sound empirical research exploring the extent to which colleges responded to the GI Bill by simply raising tuition. For a discussion of the issues raised by the most recent tax subsidies for education, see Cronin (1997).
22. See n. 11, supra.
23. U.S. Department of Education (1997b), p. 175.
24. Id.
25. In 1983, a typical public four-year university received $3,843 per student in public subsidies, compared to $1,846 for a typical public two-year college. Clotfelter (1991), p. 116.
26. For our calculations, we have used the same 2 percent real rate of interest that we have employed to determine payback obligations; see Chap. 5. The four-year total is $84,900, which has a present value (at age twenty-one) of $82,435.
27. The segregation of stakeholding dollars raises other interesting questions. For example, should a tort victim be allowed to seek damages from a defendant's stake? Should the IRS be allowed to collect from the stakes of delinquent taxpayers ? We leave these and other important details to a later stage in the stakeholding debate.
28. Of course, no legal shield will protect all underage borrowers. Loan sharks will rely on illegal means of enforcing their claims, and legal but superaggressive creditors may attempt to pressure stakeholders into "voluntarily" paying out their

stakes in order to avoid the stigma of bankruptcy. But it is utopian to suppose that all problems can be eliminated.

29. See n. 24, supra. Because we expect tuition at public universities to rise substantially, and for the reasons just discussed, tuition at the average private college is the appropriate benchmark.

30. See pp. 53–54.

31. Poor students at the most expensive colleges will continue to graduate with more substantial debts if private scholarship funds don't take up the slack. But these students will also receive the benefits of better credentials and greater social access that elite schools can provide.

32. A middle-income family will spend $300,000 to raise an only child, about $225,000 to raise a second child, and so on. Longman and Graham (1998). That figure omits foregone wages, college costs, and other added expenses, which together raise the cost of one child to a whopping $1.5 million. Id.

33. At a 2 percent interest rate, the present value of eighty thousand dollars to be received in twenty-one years is $52,782. At a 5 percent rate, the present value is $28,715.

34. See Folbre (1994), p. 115; McIntosh (1987), p. 323. The exception is former East Germany. See Buttner and Lutz (1990).

35. Oliver and Shapiro (1995), p. 7 (1987 data); compare Wolff (1996), p. 73 (in 1992, the median black household had a financial net worth of zero, and 30 percent had no positive net worth whatever).

36. Oliver and Shapiro (1995), p. 7.

37. Fuchs (1988), pp. 60–61; Goldscheider and Waite (1991), pp. 110–111; McCaffery (1993).

38. Williams (1994), p. 2242; Apter (1993), pp. 69–74.

39. See Hadfield (1993).

40. For studies of intrafamily bargaining and financial power, see Zelizer (1994), pp. 37–70; Pahl (1989).

41. The creation of such a fund would require additional revenue, which might be raised by phasing in the wealth tax more quickly than the transition to stakeholding would otherwise require. The cost would depend on the terms of the program, and we have not attempted to delineate those terms or to make a separate revenue estimate.

## Chapter 4: Profiles in Freedom

1. This estimate is based on the 1995 distribution of income among families headed by people aged twenty-five to thirty-four. Bill and Brenda earn between $15,000 and $30,000, while Mike and Mary Ann earn between $35,000 and $55,000. U.S. Bureau of the Census (1997b), p. 471, table 728.

2. Kennickell, Starr-McCluer, and Sunden (1997), p. 6, table 3. This measure excludes Social Security wealth but includes some private pension wealth. Id., p. 11, n. 12.

3. Id., p. 15, table 8 (37.9 percent of families headed by a person under age thirty-five own a primary residence).
4. U.S. Bureau of the Census (1993a), table D (1993 data).
5. In 1996, 53.1 percent of men and 62.9 percent of women aged twenty-five to thirty-four were married. U.S. Bureau of the Census (1997b), p. 56, table 59.
6. Id., p. 160, table 245.
7. In 1996, the most common occupational category for male high school graduates aged twenty-five to thirty-four was operator/fabricators. The second most common category was precision production, and third was technical, sales, and administrative work. Id., p. 415, table 648.
8. In 1996, the unemployment rate for men aged twenty-five to thirty-four was 4.9 percent. If Bill were black, his chances of being unemployed would have been even higher (10.1 percent). Id., p. 405, table 633. Unemployment among construction laborers was also relatively high (16.3 percent). Id., p. 419, table 661.
9. In 1996, the median weekly earnings of a man working as a handler, equipment cleaner, helper, or laborer were $343. The median weekly earnings of a man in sales were $589, but that figure includes the earnings of both highly paid commission salesmen and comparatively poorly paid store clerks. Id., p. 431, table 671. If Bill averages four hundred dollars a week for fifty weeks of work, he will earn twenty thousand dollars in a year.
10. In 1996, the most common occupational category for female high school graduates aged twenty-five to thirty-four was technical, sales, or administrative work; the second was the service industry, including health care. Id., p. 415, table 648. Home health care is one of the fastest-growing job categories. Id., p. 414, table 647.
11. In 1996, the median weekly earnings of a female service worker (in other than private household or protective services) were $272. Id., p. 431, table 671. But that category includes both minimum-wage workers and better-paid workers. If Brenda earns eight dollars an hour ($320 for a forty-hour week), she will make fifteen thousand dollars if she works forty-seven weeks a year.
12. In 1995, 29.2 percent of women aged twenty-five to twenty-nine had one child, 42 percent had two children, and 28.8 percent had none. Id., p. 82, table 105.
13. Even in a bad year, Bill and Brenda's income is likely to be too high to allow Peter to enroll in Head Start. See Washington and Bailey (1995), p. 36; Head Start Statistical Fact Sheet, http://www.acf.dhhs.gov/programs/hsb/factsheet.html.
14. See Edin and Lein (1997), pp. 88–119.
15. See pp. 38–39.
16. Bill and Brenda each received $21,225 on their twenty-first through twenty-fourth birthdays. (See Chap. 3.) If they have never spent any principal but have always withdrawn the investment income each year, they would have a combined principal amount of $169,800, which would generate $8,490 at 5 percent interest.
17. The remaining principal amount of $159,800 would generate interest income of $7,990 at 5 percent.

18. In 1993, only 14 percent of white renter families and 3 percent of black renter families could afford a modestly priced home (valued at between the twenty-fifth and seventy-fifth percentile) in their area. U.S. Bureau of the Census (1993b), p. 2. But with a down-payment subsidy of ten thousand dollars, 36.4 percent of all renters, and 27.2 percent of black renters, could afford to buy a house. Id., p. 4.

19. In 1996, 28.4 percent of all twenty-five- to thirty-four-year-olds had some college or an associate's degree. U.S. Bureau of the Census (1997b), p. 160, table 245.

20. For women with some college education, the most common occupational category in 1996 was technical, sales, or administrative work. Id., p. 415, table 648. The median weekly earnings of women in clerical work was $391 in 1996, or $19,550 per year. Id., p. 431, table 671.

21. In 1996, the median weekly earnings of men employed in transportation was $486 per week. Id., p. 431, table 671. Mike, who belongs to a union and earns overtime pay, makes more than that—about seven hundred dollars a week.

22. In 1995, 42 percent of women aged twenty-five to twenty-nine had two children. Id., p. 82, table 105.

23. See Mahony (1995), pp. 85–100; Apter (1993), pp. 197–198.

24. See Cancian, Danziger, and Gottschalk (1993), pp. 196, 205 (importance of women's contributions to family income in the 1970s and 1980s).

25. Assume that Mary Ann spent twenty thousand dollars at age eighteen and ten thousand dollars at age nineteen. Having spent her entire first stake payment ahead of time, she received no payment at age twenty-one, $10,612 at twenty-two, and $21,225 at both twenty-three and twenty-four. Assume that Mike spent fifteen thousand dollars of his first stake payment at age twenty-one. Both have invested the remainder at 5 percent. At age twenty-five, Mary Ann has principal plus accumulated interest of $57,972, and Mike has $77,825. The total of $135,797 would earn annual interest of $6,790 at 5 percent.

26. In 1996, the poverty rate for non-Hispanic white children was 16.3 percent; for black children, 39.9 percent; and for Hispanic children, 40.3 percent. U.S. Bureau of the Census (1997a), pp. 24–26. According to the 1990 Census, 84.5 percent of high-poverty census tracts were in cities and the remainder were in smaller towns and rural areas. Jargowsky (1997), pp. 11, 16.

27. See p. 52, supra; see also McMurrer and Sawhill (1998), p. 67 (even among students with equally high achievement-test scores, students of high socioeconomic status [SES] are more likely than low-SES students to enroll in college).

28. U.S. Department of Education (1997a), table 6 (taking into account living expenses and subtracting loans and work-study aid, the average *annual* net cost of attending a public two-year college is $4,864, the cost of attending a public four-year college is $4,922, and the cost of attending a private four-year college is $5,704; but significantly, four-year colleges, particularly private ones, require the student to take out larger annual loans).

29. Orfield (1992) (financial constraints on poor students and limited impact of financial aid).

30. In 1992, the pregnancy rate among fifteen- to seventeen-year-olds was 71 per 1,000 and the birthrate was 38 per 1,000. Henshaw (1997), p. 119.

   In 1996, 13.1 percent of adults aged twenty-five to thirty-four had not graduated from high school. U.S. Bureau of the Census (1997b), p. 160, table 245. By age thirty, 61 percent of former teen mothers had either a high school diploma or a GED. Hotz, McElroy, and Sanders (1997), p. 61.

31. About 36 percent of young noncustodial fathers are so poor that they cannot pay child support. Mincy and Pouncy (1997), p. 136.

32. The biggest occupational category for female high school dropouts is service work. U.S. Bureau of the Census (1997b), p. 415, table 648.

33. Judy's first stake payment at age twenty-one would be $21,225. Although she cannot claim the principal, she is entitled, at age twenty-two, to one year's interest at 5 percent, or $1,061.25. By age twenty-five (and thereafter), Judy's annual interest would rise to $4,245, because all four payments of $21,225 would have been deposited into her account.

## Chapter 5: Payback Time

1. See the Appendix; OMB (1997), p. 49, table 3.1 (fiscal year 1998 defense expenditures of $261 billion).

2. The GI Bill ultimately cost $14.5 billion between 1945 and 1956, with per capita expenditures of $1,858. Skocpol (1997), p. 96; Bennett (1996), p. 171. That expenditure represented nearly 5 percent of 1950 GDP of $295 billion. See BEA (1998). In 1997 dollars, the total cost would be about $84 billion (prorating the cost over the period 1945–1956) and $12,374 per person (from 1950), using inflation data from the U.S. Department of Labor (1998).

   When the GI Bill was enacted in 1944, wartime expenditures and the federal deficit were at record highs, but the debate primarily centered on America's moral debt to its young—and not on the tax cost. See Bennett (1996), p. 186; Skocpol, p. 102.

3. See OECD (1988), pp. 30–75.

4. Indeed, the Founding Fathers experimented with wealth taxes, which were imposed sporadically to finance war efforts until 1861. Ratner (1942), pp. 19, 34, 72. While an income tax was levied during the Civil War, it became a fixture of public finance only in the twentieth century with the the the passage of the Sixteenth Amendment.

5. For popular plans, including the flat tax, the USA Tax, and various national sales and value-added taxes, see Hall and Rabushka (1995); Boskin (1996).

6. See, e.g., CBO (1992). But a broad-based VAT tends to be proportional to *lifetime* income, and the tax design can be modified to mitigate the annual regressivity. See Metcalf (1994), pp. 57–61; Fullerton and Rogers (1993), pp. 228–232.

7. A universal grant financed by a regressive tax can be progressive on net. Social Security is a good example: although the payroll tax is regressive and higher earners get larger benefits, the system as a whole is progressive, because the lowest

earners receive more relative to the taxes they pay in. Similarly, if stakeholding were financed by a sales tax, the combination of a large universal benefit and a regressive tax would be progressive on a lifetime basis for a large group of poorer citizens, because the stake would represent a larger percentage of lifetime income than the tax.

8. See, e.g., Nozick (1974). In Nozick's view, succeeding generations can legitimately complain only if their predecessors made them worse off than they would have been in a world without private property and free markets. Moreover, he interprets this baseline in quite a minimalist fashion. See id., pp. 174–182.

9. In Henry Sidgwick's memorable phrase, the challenge is to adopt "the point of view (if I may so) of the Universe." Sidgwick (1906), p. 382.

10. For variations on these themes, see Parfit (1984), part 4.

11. Chap. 7 will elaborate the principles of trusteeship in connection with the problem of economic growth. For an exploration of the philosophical foundations, see Ackerman (1980), chap. 7.

12. If the stake were paid in four installments from ages eighteen to twenty-one and the real interest rate were 2 percent, the payback at age eighty would be $265,160. Recall that every stakeholder is treated *as if* she would receive her stake beginning at age eighteen, as the college-bound group would, but the non-college-bound group would receive interest to age twenty-one. See Chap. 3.

13. Researchers have found that financial links among extended families are modest at best. See, e.g., Altonji, Hayashi, and Kotlikoff (1995).

14. In 1992, the number of individuals leaving gross estates worth more than $600,000 was 60,082, or 2.76 percent of the 2.2 million U.S. deaths that year. See Eller (1996–1997), p. 9. For a discussion of the possible revenue potential of the payback requirement, see the Appendix.

15. A flat-rate consumption tax exempts from tax the yield on savings; it imposes, in effect, a zero rate of tax on income from (new) capital, under certain assumptions. See Warren (1996).

16. See Chap. 6.

17. We do so as a matter of convenience. In fact, the different system prevailing in Europe seems superior. While the Anglo-American tradition of estate taxation focuses on the donor, the Europeans commonly tax the donees of bequests, thereby avoiding a peculiarity of our system—the imposition of the same estate tax regardless of the number of children who inherit. See OECD (1988), p. 78 (in 1986, sixteen OECD countries taxed inheritance, not estates).

18. In 1999, the first $650,000 of a decedent's estate or lifetime gifts is exempt from tax. I.R.C. § 2010(c). The exclusion amount will rise to $1 million by 2006. Id. Despite the unified credit, there remains one significant advantage to giving lifetime gifts rather than bequests: tax rates in the estate tax are "tax-inclusive," meaning that the estate tax base includes the funds used to pay the tax. In contrast, gift tax rates are "tax-exclusive," meaning that gifts are in effect taxed at a lower rate. Bittker, Clark, and McCouch (1996), pp. 24–25. We would unify these two rate schedules for purposes of the payback.

19. Current law also exempts from tax gifts that are used for the payment of tuition and medical expenses. I.R.C. § 2503(e). We would maintain the status quo for the foreseeable future. In today's society, neither rich parents nor their children consider tuition payments to be "gifts"; rather, they see them as the fulfilment of an obligation akin to parents' duty to financially support their children through high school. It would cut against the grain of this perceived moral obligation to impose a hefty tax on those parents who paid college tuitions in excess of their fifty-thousand-dollar exemption.

To be sure, this will result in a stakeholding pattern at odds with the principle of equal opportunity: if children from wealthy families have their college educations paid for by their parents, they can use all of their eighty thousand dollars for other purposes; in contrast, college-bound children from the bottom 90 percent may find that much of their stake has already been exhausted by the time they reach their early twenties.

This is an injustice, but not one that seems important enough to confront at this early stage in the struggle for equal opportunity. If a generation or two of stakeholding leads to a change in expectations that release parents from a sense of social obligation as far as tuition payments are concerned, a change in the rule would be entirely appropriate. But such is not the case now.

20. See OECD (1995), p. 39 (from 1913 to 1989, U.S. labor productivity grew at an annual rate of 2.5 percent; but in recent years, annual productivity growth has slowed, to just 0.7 percent in the period 1986–1991, for example). If these recent numbers signal a long-term change in productivity growth, we would obviously change the basis of our calculations.

21. I.R.C. § 2055.

22. As under current law, the reasonable costs of supporting spouses and minor children would be exempt. Bittker, Clark, and McCouch (1997), p. 136. See also Beck and Elman (1965).

23. Two additional exceptions deserve mention. First, consider a parent who dies leaving a minor child. If the parent had lived, she could have spent almost unlimited amounts of wealth to support her young child. See n. 22, supra. To avoid treating orphans more harshly, we would defer the parental payback until the child is twenty-one. The payback obligation, with interest, would be imposed as if the parent had died then. (This exception would apply only if the parent leaves all her wealth to her child: any bequests to others, including to charity, would trigger the payback obligation under the usual rules.) In the meantime, the trustee of the parent's wealth should have the usual obligation not to dissipate funds. Current estate tax law allows the estate simply to deduct reasonable amounts for the support of minor children. IRC § 2053(a)(3); *Comr. v. Weiser,* 113 F.2d 486 (10th Cir. 1940). Second is the (rarer) case of an adult who dies leaving a dependent parent. An analogous rule would defer the payback obligation until the parent dies, provided that the parent was economically dependent on the deceased child's support.

24. Both partners' stakes would accrue interest from each person's birthdate to the death of the partner who dies last. If a husband dies at age eighty and his younger wife lives twenty years after that, to age ninety, her estate would be obliged to pay back both his stake, with one hundred years' interest, and her own stake, with ninety years' interest.

25. See n. 14, supra.

26. In effect, we would lower the exemption amount. The current-law exemption level will rise to $1 million by 2006. I.R.C. § 2010(c). Our tax, in contrast, would begin to apply to bequests over $300,000 if the taxpayer left nothing to charity and died at the age of eighty ($250,000 payback plus the $50,000 lifetime exemption).

## Chapter 6: Taxing Wealth

1. See Chap. 10.

2. See Wilhelm (1998), p. 15.

3. Id., p. 16.

4. Wolff (1998), pp. 133, 136 (net worth omits Social Security entitlements, consumer durables, and retirement wealth in excess of the cash surrender value of defined-contribution plans).

5. Wolff (1996), pp. 78–79, table A–1 (augmented wealth). Augmented wealth data are not available for more recent years.

6. Wolff (1996), pp. 23–24.

7. Id., pp. 78–79, table A–1 (augmented wealth). See also Wolff (1998), p. 135 (net worth inequality rose "steeply" in the 1980s and leveled off between 1989 and 1995). Wolff suggests that the rise in the value of stocks relative to housing in the 1990s increased wealth inequality, but that trend was offset by a decline in income concentration. Id., pp. 147–148.

   Recent studies have questioned Wolff's finding of increasing inequality during the 1980s, arguing that some technical specifications produce a flat trend instead. See Kennickell and Woodburn (1997); Weicher (1996), pp. 10–18. These revisions are also controversial, and do not suggest that wealth became *less* concentrated in the 1980s.

8. From 1983 to 1995, the average net worth for the population as a whole grew from $198,770 to $204,529. Wolff (1998), p. 135. For the definition of net worth, see n. 4, supra.

9. Id., pp. 136–137. During the 1980s, 95 percent of the growth in total net worth accrued to the top 20 percent of wealth-holders; over the same period, the bottom 60 percent saw their net worth shrink in real terms. Wolff (1996), p. 72.

10. See Weicher (1996), pp. 11–13 (treating the reduction in wealth concentration in the late 1970s as "exceptional," but finding that in 1989 the richest 1 percent owned 35 percent of total net worth and that the top 20 percent received 80 percent of the aggregate increase in net worth from 1983 to 1989).

11. See Ackerman (1980), chap. 5, and esp. pp. 180–186.

12. See Chap. 2.

13. For men aged nineteen to thirty, the difference is $26,168 versus $16,772. Mayer (1997), p. 42, table 3.1; see also Corcoran and Adams (1997), p. 19 (young men from middle-income families earn 41–63 percent more per year and 29 percent more per hour than young men from poor families). We do not have data on the earnings gap for older men or for women of any age.

14. Ten thousand dollars a year for forty years at 2 percent is $616,100.

15. High-income people can defer tax on income from capital simply by holding appreciated assets or by engaging in more sophisticated financial transactions. See I.R.C. § 1014; Graetz and Schenk (1995), pp. 159–161; Graetz and Schenk (1997), pp. 30–35. For effective tax rates on income from capital, see Gravelle (1994), pp. 131, 294, table B.1. And the tax code allows generous income tax deferrals for significant amounts of pension savings. See I.R.C. §§ 402(a), 415.

16. See Kennickell, Starr-McCluer, and Sunden (1997), p. 7, table 3.

17. For a review of the empirical evidence in support of different causal hypotheses, see Danziger and Gottschalk (1995), pp. 127–150.

18. See nn. 4–5, supra (data on wealth distribution in the absence of Social Security). These data measure the actual distribution of wealth today, not the distribution of wealth that might have occurred had Social Security never existed. The effects of Social Security on aggregate private savings and on the distribution of the foregone accumulation are controversial, and it is impossible to measure with certainty precisely how much more unequal the distribution would be had Social Security never been enacted.

19. See Caplow and Simon (1998).

20. Id.

21. Recall Aesop's classic fable: the Ants work and save while the Grasshopper plays. When winter comes, guess who is left out in the cold?

22. For the OECD countries that tax wealth, see OECD (1994), pp. 210–257; compare OECD (1988), p. 30 (eleven countries).

    In 1986, the Danish wealth tax rate was 2.2 percent of wealth in excess of the exemption level (approximately $155,000 for a married couple with two children); the Swedish wealth tax rates ranged from 1.5 to 3 percent, on wealth above $28,000. OECD (1988), pp. 34–36, tables 1.2a and 1.2b. In 1993, the Danish wealth tax rate was 1 percent. OECD (1994), pp. 218–219.

    European wealth taxes typically exempt large classes of assets and cap the wealth tax as a percentage of total income. See infra nn. 44 and 56.

23. Many politicians advocate replacement of the income tax with a "flat tax," a value-added tax, or some other kind of consumption tax—but all these "simplifications" lower taxes on the rich. See Slemrod and Bakija (1996), pp. 219–226.

24. See the Appendix.

25. See Chap. 3, pp. 58–60, for an argument that eighty thousand dollars is at least in the ballpark.

26. Individuals' wealth includes debt and equity interests in for-profit businesses. We do not propose to tax wealth held by the nonprofit sector. Churches, private universities, and other charities play crucial roles in American society; they deserve

special treatment and are worth the $9 billion in forgone revenue. See Board of Governors of the Federal Reserve System (1998), p. 109, table L100a (in 1994, nonprofit organizations had net assets of $429 billion).

Our calculations in the Appendix include the value of private pensions in which taxpayers are currently vested—i.e., the amount to which a taxpayer would legally be entitled if she were to quit her job immediately. The estimate thus excludes the value of future pension accruals. See the Appendix. The wealth tax also excludes the value of Social Security entitlements. Taking the insurance analogy seriously means treating Social Security as if it were a private pension. But for the reasons given in Chap. 8, we reject the notion that old-age benefits are merely the equivalent of private savings.

27. For example, a taxpayer who owned a $200,000 home with a $125,000 mortgage would report net wealth of $75,000.

28. Stakeholders would not be subject to income tax on their receipt of the stake, but they would be taxed on any investment income they receive.

29. Wilhelm (1998), p. 15.

30. Id., p. 18, table 2; compare Kennickell, Starr-McCluer, and Sunden (1997), p. 6 (median family wealth in 1995 of $56,400, using a narrower measure of wealth).
    The *average* household wealth is much greater: $261,187. Wilhelm (1998), p. 19. The average household size in each quintile is 2.6 people. Id., p. 16.

31. Wilhelm (1998), p. 19, table 2.

32. Id.

33. Id.

34. Similar claims are legion in estate-tax debates, although the tax in fact affects only a small percentage of small businesses, and most have liquid assets sufficient to pay the tax, often through life insurance. See Burman (1997).

35. See the Appendix.

36. The income tax takes similar measures. See IRC § 151(d)(2) (no personal exemption for dependent children).

37. Continued joint filing in the income tax raises questions of transition or long-term coordination. The income tax might adopt individual filing as well, as many commentators have urged. See, e.g., Zelenak (1994); McCaffery (1997). But income-tax reform is not essential: without it, a couple would file three returns instead of two (i.e., two separate wealth tax returns and one joint income tax return, rather than two integrated income-and-wealth-tax returns).

38. According to the OECD, member countries with a net wealth tax aggregate spouses' wealth for purposes of the tax. OECD (1988), p. 39. Some countries, however, impose income taxation on individuals, and their experience provides some guide to analogous issues in wealth taxation. See generally Gann (1980); Munnell (1980).

39. In a more sophisticated scam, they might borrow heavily in the United States, thus reducing their taxable *net* wealth, and then hide the proceeds abroad.

40. Kennickell, Starr-McCluer, and Sunden (1997), p. 12, table 7 (in 1995, 65.9 percent of assets owned by U.S. families were nonfinancial assets, including vehicles, homes, investment real estate, and non-publicly-traded business assets).

41. Id.
42. See OECD (1988), pp. 61–74.
43. See id., pp. 71–73. There are clear advantages to collecting wealth taxes on business assets (whether privately or publicly held) at the entity level. The corporation (or partnership) would determine the value of owners' interests and remit the wealth tax on their behalf. Individuals would then report the value of their holdings on their own wealth-tax returns, claiming a credit for tax "withheld" at the corporate level. This model would help ensure that individual taxpayers pay their taxes and would, in the end, collect only one level of tax on business assets. For analogous proposals and other variations in the income-tax context, see Warren (1993); U.S. Department of the Treasury (1992).
44. OECD (1988), pp. 44–61. All countries give some exemption for household and personal effects and pension rights, while some also exempt small savings, life insurance, works of art and collections, and homes. Id., p. 45.
45. Wilhelm (1998), p. 15.
46. The growing trend toward defined contribution pensions assists valuation, since, in general, the value of a defined contribution plan is the current account balance. Defined benefit (DB) plans pose greater challenges, because benefits change with length of tenure and salary and employers sometimes underfund their DB plans. Entity-level taxation is one possible, albeit imperfect, solution: it has the advantage of taxing directly only the assets in the plan, but it would indirectly overtax some individuals by not allowing a personal exemption. Another option would require plan sponsors (companies and unions) to disclose to the IRS and to individuals the accrued value of individuals' pension rights. This method could provide useful information to employees as well as to the tax authorities.
47. See the Appendix. The revenue estimate is static; the 21 percent "cushion" also leaves room for behavioral responses to the tax, as discussed in Chap. 7.
48. The consensus view in Europe is that net wealth taxes aid in income tax administration. See OECD (1988), p. 163. In the United States, potential gains from coordinated administration include enhanced information reporting for both the wealth tax and the income tax. The adoption of a U.S. wealth tax might also encourage greater cooperation among national tax authorities. Expanded reporting systems may help prevent income-tax evasion, as taxpayers would find it more difficult to escape a dual system and the IRS could begin to use wealth data to cross-check for unreported income.
49. Interest on state and local bonds is excluded from tax. I.R.C. § 103. Long-term capital gains are taxed at reduced rates (I.R.C. § 1[h]), and the "realization requirement" permits taxpayers to defer tax on a variety of gains until the asset is sold. See generally *Eisner v. Macomber,* 252 U.S. 189 (1920). Imputed income on owner-occupied housing is excluded. See Chirelstein (1997), pp. 22–25.
50. Jane Gravelle estimates that in 1989, when the top statutory individual rate was 28 percent, the effective marginal tax rate was 22 percent on noncorporate capital and only 4 percent on owner-occupied housing. Gravelle (1994), p. 294, table B.1. The effective marginal tax rate on capital gains depends on the holding pe-

riod and the rate of inflation, with the rate dropping to zero for assets held until death. Id., p. 131. In contrast, the effective marginal tax rate was 43 percent on corporate capital. Id., p. 294. But that is a product of the "two-tier" corporate tax system. Although our system would preserve the corporate *income* tax, it would tax wealth only once. See n. 43, supra.

51. Like a comparable income tax, an annual wealth tax reduces the (after-tax) return on savings. But a wealth tax is not identical to an income tax, since its net impact depends on the taxpayer's overall rate of return. If an investor earns 10 percent on her capital, our wealth tax is equivalent to a 20 percent income tax; for a taxpayer earning a 5 percent return, it is equivalent to a 40 percent income tax.

52. State and local real property taxes also create the potential for multiple taxation of the same asset. While the states may fear that the federal tax will limit their ability to tax wealth, they should consider that their treasuries will also gain billions each year as stakeholding allows them to cut their subsidies to higher education. See the Appendix.

53. The calculation in the text assumes that the state tax is 12 percent, or $6. The federal income tax is 39.6 percent of $44 ($50, less the deductible state tax), or $17. The wealth tax is 2 percent of $1,000 (assume that all income is spent), or $20. The total ($6 plus $17 plus $20) is $43.

54. High marginal rates also exacerbate concerns as to the impact of our tax on savings and investment. We consider this problem at length in Chap. 7.

55. See Bittker and Lokken (1992), 111–88 to 111–92 (the alternative minimum tax).

56. Many European countries take just the opposite approach. They set a ceiling on the combined rate of income and wealth taxation, expressed as a maximum *income* tax rate. See OECD (1988), pp. 40–43. If, for example, a taxpayer has taxable wealth of one thousand dollars and income of one hundred dollars, her combined income and wealth tax could not exceed (say) 70 percent of her income, or seventy dollars. We reject this approach as precisely backward: it extends, rather than offsets, many of the income tax's special preferences. When the ceiling is a percentage of income, taxpayers with excludable income pay less income *and* wealth tax than those with fully taxable income.

57. Table 4 provides a simple example, in which the 2 percent wealth tax happens to offset the effect of a tax preference in a 40 percent income tax, assuming a 5 percent rate of return.

Table 4.  Coordinating the Income Tax and the Wealth Tax

| Asset type | Income tax (40%) | Wealth tax (2%) | Total tax |
|---|---|---|---|
| Taxable $1,000 bond, yielding 5% (pretax) | $20 | $0 ($20 − $20) | $20 |
| Tax-free $1,000 bond, yielding 5% (pretax) | 0 | $20 | $20 |

58. Tables 5 and 6 illustrate the tax treatment prevailing under an integrated system.

**Table 5.  An Integrated Income and Wealth Tax, at Various Rates of Return**

| Bond yield (pre-tax), on a $1,000 bond | Income tax alone (40%) | Wealth tax alone (20%) | Combined income plus wealth tax, with no integration | Combined tax, if income tax is subtracted from wealth tax (with wealth tax not less than zero) |
|---|---|---|---|---|
| $20 (2%) | $ 8 | $20 | $28 | $20 |
| $40 (4%) | $16 | $20 | $36 | $20 |
| $80 (8%) | $32 | $20 | $52 | $32 |
| $100 (10%) | $40 | $20 | $60 | $40 |

Note: For a taxable investment, the integrated income-wealth tax imposes the wealth tax on low-yielding assets and the income tax on high-yielding assets.

**Table 6.  Tax-Preferred Assets in an Integrated System**

| Asset type (subject to income tax or not) | Pretax yield (%) | Unintegrated wealth and income tax ($) | Integrated wealth and income tax ($) |
|---|---|---|---|
| Tax-exempt | 4 | 20 | 20 |
| Taxable | 4 | 28 | 20 |
| Tax-exempt | 10 | 20 | 20 |
| Taxable | 10 | 60 | 40 |

Note: The integrated income-wealth tax closes but does not always eliminate the gap between income-tax preferred assets and highly taxed assets.

59. Any practical integration system would make some simplifying adjustments. For example, the system might allow a credit only for categories of income that are generally taxed at relatively high rates, including taxable interest and dividends and those rents and royalties subject to current taxation at the statutory rate. In contrast, the system should not allow a credit for those items of income, like capital gains, that are taxed at substantially reduced rates.

Even this streamlined system would also have to associate deductions with items of income, to prevent taxpayers with large deductions from being awarded excessive credits. Some simplifying presumptions might be adopted to help out average taxpayers, who generally do not have significant amounts of deductible interest expense (other than on home mortgages), percentage depletion, and so on. The goal, at least for typical wealth-holders, would be a rough equity, not precision.

These income categories are an imprecise way of identifying tax-preferred income, with the result that some kinds of income (e.g., capital gains resulting from very short-term holding periods) would still be subject to high rates of tax. But the coordination rules can still provide rough justice, which is all that can be expected given the complex pattern of tax preferences established by the existing income tax.

One downside is that the coordination rule—like many other partial limitations on tax preferences—could encourage sophisticated taxpayers to play games. One early strategy would be to cross boundary lines: by recharacterizing ineligible income (say, rent) as interest or dividends, the taxpayer could claim an undeserved credit. Another potential abuse would be the manipulative apportionment of total income taxes paid between creditable and noncreditable items in order to maximize the wealth-tax credit. Both of these games are already wearily familiar in the income tax, which fights an unending battle against taxpayers' ingenuity.

60. See the Appendix.

61. Just as in the income tax, this approach requires some method of avoiding double taxation in instances where other countries also impose a wealth tax on assets located abroad. The current solution in the U.S. income tax is a foreign income tax credit; a foreign wealth tax credit would be the analogue.

62. I.R.C. §§ 871, 881. Just as in the domestic context, a corporate-level collection mechanism would help ensure compliance. See n. 43, supra.

63. European countries typically tax the wealth of nonresidents located in their country; a majority limit the wealth tax on foreigners to real property and businesses physically located in the country. See OECD (1988), pp. 38–39.

64. The income-tax analogue is the "effectively connected" or "permanent establishment" standard. See I.R.C. §§ 871(b), 882; United States Model Income Tax Convention of 1996, Article 5, reprinted in Gustafson, Peroni, and Pugh (1996).

65. See the Appendix.

66. We discuss this point further in Chap. 10.

67. To be sure, every expatriate should be given an opportunity to establish, by convincing evidence, that his decision was not motivated by tax considerations.

In any event, expatriation should not be tax-free. First, expatriate stakeholders should be required to pay back their stakes, with interest, under the same rules that apply to decedents, and regardless of their motives for expatriation. Second, all expatriates should be required to continue paying U.S. wealth taxes for ten years on wealth remaining in the country, including stocks and bonds in U.S. companies. This regime might be patterned on current I.R.C. § 877, which extends the U.S. income tax for ten years to expatriates. Like § 877, the ten-year tax might apply only to expatriates who fail to establish that they have a good nontax reason for leaving.

The § 877 tax is sometimes portrayed as an antiabuse rule responding to deferral possibilities in the income tax. The rationale for the ten-year wealth tax is slightly different: when people have benefited from living as citizens in a stakeholder society (even if they are not stakeholders themselves), on the understanding that a lifelong wealth tax is an intrinsic part of the justice of that society, a ten-year antiabuse rule discourages them from evading their obligations by expatriating, say, just before their peak wealth-holding years.

68. Robert Bork, for example, likens it to a "provision that is written in Sanskrit or is obliterated past deciphering by an ink blot," which "has, quite properly, remained a dead letter." See Bork (1990), p. 166.

69. This has been the approach traditionally taken by the Supreme Court when it has construed the meaning of the clause. See the Slaughterhouse Cases, 83 U.S. 36 (1873). But the Court would undoubtedly uphold Congress's authority to take a much broader view of the matter in the exercise of its power to tax and spend for the "general welfare." See Chap. 7.

70. See Amar (1998), chap. 9.

71. See Black (1997).

## Chapter 7: The Limits of Growth—and Other Objections

1. See Chap. 5.

2. See Chap. 5.

3. For further elaboration, see Ackerman (1980), chap. 7.

4. From 1973 to 1997, the average annual growth in real GDP was 2.728 percent. See Council of Economic Advisors (1998), p. 285, table B–4; compare id., pp. 78, 86–87 (predicting future real GDP growth of 2.4 percent per year).

   With a real growth rate of 2 percent, GDP would grow from its 1996 level of $7.576 trillion to about $27 trillion in 2060 (in 1997 dollars). See U.S. Bureau of the Census (1997b), p. 447, table 692. Even if the growth rate falls to just 1 percent, real GDP in 2060 would be about $14 trillion.

   The U.S. population in 2050 (the latest date for which we could find a standard projection) is estimated to be 393.931 million, compared to the 1996 population of 265.284 million. Statistical Abstract (1997), p. 16, table 16; p. 17, table 17 (middle series).

   In 1996, real GDP per capita was $28,558. Despite the population growth over time, real GDP per capita will be higher in 2060 whether we assume a 2 percent growth rate ($68,301 in 1997 dollars) or a 1 percent growth rate ($36,357).

5. For example, if the rate of return on an eighty-thousand-dollar investment made for forty years fell from 2 percent to 1.5 percent, the accumulated sum would drop from $176,643 to $145,121—or a 41 percent reduction in the total return.

6. See Wolff (1998), pp. 136–137 (from 1983 to 1995, wealth increased only for the richest 5 percent of U.S. households); Blank (1997), pp. 53–56 (noting that the

economic expansions of the 1980s and 1990s failed to produce substantial declines in poverty).

7. See Chap. 6, p. 99.

8. See, e.g., Sandmo (1985), pp. 281–283; Boadway and Wildasin (1994), pp. 33–35; Randolph and Rogers (1995), pp. 432–434.

9. Because the stake is universally available, it is essentially a lump-sum transfer and so should have virtually no substitution effects, other than to encourage young people to become U.S. citizens and to graduate from high school.

10. For evidence on the income (and substitution) effects of current income transfers, see Moffitt (1992) (finding "nontrivial" work disincentives in Aid to Families with Dependent Children). But these studies are unlikely to tell us much about stakeholding, for they examine only poor people and their response to small, income-tested, annual transfers.

11. See, e.g., Cowell (1997); Whitney (1997).

12. See Garrett (1998). See also Atkinson (1995b) (conventional economic complaints about the welfare state are often undertheorized and unsupported by empirics).

13. In 1994, U.S. taxes at all levels were $1.885 trillion, or 27 percent of GDP of $6.936 trillion. U.S. Bureau of the Census (1997b), pp. 447, 844, tables 692, 1358. Adding $255 billion in new revenues for stakeholding (see Appendix) would mean a total tax burden of $2.14 trillion, or 31 percent of GDP. In 1995, the OECD average tax burden was 37.4 percent of GDP, and several nations—including Sweden (49.7 percent), France (44.5 percent), Italy (41.3 percent), and the Netherlands (44.0 percent)—were well above that level. OECD (1997), p. 74.

14. See Slemrod and Bakija (1996), pp. 103–112; Rosen (1992), pp. 431–432.

15. Rosen (1992), p. 432; Gravelle (1994), pp. 27–28, 40–41. Compare Boskin (1978) with Hall (1988). Feldstein (1995), pp. 405–408, acknowledges the emerging consensus but argues on methodological grounds that we should disregard most of the evidence and rely instead on studies that show greater responsiveness to Individual Retirement Account rules.

16. See Rosen (1992), p. 418; MacCurdy, (1992), pp. 243, 248. Even high-income labor supply appears to be quite inelastic. See Moffitt and Wilhelm (1998). For divergent views, compare Feldstein and Feenberg (1993) with Gravelle (1993).

17. In general, married women's labor supply is more elastic; see Eissa (1996).

18. Even if we had uncontested studies measuring the effects of existing taxes on savings and the labor supply, we could not jump to any conclusions about the overall effects of the wealth tax. The wealth tax is not a straightforward reduction in the rate of return on capital or the wage, and its effects vary by taxpayer, by investment, and with changes in market interest rates. Because the wealth tax would be so complex and large a change, it would be simpleminded to predict its effects on savings, for example, by assuming a standard rate of return and multiplying the change by the chosen elasticity.

19. In 1995, foreign investment in the United States exceeded U.S. investment abroad by $774 billion. U.S. Bureau of the Census (1997b), p. 791, table 1295

(market value of assets). In 1994, U.S. affiliates of foreign companies had assets worth $2.2 trillion in the United States. Id., p. 792, table 1298. In 1996, the United States had a significantly larger stock of foreign direct and portfolio investment (in absolute dollars) than did other industrialized countries, including the United Kingdom, Canada, Australia, France, Germany, and Japan. International Monetary Fund (1997), pp. 48, 143, 285, 301–302, 403, 845–846, 853.

20. For the latest round in this debate, see McCaffery (1994), Alstott (1996), and Holtz-Eakin (1996).

21. See Holtz-Eakin (1996); Alstott (1996), pp. 383–394; Graetz (1983), pp. 278–283. For debate on the importance of inherited wealth in the U.S. capital stock, see Kotlikoff (1988); Modigliani (1988); Kessler and Masson (1989).

22. For a more elaborate analysis of the constitutional issues, see Ackerman (1999). Calvin Johnson (1998) has reached similar conclusions through different arguments. An opposing view is presented by Jensen (1997).

23. 158 U.S. 601, 684 (1895).

24. 514 U.S. 549 (1995).

## Chapter 8: From Worker to Citizen

1. For critiques of Social Security's treatment of women, see Pateman (1988), Becker (1989). For a dramatic illustration of the very contingent benefits a woman will receive, depending on her marital status, her earnings, and the earnings of her partner, see Holden (1997), p. 97, table 6.3.

2. See Kingson and Schulz (1997), p. 43.

3. See infra pp. 145–149.

4. World Bank (1994), p. 357, table A.4. Some of these countries also include a means-tested benefit and / or a contribution-related benefit. Canada, Denmark, Iceland, and Norway provide all three types; Finland provides a universal, flat benefit and a contribution-related benefit.

5. For the calculation of the benefit level, see the Appendix.

   The citizen's pension, like current Social Security benefits, would be tax-free for the great majority of recipients. See U.S. House of Representatives (1998), pp. 851–852.

6. We estimate that the present value of current social insurance ranges from $21,000 to $77,000 for a twenty-one-year-old man and from $32,000 to $112,000 for a twenty-one-year-old woman. These estimates include Social Security, Medicare, and a number of welfare programs. The lower end of the range reflects a discount rate of 6 percent, while the high end reflects a discount rate of 2 percent. See Madison (1997).

   These findings are roughly compatible with other estimates. Compare Steuerle and Bakija (1994), pp. 99, 278, 282 (discounting to age twenty-one at 2 percent, the present value of Social Security and Medicare benefits is $162,497 to a twenty-one-year-old wife in a two-earner couple); Kotlikoff (1993), pp. 116–119 (using a discount rate of 6 percent, in 1989, total Social Security, Medicare, and certain welfare benefits had a present value of $21,600 to a twenty-year-old man and $33,600 to a twenty-year-old woman).

7. See Ackerman (1997).

8. Kingson and Schulz (1997), pp. 59–60, n. 6.

9. On the problems of adverse selection in private markets for health insurance, see, e.g., Cutler and Zeckhauser (1997). On mandatory social insurance, see Rosen (1992), pp. 204–205.

10. But perhaps significant numbers of women would also like to buy "divorce insurance" in order to protect themselves against becoming displaced homemakers— raising similar questions and perhaps the prospect of a separate insurance scheme.

11. Higher-wage workers get higher absolute benefits but a smaller benefit per dollar of contribution. See U.S. House of Representatives (1998), pp. 25–27, table 1–17; for empirical studies, see Chen and Goss (1997), pp. 82–83.

   The system also redistributes from two-earner to single-earner couples and from shorter- to longer-lived people. These redistributions partly counteract the progressive income redistribution, since single-earner couples cluster at the top and bottom, and richer people are healthier. See Rosen (1992), pp. 210–214.

12. See Steuerle and Bakija (1994), pp. 106–112.

13. We do not address the question of whether citizens' pensions ought to be financed on a pay-as-you go basis or through advance funding; the system that we describe could be funded either way.

14. See Mashaw and Marmor (1996).

15. See Chen and Goss (1997).

16. For the exact figures from the Social Security Administration (1997), tables 5.A1 and 5.A7, see Table 7.

**Table 7. Social Security Benefits Status of Elderly Women in 1996**

|  | Number of women | Percentage of total |
|---|---|---|
| Received benefit based solely on own work history | 7.369 million | 36 |
| Had own work history, but received a higher spousal benefit | 5.518 million | 27 |
| Received retirement benefit solely as a spouse | 2.877 million | 14 |
| Received survivor's benefit based on husband's work history | 4.980 million | 24 |
| Total | 20.734 million | 100 |

Note: Percentages do not add to 100 due to rounding.

17. See Ferber (1993), pp. 43–44.

18. For a vivid illustration, see Holden (1997), p. 97, table 6.3.

19. 42 U.S.C. § 401(b).

20. 42 U.S.C. § 416(d).

21. See Ferber (1993), pp. 38–40, 43 (even women who work full-time, and continuously, have lower lifetime earnings than men; and noting women's lower average Social Security benefit).

22. U.S. House of Representatives (1996), p. 4 (1996 retirees). Today's retirees are eligible for full benefits at age sixty-five, but the retirement age is scheduled to rise to age sixty-seven by 2027. See the Appendix, n. 42. Our program would adopt the same approach.

23. In 1996, almost 30 percent of all retirees, and 44 percent of elderly women, received less than $550 per month. Social Security Administration (1997), p. 212, table 5.B9; see also id., p. 202, table 5.A16 (average benefit for wives of retired workers in 1996 was $385).

24. Social Security Administration (1997), p. 212, table 5.B9 (39.4 percent). The percentages may be even greater, as we have not counted people who receive more than $650 but less than $670 per month.

25. Id., p. 212, table 5.B9, and p. 228, table 5.F11 (40.5 percent). This figure is necessarily imprecise, given the limitations of available data. It is slightly overstated, since not all wives are sixty-five or older; it is also understated, since it shows the percentage of retired workers and wives who jointly receive less than $1,300, rather than the higher $1,340 that two citizens' pensions would provide.

26. See id., p. 236, table 5.H3 (51.4 percent). The enactment of citizens' pensions would allow a significant reorganization of the Supplemental Security Income (SSI) program, which pays maximum benefits of $470 per individual ($705 per couple) to elderly beneficiaries with low incomes, at an annual cost of more than $4 billion. House of Representatives (1996), pp. 263, 291–292, tables 4–11 and 4–12 (in 1995, 1.455 million elderly SSI recipients received an average annualized SSI benefit of $3,002, or $250.21 per month). Total annualized expenditures were thus $4.369 billion.

27. A wife is automatically entitled to a spousal benefit equal to 50 percent of her husband's basic pension; she receives that benefit unless her own work history entitles her to a larger one. 42 U.S.C. § 401(b). The same spousal benefit is available to husbands, too, but in practice it has usually been claimed by wives.

28. See pp. 137–138, supra.

29. For evidence on the availability of and economic returns on private life annuities, see Mitchell, Poterba, and Warshawsky (1997) (finding that life annuities offer a below-market rate of return, reflecting transactions costs and adverse selection, but that returns have improved since the 1980s). See also Poterba (1997b) (on long-term growth in the private annuity market).

30. For a discussion of the partial wage-replacement that Social Security provides, see Moon (1997), pp. 63–65.

31. See Graetz (1987), pp. 855–856 ("Replacement of some significant portion of preretirement wages must be the fundamental goal of retirement security policy. . . . The replacement of preretirement labor income will generally ensure against an abrupt decline in a retiree's lifestyle").

32. It is not clear whether workers view the payroll tax as a "payment" for future benefits or as a "tax" that reduces current earnings. The smaller the psychological linkage between current taxes and benefits, the smaller the impact of our plan. Many young workers today doubt that the Social Security system will deliver on its promises to them. See Reno (1997), pp. 184–186.

33. This situation occurs when the wife's own benefit is less than 50 percent of her husband's benefit. 42 U.S.C. § 401(b). Although today more wives have longer work histories, many working wives will still receive only a spousal benefit after retirement because they will have earned significantly less and worked fewer years than their husbands did. In 1996, for example, 43 percent of female retired workers entitled to their own Social Security benefits were also entitled to a higher spousal benefit. See Social Security Administration, Social Security Bulletin, Annual Statistical Supplement (1997), table 5.G2.

    For an extended discussion with many examples, see Ross and Upp (1993). Unless a wife earns at least one-third of the couple's total lifetime income, she will receive a higher benefit as a spouse than she would as an earner. Id., p. 59. By 2015, 60 percent of retired wives will claim earned benefits rather than spousal benefits, but even for this group, the marginal gain over the spousal benefit may be small. Fierst (1996).

34. For ease of comparison, we have assumed that citizens' pensions would be financed on a pay-as-you-go basis, just as the current Social Security system is. There is currently much controversy over whether this system should be replaced by one that funds pensions in advance. It suffices to say that our program could be easily adapted to accommodate advanced funding. This change would impose some hardship on the transition generation, who would have to fund their parents' retirement and their own. But reforming the existing Social Security system would raise precisely the same issue.

35. We have been confining our discussion to the cash income necessary for a dignified old age. The design of an appropriate health insurance package raises empirical and normative questions beyond the scope of this book. The following discussion assumes the continuation of current Medicare, without critical scrutiny of this premise.

36. Although poverty rates among the elderly have fallen dramatically over the long term, they remain significant. See Moon (1997), p. 69.

37. In 1995, 1.446 million elderly people received ssi (described in n. 26, supra). Thirty-eight percent of these also received Social Security, but in such small amounts that they remained eligible for ssi. U.S. House of Representatives (1998), pp. 264–265, table 3–1. The number of elderly ssi recipients has fallen since 1974. Id.

38. Our calculations assume the same retirement age as that currently required by the Social Security program—age sixty-five, rising to age sixty-seven for those born after 1959. Id., p. 17. For the calculations that support the $670 monthly benefit, see the Appendix.

39. See Ruggles (1990) pp. 3–6, 33–62; see also Mayer and Jencks (1989).

40. Consider how a blue-collar worker might view the problem: on one hand, he will sympathize with the plight of the next generation of low-skilled workers as they face the uncertainties of old age; but on the other, a large stake may provide his best chance to buy a decent house. At the other end of the economic spectrum, the Wall Street lawyer might also lack clear priorities: on one hand, he may not share others' anxieties about having a dignified retirement, but he may not place such a compelling value on a high stake for young adults. There is, in short, no particular reason to suppose that this new choice will divide Americans neatly along class lines.

41. The Orshansky measure was never intended to support judgments about individual families' eligibility for assistance. See Orshansky (1988).

42. See, e.g., Edin and Lein (1997).

## Chapter 9: Taxing Privilege

1. In 1960, workers and employers each paid 3 percent of the first $4,800 of wages; in 1997, the tax rate was 7.65 percent on the first $65,400 of wages. U.S. House of Representatives (1998), p. 59, table 1–35.

2. OMB (1997), pp. 29–30, table 2.2.

3. Only federal excise taxes are more regressive. See U.S. House of Representatives (1993), pp. 1516–1518, table 26 (1994 estimates). Although payroll tax rates are proportional, the tax burden is mildly progressive at the very lowest income levels because of low rates of labor-force participation. If we treat the earned income tax credit (EITC) as part of the payroll tax system, it would be even more progressive at low income levels. But the EITC is not formally integrated into the payroll tax and does not reduce payroll tax revenues. And the expanded EITC of the 1990s has been promoted as serving so many functions—as an earnings subsidy, as a child care subsidy, and so on—that its progressivity cannot be claimed solely for the payroll tax.

    As far as the top earners are concerned, the regressive character of the Social Security payroll tax is indisputable. In 1994, 5.4 percent of workers had earnings above the cap, and 13.9 percent of wages were above the cap. Social Security Administration (1997), tables 4.B1, 4.B4. In 1994, the tax cap was eliminated for the Hospital Insurance (HI) portion of the payroll tax, which funds Medicare. I.R.C. §§ 3101, 3111. While the distributional tables described above do not reflect that change, the unlimited HI tax is only 2.9 percent of the total 15.3 percent combined payroll tax.

4. Workers and their employers each pay the Social Security payroll tax of 7.65 percent on wages up to $65,400, but wages above that amount are subject only to the

HI tax of 1.45 percent. For an explanation of terms and the law, see the preceding note.

5. See Pechman (1989), p. 181; JCT (1993), pp. 41–43.

6. On wages of $200,000, and counting both the worker's and the employer's share, the total Social Security and Medicare (OASDHI) tax is $13,909.60, or 6.95 percent. The Social Security (OASDI) portion of the tax is $8,109.60 (12.4 percent of $65,400), and the HI tax is $5,800 (2.9 percent of $200,000).

7. If the couple earns $80,760, their income tax of $12,357 will just exceed their payroll tax (OASDHI) of $12,356. This 1997 calculation includes the employer's and worker's share of the payroll tax and assumes that neither the husband nor the wife individually earns more than the Social Security wage base of $65,400. It assumes that the couple takes the standard deduction of $10,600 and four personal exemptions of $2,650, and it treats the earned income tax credit as a reduction in the income tax, not in the payroll tax. At an income of $80,000, this couple is well above the median family income of $38,782. U.S. Bureau of the Census (1997b), p. 471, table 727. At current rates, even a one-earner couple would have to earn more than $75,000 before their income tax exceeded their payroll tax.

8. See, e.g., Pechman (1989), p. 37 (the tax system—federal, state, and local—became less progressive from 1966 to 1985 because of increasing reliance on the payroll tax and decreasing reliance on corporate and property taxes).

9. See Chap. 2.

10. Our proposal is distantly related to the idea of "endowments taxation" in the economics literature (see Mirrlees [1971], pp. 202–208), but it differs in two significant respects. First, an endowments tax attempts to measure an individual's market earnings capacity, without considering whether these capacities are based on differences in genetics, parental or individual values, or social privilege. Our proposal aims only at differences rooted in social privilege. Second, endowments taxation focuses on the market value of an individual's earning power. We are interested in the market advantages that privilege confers but also, more broadly, in its intangible social and psychological advantages.

11. To be sure, the value of childhood privilege does not disappear with the onset of old age. But here the principle of intrapersonal trusteeship comes into play. (See Chap. 8.) Assessing the privilege tax against the elderly could deprive some of them of their minimum guaranteed pension—leaving them, once again, at the mercy of their younger selves.

12. See the Appendix.

13. U.S. House of Representatives (1998), p. 24, table 1–15 (average earnings of $25,724 multiplied by 15.3 percent employer and employee OASDHI payroll tax rate). Our calculation does not replace the FUTA tax that is used to fund unemployment insurance. As Chap. 8 explains, the rationale for UI is different from the rationale for citizens' pensions, and payroll taxation may be appropriate.

Because the distribution of earnings is unequal, the median taxpayer earns less (and pays less tax) than the average. But any median based on actual earnings would also be skewed downward because of the significant number of part-time workers: part of the goal of the privilege tax is to shift the base of taxation away from work choices of this kind.

14. See Senesky (1998) (distributing privilege tax burdens by income and educational achievement; showing that low-privilege-bracket taxpayers are concentrated in low-income and low-educational-achievement groups and that the same holds true for high-privilege taxpayers in high-income and high-achievement groups).

15. See, e.g., Mayer (1997), p. 42, table 3.1; Haveman and Wolfe (1994), pp. 106–107 (correlation between childhood poverty and lower educational achievement as adults). For a careful review of a large number of studies, see Haveman and Wolfe (1995). According to Mayer's data, the high school dropout rate is 34.1 percent for children from the poorest 20 percent of households but only 6.5 percent for children from the richest 20 percent. The percentage of girls who become teen mothers is 40 percent in the lowest childhood-income quintile but only 4.9 percent in the top quintile.

16. Jencks (1992), pp. 175–177 (in 1970–1982, the rate of high school dropout for children of dropouts was 17.4 percent for whites and 18.9 percent for blacks, while in contrast, the dropout rate among children whose parents attended college was 2.6 percent among whites and 6.3 percent among blacks; but over time, family background has had a declining impact on black educational attainment); Haveman and Wolfe (1994), pp. 246–251 (finding a strong and statistically significant correlation between parental education and children's rates of high school graduation, years of schooling, likelihood of a teen birth, and economic inactivity in young adulthood).

17. Mayer (1997), p. 42, table 3.1.

18. We discuss the causation issue infra at p. 161. A variety of studies confirm that parental income—or, in some cases, poverty—is correlated with impaired physical health and cognitive development during childhood *and* with lower economic success in adulthood. See Brooks-Gunn, Duncan, and Maritato (1997), pp. 9–13; Korenman and Miller (1997).

19. See Sturm and Guinier (1996), pp. 988–992.

20. See id. for a discussion of coaching and the effects of coaching on SAT scores.

21. Id., p. 990 ( graduate admissions policies that discount grades from community colleges and state schools); U.S. Department of Education (1990), pp. 44–45 (enrollment patterns by income and parental education).

22. See pp. 1–2.

23. For studies of occupational mobility, see McMurrer, Condon, and Sawhill (1997), pp. 9–19; Hout (1988), pp. 1381–1389; Biblarz, Bengtson, and Bucur (1996), pp. 197–198. These studies find that, although circulation mobility (the lack of correlation between family background and sons' occupational status) increased from the mid-1960s to the mid-1980s, circulation mobility is greatest for college graduates and decreases at lower educational levels. This trend in circulation mobility has not been sufficiently well explained for us to know whether non–college graduates are benefiting or whether the trend will continue in the future. Hout's analysis suggests that a significant part of the positive trend may be attributable to

the rising percentage of college graduates in the population, but data from the 1960s and 1970s raise the possibility that circulation mobility may be increasing due to other unspecified factors as well. Hout (1988), pp. 1384–1386. Others hypothesize that factors like increasing rates of family disruption may have helped weaken the link between class origins and eventual success. Biblarz, Bengtson, and Bucur (1996), p. 197.

Studies of intergenerational *income* mobility find that there is a significant correlation between fathers' and sons' earnings. See, e.g., McMurrer, Condon, and Sawhill (1997), pp. 19–21; Solon (1992). For one study of intergenerational *wealth* mobility, see Menchik (1979), p. 360 (finding significant wealth immobility but noting, once again, that imputing causation is difficult because children may inherit earnings capacity as well as material wealth).

24. McMurrer, Condon, and Sawhill (1997), p. 20.
25. Mayer (1997), p. 42, table 3.1; see also Chap. 6, n. 13. See also Haveman and Wolfe (1995), pp. 1855–1856 (evidence on the correlation between parental income and children's labor-market outcomes).
26. See Duncan and Brooks-Gunn (1997), pp. 601–605; Mayer (1997), pp. 55–78, 143. Others dispute these revisionist claims. See Brooks-Gunn and Duncan (1997); see also Corcoran and Adams (1997), p. 17.
27. See McMurrer and Sawhill (1998), pp. 75–76.
28. In *The Bell Curve,* Herrnstein and Murray (1994) attribute poverty to low inherited intelligence. But, as many critics have pointed out, this thesis is based on biased data and unscientific methods. See, e.g., Gould (1994). While few would deny that inherited intelligence plays some role in economic outcomes, Herrnstein and Murray's argument contains at least three glaring errors. First, they use a single measure of general intelligence, ignoring a significant academic controversy over the nature and measurement of intelligence. Gardner (1994). Second, they treat intelligence as strongly the product of heredity, underestimating the contribution of environment and overlooking a substantial body of contrary evidence. See Kaus (1995); Sowell (1995). Finally, they argue that intelligence is a major predictor of economic success, without examining carefully the causal role of social and economic background and public policies. See Fischer et al. (1996), pp. 70–93.
29. See supra, n. 5 (on the incidence of the "employer's" share of the tax). For concern about increasing payroll taxes in the context of Social Security reform, see Sass and Triest (1997), pp. 38–39; for an argument that repealing the payroll tax would spur economic growth, see Drayton (1997).
30. Recent empirical evidence suggests that the net disincentive effect may not be large. See Chap. 7.
31. To be sure, strict neutrality must sometimes give way to higher purposes. Our wealth tax, for example, tolerates nonneutralities between spenders and savers as a means to a fairer distribution of initial opportunity for all. But—without relying on a misleading insurance analogy—no one has yet made a convincing case for the fairness of a regressive wage tax.

32. See infra, p. 167.
33. Consider, for example, how parents of a five-year-old might assess the dollars and cents of the problem. On one hand, if they seek to maintain their high salaries, their child will be pushed into the high-privilege tax bracket, obliging him to pay seventeen hundred dollars more a year throughout his lifetime. Assume, moreover, that our hypothetical parents are perfectly altruistic and treat this cost as if they themselves were paying it. Even then, the total cost of the extra privilege tax is only about thirty-seven thousand dollars once the stream of payments is discounted to present value. But to escape the tax, they will have to sacrifice lots of *immediate* income for seven or more years to keep the family out of the top privilege bracket while the child is growing up. These parents will most likely decide that these cuts in family income won't be in the child's overall self-interest, especially since the privilege-tax laws might change radically over the child's long lifetime, making the sacrifice utterly pointless.

    The system should also be designed to make it hard for parents to predict the precise dollar cutoff points for privilege tax brackets, making their tax-gaming possibilities especially risky. If they fail to cut back their income enough, they may still fall within the top bracket, despite their efforts to save their children from the extra tax bite.
34. See supra, pp. 160–161.
35. See Haveman and Wolfe (1994), pp. 76–79, 251.
36. In 1994, 107 million federal income tax returns were filed. See Keenan and Curry (1995), p. 21, table 1. Of these, 44 million were joint returns, which represent two adults, for a total of 151 million individuals. Although some portion of total returns are filed on behalf of minor children, the number cannot be determined from the available data.
37. Parents with very high incomes lose the value of the personal exemption. See I.R.C. § 151(d)(3). It might be wise to revisit this policy, for the opportunity for a full, current deduction might discourage evasion of the privilege tax; enforcing the privilege tax may also require other measures, already begun under current law, to encourage early matching of parents and children by taxpayer identification number. See, e.g., I.R.C. § 32(c).
38. We used data from the Panel Study of Income Dynamics to derive this result. See Senesky (1998).
39. See id.
40. Welfare records are kept by states and sometimes by localities; their degree of computerization and compatibility varies. One bright spot is that a large number of low-income workers (18 million in 1996) file income-tax returns to claim the earned income tax credit. See U.S. House of Representatives (1998), p. 871.
41. See supra, p. 167.
42. A tiebreaker of some kind would be needed for the very rare child who spends nine or more years in the high-income group and seven or more in the low-income group. Not a single child fell into this category in a study based on a large, representative sample. See Senesky (1998), p. 6.

43. The following list (derived from U.S. Bureau of the Census [1997b], p. 471, table 728) shows median family income by age in 1995.

Fifteen to twenty-four: $18,756
Twenty-five to thirty-four: $36,020
Thirty-five to forty-four: $46,527
Forty-five to fifty-four: $55,029
Fifty-five to sixty-four: $45,265
Over sixty-five: $28,301

44. One approach would be to include no adjustments at all for family size, on the ground that parental income serves as a proxy for benefits that children receive (including social status and economic security) that are largely independent of family size. We have chosen this approach in simulating the privilege tax. See Senesky (1998). But it would also be plausible to incorporate some modest adjustment for family size, as very large differences in family size could well affect a family's class status and economic security. Senesky (1998) provides data using such an adjustment patterned after the official poverty measure. An extreme form of adjustment (for example, dividing total income by number of family members, ignoring economies of scale) would be inappropriate. For a general discussion of the issues involved in constructing equivalence scales, see Ruggles (1990), pp. 63–88.

Another classic question: should families with a stay-at-home parent—usually the mother—be deemed to have extra "imputed income" from her valuable, but usually untaxed, services? See generally Chirelstein (1997), pp. 22–25. For one proposal, see Staudt (1996). For our part, we doubt that the extra precision is worth the effort.

45. Under one approach, the child would be credited with the income of the custodial household (custodial parent plus stepparent, if there is one) *plus* child support received from the noncustodial parent. This approach could be under-inclusive, as it ignores time spent in the noncustodial parent's home. A second alternative takes this point into account by treating the child as if he or she were living in a household with the *average* income of the custodial and noncustodial parents. But this approach is likely to be dramatically overinclusive, because the noncustodial parent may not in fact be sharing resources with the child. In 1991, for example, 25 percent of noncustodial parents ignored their child support obligations entirely, and nearly 50 percent paid less than the full amount due. See U.S. Bureau of the Census (1997b), p. 389, table 609. All in all, we favor the first approach, particularly if "child support" is construed broadly to include cash "gifts" used to pay for school tuition, expensive travel, and so on.

46. Some of these items (e.g., deferred compensation) are now reported by employers though not taxed. I.R.C. § 6051.

47. The unpaid tax would be forgiven once the conditions of the escape hatch were satisfied. In the interim, we would be inclined to allow the tax authorities to pursue the usual remedies for collecting unpaid taxes—putting liens on assets, and so on. An alternative rule would allow the unpaid tax to accrue, with interest, for

some period. This would give people some time either to get back on their feet or to drop down a bracket, but at the cost of creating an accruing debt that might unduly discourage them from going back to work.

48. Some students will have trouble paying their privilege tax during their school years. Although the life-cycle adjustment described above would minimize the problem, we might also permit elective deferral—with interest accruing at a market rate—for students.

49. The Supreme Court has ruled that couples residing in community-property states must report half of their joint income on each individual return. In contrast, couples who live in common-law states must report each individual's separate income on his or her return. *Poe v. Seaborn,* 282 U.S. 101 (1930); Gann (1980), pp. 62–65. The solution suggested in the text would override *Poe* (for purposes of the escape hatch) and treat all married couples, regardless of their state of residence, as if they each earned half the joint income.

50. Even if a wealth tax were not enacted, we might require reporting of municipal-bond interest, which is already used for purposes of some tax rules. See, e.g., §§ 32(i), 86(b)(2) (including tax-exempt interest in income for purposes of determining EITC eligibility and the taxable portion of Social Security benefits).

51. In 1996, the poverty line for an individual without children was $7,995; 175 percent of that amount is $13,991. U.S. Bureau of the Census (1997a), p. 1. In 1991, a 1.75 threshold would have encompassed families in the first and second income deciles (mean income of 0.47 and 1.14 of the poverty line, respectively) and part of the third (mean income of 1.72). Danziger and Gottschalk (1995), p. 53, table 3.3. This is a single-year snapshot; a multiyear threshold would include fewer people. As Chap. 8 explains, the official poverty thresholds are deeply flawed, but they are our best measures at present.

52. A related objection asserts that the privilege tax interferes with the liberty of privileged children to pursue low-paying careers. But this gets the point precisely backward: the obligation to contribute to society in accordance with privilege is *prior to* one's liberty to choose careers.

53. The low-bracket privilege tax of $360 equals a 15.3 percent payroll tax on just $2,353 of salary; anyone in the low-privilege bracket who earns more than that will pay less than he or she would today.

54. Mashaw and Marmor (1996).

55. Our discussion assumes the current practice of requiring each generation to pay for the retirement of its successor. The first stakeholders continue to pay payroll taxes to support their parents' Social Security benefits; the second generation of stakeholders will pay privilege taxes to fund their predecessors' citizens' pensions; and so on. Depending on the actuarial tables, the transition may bite a bit harder on the second generation of stakeholders, who will continue to labor under a gradually diminishing payroll tax *and* a gradually increasing privilege tax after retirement. But if this imbalance proves to be a political stumbling block, one alternative would be to shift some of the burden to the first generation of stakeholders by introducing the privilege tax at an earlier point.

## Chapter 10: Ideals

1. Paine (1797), in Foner (1995), p. 410.
2. Id., p. 400. (We have eliminated the erratic italics and capitalizations of eighteenth-century typography.)
3. Id., p. 410. As a token of his universalistic aspirations, Paine made the following offer: "I have no property in France to become subject to the plan I propose. What I have, which is not much, is in the United States of America. But I will pay one hundred pounds sterling towards this fund in France, the instant it shall be established, and I will pay the same sum in England, whenever a similar establishment shall take place in that country" (id.).
4. Id., p. 402.
5. For a useful survey of historical antecedents, see Van Parijs (1992).
6. 2 Farrand, The Records of the Federal Convention of 1787 203 (August 7, 1787) (1911).
7. Id., p. 204.
8. See Chap. 1 and Ackerman (1984).
9. Aristotle's *Politics,* edited by McKeon (1941); Harrington (1992). Martin Diamond (1986) has written a particularly fine essay on the relationship between property and virtue in American constitutionalism.
10. See, e.g., Glendon (1991). This tendency is by no means universal in communitarian thought. For a notable exception, see Barber (1984).
11. In 1995, the median household headed by a thirty-five- to forty-five-year-old had net wealth of $66,500. Wilhelm (1998), p. 15.
12. Parents from the upper middle classes might already be intending to spend eighty thousand dollars of their own money on each child's higher education. While these people might also pay hefty wealth taxes, the sting might be ameliorated by the consideration that stakeholding will allow them to reduce their own expenditures on their college-age children.
13. See Walzer (1983); Radin (1996).
14. See, e.g., Rawls (1971), whose talent-pooling premises have been attacked by a long line of critics, including Nozick (1974), Sandel (1982), and Kronman (1981). Utilitarian theories of redistribution have proved even more vulnerable to criticism. For the best critique of the ideal of self-ownership, see Cohen (1995).
15. See Ackerman (1980), chaps. 4–6.

## Chapter 11: Alternatives

1. See Chaps. 2 and 3, pp. 38–39, 49–51.
2. See Graetz (1997), p. 48. As Graetz points out, the 1986 reforms were a political compromise that fell well short of perfection, but they did accomplish some significant changes. Id., pp. 130–139.
3. The Taxpayer Relief Act of 1997 included a cut in the capital gains tax, an increase in the estate and gift tax unified credit, and new tax credits for education

and children. See Chirelstein (1997) (Supplement). The top 1 percent of taxpayers will gain about 32 percent of the tax cuts in the legislation. See CBPP (1997).

4. See JCT (1997), p. 205 (during a ten-year period, IRA expansion cost $20 billion,
   and capital gains tax relief, including the homeowner provision, cost $21 billion).
5. There are no official, published estimates of the separate distributional effects of
   these programs. But an analysis by the Center on Budget and Policy Priorities
   suggests that the expanded IRAs provided benefits primarily to people well within
   the top half of the income distribution. See Greenstein (1997).
6. See JCT (1997), p. 38 ($183 billion over five years).
7. See Lav (1997). The only serious redistributive initiative in recent years has been
   the earned income tax credit. See Alstott (1995). We discuss it further at n. 46
   infra.
8. For a thorough analysis of the cumulative impact of government policies and
   business flight that lie at the source of present pathologies, see Wilson (1996).
9. The tax breaks include access to tax-exempt financing, a tax credit for firms that
   hire zone residents, and quicker tax deductions for business investment. I.R.C.
   §§ 1391–1397D.
10. Ladd (1994).
11. See Chirelstein (1997) (Supplement), pp. 19–26.
12. A parent with two children in college may be able to take a fifteen-hundred-
    dollar credit for one child and a one-thousand-dollar credit for the other. Id.,
    pp. 22–23.
13. See Chap. 3.
14. See I.R.C. § 1(h) (maximum rate of 20 percent on long-term capital gains); § 2010
    (raising to $1 million by 2006 the exemption level for the estate and gift tax).
15. See 42 U.S.C. § 601 et seq.
16. Blank (1997), pp. 80–81; Burtless (1997), p. 44.
17. Hershey and Pavetti (1997), pp. 78–81; Edin and Lein (1997), pp. 65–69.
18. Recent studies confirm that the economic recovery is largely responsible for the
    drop in welfare caseloads. See CEA (1997); Ziliak et al. (1997).
19. See McMurrer and Sawhill (1998), pp. 85–89.
20. See Wilson (1996), pp. 25–50.
21. See Blank (1997); Handler and Hasenfeld (1997).
22. See the Appendix.
23. See Report of the 1994–1996 Advisory Council on Social Security (1996),
    1:28–34.
24. Ball et al. (1996), pp. 69–72; Fierst (1996), p. 150.
25. See Chap. 8.
26. Kaus (1992).
27. In 1996, there were 1,471,700 active-duty military personnel. U.S. Bureau of the
    Census (1997b), p. 363, table 564. Of these, 69,300 were recruits. In that year,
    the military also employed 732,000 civilians and 1,464,000 reserve and National
    Guard positions. Id., p. 355, table 548. Assuming (optimistically) that untrained
    civilians could fill all the positions for recruits and replace 10 percent of the civil-

ian workforce and the reserve and National Guard positions, that would create 288,900 jobs—enough to employ 8 percent of the 3,570,000 eighteen-year-olds in 1996. Compare Kaus (1992), p. 80 (estimating that, in 1995, the military could employ 11 percent of America's draft-age *men*).

28. Kaus (1992), p. 81.

29. Id., p. 83.

30. See Moynihan (1969).

31. Phelps (1997).

32. Id., pp. 145–146.

33. Compare Card and Krueger (1995) with Shaviro (1997), pp. 407, 414–419.

34. Phelps (1997), pp. 113–114.

35. Id., pp. 110, 115–116.

36. U.S. Bureau of the Census (1997a), p. 1.

37. Phelps (1997), p. 116.

38. Id., pp. 16–26.

39. Id., pp. 134–143.

40. Id., p. 24 (in the late 1980s, the bottom 30 percent of male workers earned seven dollars an hour or less).

41. For example, in Phelps's plan, the subsidy could be received only by full-time workers. Phelps (1997), p. 108. He does not discuss the child care needs and other difficulties that working mothers face.

42. Id., pp. 38–50.

43. Id., pp. 126–128.

44. In purely financial terms, Phelps's subsidy can be worth more than stakeholding under certain stringent conditions. This is true if a worker qualifies for the maximum annual subsidy of six thousand dollars (three dollars an hour multiplied by two thousand work hours), receives no raise during his or her entire working life, and works full-time, year-round, from age eighteen until age sixty-five. At a 5 percent (nominal) interest rate, an eighty-thousand-dollar stake could buy an annuity, payable from ages twenty-one to sixty-five, of $4,314—less than the $6,000 per year for forty-seven years payable under Phelps's plan. But, of course, these are special conditions indeed; the majority are likely to gain much more from stakeholding.

45. Burkhauser, Couch, and Glenn (1995).

46. Like Phelps's more ambitious plan, the earned income tax credit (EITC) is not properly viewed as an alternative to stakeholding. While the EITC has some comparative advantages over Phelps's plan as an incrementalist means of raising wages at the bottom, stakeholding, as we have emphasized, has a different aim.

47. Phelps would finance the wage subsidy with an increase in the payroll tax. Phelps (1997), pp. 116–118.

48. See Van Parijs (1995).

49. See Van Parijs (1992), p. 3.

50. For the economist's take on the basic income, see, e.g., Atkinson (1995a); Bankman and Griffith (1987). For a philosopher's take, see Van Parijs (1995).

51. See Van Parijs (1995); Offe (1997).

52. The distribution of net benefits would depend on the tax base and rate structure used to finance the program.

53. Some economists will be tempted to say that the initiative "distorts" the money-leisure tradeoff for those at the top who have to pay higher taxes to fund the program. But no one has an unconditional right to her pretax income stream or to her pretax labor-leisure tradeoff. In a liberal regime, everyone's legitimate claims are limited by background conditions of justice—including the basic income and the tax structure that finances it. Put another way, the obligation to contribute to a just system for sharing resources trumps the "rights" of rich people to spend "their" income.

54. To make our basic point, we have presented an extremely simple and stark version of the discontinuous view of the self. Because serious philosophers of discontinuity have more nuanced views, their assessment of the case for a basic income would be more nuanced. This intersection has yet to be explored, and we leave the task to others more persuaded of discontinuity's fundamental value. For present purposes, it is enough to refer the reader to representative works from different traditions that have recently been tending toward discontinuity: see Butler (1990); Lyotard (1984); Parfit (1984).

   This is hardly the place to defend at length our own view of the self. For further elaboration, see Ackerman (1997). For the historical and philosophical roots, see Taylor (1989).

55. See Lehman (1997); Rich (1997); Stranahan (1997).

56. Unger (1996), pp. 14–15 ("social-endowment accounts"); Tobin (1968), pp. 92–93 (national youth endowment of five thousand dollars); Haveman (1988), pp. 168–171; (a universal personal capital account for youth of twenty thousand dollars each); Klein (1977) (universal personal capital accounts).

57. They may, however, be disadvantaged by the fact that colleges would be more likely to raise tuition under the restricted plan, since stakeholders could not respond by using their money on competitive activities. See Chap. 3.

58. See Chap. 4.

## Appendix: Funding the Stakeholder Society

1. This number is based on Census Bureau data for the 1994 election. We estimated the number of eighteen-year-old citizens in 1994 (and thus twenty-one-year-old citizens in 1997) by subtracting the number of eighteen-year-olds who reported that they were not citizens (245,000) from the total number of eighteen-year-olds surveyed (3.437 million). This yields an estimate of 3.192 million. See http://www.census.gov/population/socdemo/voting/ work/tab01.txt. The true number of citizens is probably smaller, since the survey reports that a large number of respondents did not answer or said "don't know." If these are all counted as noncitizens, we get a lower-bound estimate of 2.884 million. The estimate of 3.1 million used in the text is thus a conservative figure close to the upper bound.

2. See Chap. 3.
3. See Chap. 5. Thus every stakeholder notionally receives an account into which the government makes four annual payments of twenty thousand dollars beginning at age eighteen. If the stakeholder doesn't draw down the funds (because, say, she has chosen not to go to college and therefore doesn't use the money for tuition), the funds earn interest. But every stakeholder has a payback obligation that begins at age eighteen (for the first payment of twenty thousand dollars), is increased at nineteen (for the second payment), and so on.
4. To put the point another way, $82,435 is also the value, with accrued interest, of what a twenty-one-year-old would have if he or she had deposited twenty thousand dollars in a bank account each year beginning at age eighteen.
5. This is the proportion of twenty-five- to twenty-nine-year-olds in 1997 with four-year college degrees. U.S. Department of Education (1997b), table 8 (27.1 percent). This overstates the number of eighteen- to twenty-one-year-olds in college, since some graduates start or finish school at earlier or later ages. See id., table 176. But the estimate also understates the number of early stake claimants, since it does not take into account the eighteen- to twenty-one-year-olds who will withdraw funds in order to enroll in two-year colleges or vocational educational programs.
6. Id., table 312.
7. Table 8 illustrates the calculations behind our estimate that the cost of stakeholding in 1997 would have been $255 billion. Population numbers are taken from U.S. Bureau of the Census (1997b), p. 16, table 16, with each age cohort in 1996

Table 8.  Estimated Revenue Cost of Stakeholding for 1997

| Age group | Number of residents (millions) | Number of citizens (millions) | Number of stake claimants (millions) | Payment per person ($) | Total cost ($, in billions) |
|---|---|---|---|---|---|
| 18 | 3.729 | 3.237 | 0.877 | 20,000 | 17.540 |
| 19 | 3.570 | 3.099 | 0.840 | 20,000 | 16.800 |
| 20 | 3.752 | 3.257 | 0.883 | 20,000 | 17.660 |
| 21 | 3.571 | 3.100 | 0.840 (college) | 20,000 (college) | 16.800 |
| | | | 2.260 (noncollege) | 21,225 (noncollege) | 47.969 |
| 22 | 3.545 | 3.077 | 2.243 | 21,225 | 47.608 |
| 23 | 3.369 | 2.925 | 2.132 | 21,225 | 45.252 |
| 24 | 3.403 | 2.954 | 2.153 | 21,225 | 45.697 |
| Total | n/a | n/a | 12.229 | n/a | 255.348 |

treated as one year older in 1997. Numbers of citizens are estimated by applying to each age cohort the population ratio derived from the data in n. 1 supra. In 1997, there were 3.1 million citizens and 3.571 million residents, for a ratio of 86.81 percent. (Because the citizenship data are based on voting in 1994, we cannot directly measure the citizenship ratio for groups younger than twenty-one in 1997.)

8. For this group of stakeholders, a fund of $320 billion represents eighty thousand dollars per person. But once again, the real costs will be a bit more because of the interest paid to non-college-bound stakeholders, with the precise cost depending on the proportion of college-bound and non-college-bound stakeholders.

9. The current baby boomlet raises the question of how to adjust the size of the stake so that blips in demographics do not dramatically increase the cost burden or reduce the size of the stake. This is actuarially possible and probably desirable. Like the Social Security trust funds, the stakeholding fund could periodically accumulate surpluses or deficits according to projected taxes and benefits.

10. OMB (1997), p. 20, table 1.1.

11. See Chap. 3, nn. 10–12 (1990–1991 and 1998 data).

12. In 1994, state and local property taxes raised $197 billion. Statistical Abstract (1997), p. 304, table 484. The extent to which a federal wealth tax would reduce property-tax revenues is unknowable and would depend on taxpayers' behavioral adjustments as well as political dynamics.

13. See Chap. 7, pp. 119–120.

14. Wilhelm (1998), p. 18.

15. The SCF, a survey of U.S. households, contains detailed information about financial and nonfinancial wealth. The SCF sample is nationally representative but also oversamples high-income households, permitting an accurate analysis of the top 5 and 1 percent. Wilhelm (1998), p. 2.

16. An additional wrinkle is that non-college-bound stakeholders will receive interest on their stakes and will ultimately collect four payments of $21,225, or $84,900 (see Chap. 3). The wealth-tax exemption could be raised to eighty-five thousand dollars with only a trivial revenue loss. See Wilhelm (1998), p. 20 (total revenue of $372.4 billion).

17. In another conservative move, we subtract all debt from net assets, even though some of it may finance consumer durables that are not in the SCF wealth base. Id., p. 5.

18. See Chap. 6, p. 106.

19. Wilhelm (1998), pp. 6–9. Because this amount includes future payouts (discounted at 2 percent and deflated at 3 percent per year), it is greater than the "cash surrender value," or the amount of cash into which the pension could be converted immediately. But the wealth tax is not restricted to liquid assets, and so we rejected the cash-surrender approach.

20. See Chap. 6, n. 26.

21. See Chap. 6, p. 105.

22. See Wilhelm (1998), p. 10.

23. Data are taken from http://www.dowjones.com/, the website for Dow Jones and Company.

24. From 1989 to 1995, the percentage of families owning stock (either directly, or indirectly through a pension plan or mutual fund) grew from 31.7 percent to 41.1 percent. But even so, in 1995, 83.9 percent of families earning $100,000 or more owned stock (either directly, or indirectly through a pension plan), whereas only 47.7 percent of families in the $24,000–$49,000 range held stock. And the median value of the high-income group's stock holdings was $90,800, compared to only $8,000 for the middle-income group. Kennickell, Starr-McCluer, and Sunden (1997), pp. 11–12.

25. See Chap. 6, pp. 108–109.

26. Board of Governors of the Federal Reserve System (1998), p. 69, table L.107.

27. In other words, $1.719 trillion (foreigners' U.S. corporate equities and foreign direct investment) divided by $4.654 trillion (total foreign assets) yields .3694, or about 37 percent of total foreign assets. Multiplying that ratio by the total liabilities of $2.267 billion yields deductible debt of $837 billion.

28. I.R.C. §§ 871, 881.

29. See Chap. 6, n. 43.

30. This calculation may also understate foreigners' U.S. wealth, because the Flow of Funds table appears to omit investments in U.S. real estate that are not part of foreign direct investment. See Board of Governors of the Federal Reserve System (1998), p. 69, table L107.

31. Internal Revenue Service (1997), p. 136, table 1. The calculation omits net income from estates and trusts, because there is no breakdown by income type. The calculations treat income from partnerships and S corporations as earnings rather than capital income, although there is no clear way of separating them in this context.

32. In 1994, the average tax rate for all taxpayers was 14.3 percent. Cruciano (1997), pp. 7–8, figure A. But because owners of capital income tend to be somewhat richer than average, we have chosen 20–25 percent as an approximate effective rate.

33. See Chap. 5, n. 18.

34. See Chap. 5, pp. 89–93.

35. Eller (1996–1997), p. 42, table 1d (69,772).

36. In estimating what this group would have paid back into the stakeholding fund, we have ignored the possibility of charitable gifts, debts exceeding $300,000 (the amount necessary to leave an estate of $600,000 or more with less than the $250,000 payback plus the $50,000 exemption), and deductible bequests to surviving spouses. See Chap 5, pp. 89–93. On actual estate tax revenue in 1995, see Eller (1996–1997), p. 46, table 1d.

37. U.S. Bureau of the Census (1997b) (1.926 million deaths in 1995).

38. One might begin with the much more detailed scf wealth data and then simulate annual death rates, but we have not done so. Compare Poterba (1997a), pp. 14–19.

39. Ten percent of 1995 deaths would be 192,600 people; if each owed (and paid) $250,000, the total would be $48.15 billion.
40. Poterba (1997a), p. 25.
41. See Chap. 9, p. 176.
42. The retirement age will be sixty-seven for people born after 1959. U.S. House of Representatives (1998), p. 16. Those born in 1960 will be sixty-seven in 2027.
43. In calculating the total retirement and survivors' benefits paid in 1996, we have omitted the benefits paid to early retirees. For the average monthly benefit, see Social Security Administration (1997), table 5.A16 (31,667,000 recipients, ages sixty-five or older, in all categories, received an average benefit of $717.67 monthly, or $8,612 per year). The total expenditure is the number of beneficiaries multiplied by the average annual benefit, or $272.717 billion.
44. U.S. Bureau of the Census (1997b), p. 16, table 16 (33.861 million). This is the number of U.S. residents, not the number of U.S. citizens, because citizens' pensions (despite their name) would be payable to all permanent residents. See Chap. 8, pp. 149–150.
45. $272.717 billion divided by 33.861 million is $8,054.01.
46. See OMB (1997), p. 252, table 13.1.
47. Report of the 1994–1996 Advisory Council on Social Security (1996), 1:11.
48. In 1996, OASI payroll taxes raised $311.869 billion, while benefits cost $299.985 billion. OMB (1997), p. 252, table 13.1. The ratio is $311.869 divided by $299.985, or 1.0396.
49. Multiplying the 1996 cost of citizens' pensions by the ratio of 1996 benefits to taxes implicitly includes a proportionate share of administrative costs and other trust-fund expenses, as well as the excess amounts left to accumulate in the trust fund.
50. U.S. Bureau of the Census (1997b), p. 16, table 16 (151.481 million).
51. Though arbitrary, the assumption of proportional default seems pretty reasonable. While taxpayers in the low-privilege bracket may be least able to pay, they also owe the least. High-bracket taxpayers and mid-bracket taxpayers may have, on average, greater ability to pay, but their tax liability is significantly greater.
52. If $x$ is the highest privilege tax, we have assumed that the low-privilege group pays $0.1x$ and that the middle group pays $yx = (.1x + x + y) / 3$, or $y = .5494x$.
53. The total revenue is ($3,800 × 27.267 million = $103.615 billion) + ($2,090 × 81.8 million = $170.962 billion) + ($380 × 27.267 million = $10.362 billion) = $284.939 billion.
54. Report of the 1994–1996 Advisory Council on Social Security (1996), 1:11. While these calculations assume that the OASDI system has been placed on an actuarially sound foundation, they do not address the predictable fiscal gap in Medicare or how it should be filled.
55. For the taxable payroll in 1996, see U.S. House of Representatives (1996), p. 68. To estimate the additional revenue, we multiplied the 1996 taxable payroll ($3.05 trillion) by 2.17 percent (the percentage-point increase in the payroll tax) for a total of $66.185 billion.

56. In December 1996, total (annualized) OASDI outlays for all beneficiaries were $340.632 billion (40.631 million beneficiaries × [$698.63 × 12) annualized average benefit). Social Security Administration (1997), table 5.A16. Of that amount, 80.06 percent, or $272.717 billion (see supra, n. 43), was paid to recipients age sixty-five or older.

57. More precisely: 80.06 percent of $66.2 billion is $53 billion. Added to the current tax cost of $283.517 billion (see supra, nn. 48–49), the total is $336.517 billion.

58. The total revenue is ($4,500 × 27.267 million = $122.702 billion) + ($2,475 × 81.8 million = $202.455 billion) + ($450 × 27.267 million = $12.270 billion) = $337.427 billion. We have rounded numbers for ease of presentation in the text.

59. In 1996, OASDHI payroll tax revenues were $472.489 billion. OMB (1997), pp. 252–253, table 13.1. (OASI taxes of $311.869 billion plus DI taxes of $55.623 billion plus HI taxes of $104.997 billion.) $472.489 billion current revenues – $283.517 billion replaced by the privilege tax = $188.972 billion.

60. As in the preceding note, in 1996, OASDHI payroll tax revenues were $472.489 billion. As described in n. 55, the total payroll-tax increase needed to put the Social Security system on an actuarially sound footing is $66.185 billion, for a total of $538.674 billion. The privilege tax would replace $336.517 billion, leaving $202.184 billion.

61. See supra, n. 59.

62. The total revenue is: ($6,300 × 27.267 million = $171.782 billion) + ($3,465 × 81.8 million = $283.437 billion) + ($630 × 27.267 million = $17.178 billion) = $472.397 billion.

# Bibliography

Ackerman, Bruce. Taxation and the Constitution, Colum. L. Rev. (forthcoming, Jan. 1999).

———. Temporal Horizons of Justice, 94 J. Phil. 299 (1997).

———. Crediting the Voters: A New Beginning for Campaign Finance, The Am. Prospect 71 (Spring 1993).

———. Reconstructing American Law (Cambridge: Harvard Univ. Press, 1984).

———. Social Justice in the Liberal State (New Haven: Yale Univ. Press, 1980).

Alstott, Anne L. The Uneasy Liberal Case Against Wealth Transfer Taxation, 51 Tax L. Rev. 363 (1996).

———. The Earned Income Tax Credit and the Limitations of Tax-Based Welfare Reform, 108 Harv. L. Rev. 533 (1995).

Altonji, Joseph G., Fumio Hayashi, and Laurence Kotlikoff. Parental Altruism and Inter Vivos Transfers: Theory and Evidence, NBER Working Paper No. 5378 (Dec. 1995).

Amar, Akhil. The Bill of Rights: Creation and Reconstruction (New Haven: Yale Univ. Press, 1998).

Apter, Terri. Working Women Don't Have Wives (New York: St. Martin's Press, 1993).

Atkinson, Anthony B. Public Economics in Action (Oxford: Oxford Univ. Press; New York: Clarendon Press, 1995a).

———. The Welfare State and Economic Performance, 48 Nat'l Tax J. 171 (1995b).

Ball, Robert M., et al. Social Security for the Twenty-First Century. In 1994–1996 Advisory Council on Social Security, vol. 1, 59 (1996).

Bankman, Joseph, and Thomas Griffith. Social Welfare and the Rate Structure: A New Look at Progressive Taxation, 75 Cal. L. Rev. 1905 (1987).

Barber, Benjamin. Strong Democracy: Participatory Politics for a New Age (Berkeley: Univ. of California Press, 1984).

Beck, David, and Sheldon V. Ekman. Where Does Support End and Taxable Gift Begin? 23 NYU Inst. on Fed. Tax'n 1181 (1965).

Becker, Mary E. Obscuring the Struggle: Sex Discrimination, Social Security, and Stone, Seidman, and Tushnet's Constitutional Law, 89 Colum. L. Rev. 264 (1989).

Bennett, Michael J. When Dreams Came True (Washington, D.C.: Brassey's, 1996).

Biblarz, Timothy J., Vern L. Bengtson, and Alexander Bucur. Social Mobility Across Three Generations, 58 J. Marriage and the Family 188 (1996).

Bittker, Boris I., Elias Clark, and Grayson M. P. McCouch. Federal Estate and Gift Taxation, 7th ed. (Boston: Little, Brown, 1996).

Bittker, Boris I., and Lawrence Lokken. Federal Taxation of Income, Estates, and Gifts (Boston and New York: Warren, Gorham, and Lamont, 1992).

Black, Charles. A New Birth of Freedom (New York: Grossett, Putnam, 1997).

Blank, Rebecca. It Takes a Nation (New York: Russell Sage Foundation; Princeton, N.J.: Princeton Univ. Press, 1997).

Blau, Francine, and Adam J. Grossberg. Maternal Labor Supply and Children's Cognitive Development, 74 Rev. Econ. and Stat. 474 (1992).

Boadway, Robin, and David Wildasin. Taxation and Savings: A Survey, 15 Fiscal Stud. 19 (1994).

Board of Governors of the Federal Reserve System. Flow of Funds Accounts of the United States: Level Tables, http://www.bog.frb.fed.us/releases/Z1/Current (1998).

Bork, Robert. The Tempting of America (New York: Free Press, 1990).

Boskin, Michael J. (ed.). Frontiers of Tax Reform (Stanford, Calif.: Hoover Institution Press, 1996).

———. Taxation, Saving, and the Rate of Interest, 86 J. Pol. Econ. S3 (1978).

Brooks-Gunn, Jeanne, and Greg J. Duncan. The Effects of Poverty on Children, 7 Children and Poverty 55 (1997).

Brooks-Gunn, Jeanne, Greg J. Duncan, and Nancy Maritato. Poor Families, Poor Outcomes: The Well-Being of Children and Youth. In Consequences of Growing Up Poor 1 (Duncan and Brooks-Gunn, eds.) (New York: Russell Sage Foundation, 1997).

Brown, William S., and Clive S. Thomas. The Alaska Permanent Fund: Good Sense or Political Expediency? 37 Challenge 38 (1994).

BEA (Bureau of Economic Analysis). Table 1: Gross Domestic Product, http://www.bea.doc.gov/bea/dn/0897nip2/tab1.htm (May 29, 1998).

Burkhauser, Richard V., Kenneth A. Couch, and Andrew J. Glenn. Public Policies for the Working Poor: The EITC Versus Minimum Wage Legislation, IRP Discussion Paper No. 1074–95 (1995).

Burman, Leonard E. Estate Taxes and the Angel of Death Loophole, 76 Tax Notes 675 (Aug. 4, 1997).

Burtless, Gary. Welfare Recipients' Job Skills and Employment Prospects, 7 The Future of Children 39 (1997).

Butler, Judith. Gender Trouble (New York: Routledge, 1990).

Buttner, Thomas, and Wolfgang Lutz. Estimating Fertility Responses to Policy Measures in the German Democratic Republic, 16 Pop. and Dev. Rev. 539 (1990).

Cancian, Maria, Sheldon Danziger, and Peter Gottschalk. Working Wives and Family Income Inequality Among Married Couples. *In* Uneven Tides (Danziger and Gottschalk, eds.) (New York: Russell Sage Foundation, 1993).

Caplow, Theodore, and Jonathan Simon. Understanding Penal Policy. *In* Crime and Justice: Prison Issue (Joan Petersilia and Michael Tonry, eds.) (Chicago: Univ. of Chicago Press, forthcoming 1999).

Card, David, and Alan B. Krueger. Myth and Measurement: The New Economics of the Minimum Wage (Princeton, N.J.: Princeton Univ. Press, 1995).

CBPP (Center on Budget and Policy Priorities). Distribution of Budget Agreement's Tax Cuts Far More Similar to Congressional Bills Than to President's Plan (July 31, 1997).

Chen, Yung-Ping, and Stephen C. Goss. Are Returns on Payroll Taxes Fair? *In* Social Security in the Twenty-First Century 76 (Eric R. Kingson and James H. Schulz, eds.) (New York: Oxford Univ. Press, 1997).

Chirelstein, Marvin A. Federal Income Taxation, 8th ed. (Westbury, N.Y.: Foundation Press, 1997).

Choy, Susan P. Public and Private Schools: How Do They Differ? *In* Condition of Education 1997 (Washington, D.C.: U.S. Department of Education, 1997).

Clotfelter, Charles T. Economic Challenges in Higher Education (Chicago: Univ. of Chicago Press, 1991).

Cohen, G. A. Self-Ownership, Freedom, and Equality (Cambridge: Cambridge Univ. Press, 1995).

CBO (Congressional Budget Office). Effects of Adopting a Value-Added Tax (Mar. 17, 1992), reprinted in 92 Tax Notes Today 60–11 (LEXIS).

Corcoran, Mary, and Terry Adams. Childhood Poverty, Childhood Welfare, Environmental Disadvantages, and Men's Earnings, mimeo, Univ. of Michigan (Mar. 5, 1997).

CEA (Council of Economic Advisors). Economic Report of the President (Washington, D.C.: The White House, 1998).

———. Technical Report: Explaining the Decline in Welfare Receipt 1993–1996, available at http://www.whitehouse.gov/WH/EOP/CEA/Welfare/Technical_Report.html (May 9, 1997).

Cowell, Alan. It's Young Versus Old in Germany as the Welfare State Fades, New York Times, p. A1 (June 4, 1997).

Cronin, Julie-Anne. The Economic Effects and Beneficiaries of the Administration's Proposed Higher Education Tax Subsidies, 50 Nat'l Tax J. 519 (1997).

Cruciano, Therese. Individual Income Tax Rates and Tax Shares, Statistics of Income Bulletin (Spring 1997).

Cuccaro-Alamin, Stephanie. Postsecondary Persistence and Attainment, Condition of Education 1997 (Washington, D.C.: U.S. Department of Education, 1997).

Cutler, David M., and Richard J. Zeckhauser. Adverse Selection in Health Insurance, NBER Working Paper No. 6107 (July 1997).

Danziger, Sheldon, and Peter Gottschalk. America Unequal (New York: Russell Sage Foundation; Cambridge: Harvard Univ. Press, 1995).

Diamond, Martin. Ethics and Politics: The American Way. In The Moral Foundations of the American Republic (Robert Horwitz, ed.) (Charlottesville: Univ. of Virginia Press, 1986).

Drayton, William. The Hidden Jobless, 77 Barron's 58 (Feb. 24, 1997).

Duncan, Greg J., and Jeanne Brooks-Gunn. Income Effects Across the Life Span: Integration and Interpretation. In Consequences of Growing Up Poor 596 (Duncan and Brooks-Gunn, eds.) (New York: Russell Sage Foundation, 1997).

Dworkin, Ronald. What Is Equality? Part 1, 10 J. Phil. & Pub. Affairs 185 (1981a).

———. What Is Equality? Part 2, 10 J. Phil. & Pub. Affairs 284 (1981b).

Edin, Kathryn, and Laura Lein. Making Ends Meet: How Single Mothers Survive Welfare and Low-Wage Work (New York: Russell Sage Foundation, 1997).

Eissa, Nada. Labor Supply and the Economic Recovery Tax Act of 1981. In Empirical Foundations of Household Taxation 5 (Martin Feldstein and James M. Poterba, eds.) (Chicago: Univ. of Chicago Press, 1996).

Eller, Martha B. Federal Taxation of Wealth Transfers 1992–1995, Statistics of Income 8 (Winter 1996–1997).

Engen, Eric M., and William G. Gale. Effects of Social Security Reform on Private and National Saving. In Federal Reserve Board of Boston, Social Security Reform: Conference Proceedings, Conference Series No. 41 (June 1997).

Feldstein, Martin. Fiscal Policies, Capital Formation, and Capitalism, 39 Eur. Econ. Rev. 399 (1995).

Feldstein, Martin, and Daniel Feenberg. Higher Tax Rates with Little Revenue Gain: An Analysis of the Clinton Tax Plan, 64 Tax Notes 1653 (1993).

Ferber, Marianne A. Women's Employment and the Social Security System, 56 Soc. Sec. Bull. 33 (1993).

Fierst, Edith U. Supplemental Statement. In Report of the 1994–1996 Advisory Council on Social Security, vol. 1, 135 (1996).

Fischer, Claude S., et al. Inequality by Design: Cracking the Bell Curve Myth (Princeton, N.J.: Princeton Univ. Press, 1996).

Flynn, Rob. Political Acquiescence, Privatisation, and Residualisation in British Housing Policy. In Privatization and Its Alternatives (William T. Gormley, Jr., ed.) (Madison: Univ. of Wisconsin Press, 1990).

Folbre, Nancy. Who Pays for the Kids? (New York: Routledge, 1994).

Fuchs, Victor R. Women's Quest for Economic Equality (Cambridge: Harvard Univ. Press, 1988).

Fullerton, Don, and Diane L. Rogers. Who Bears the Lifetime Tax Burden? (Washington, D.C.: Brookings Institution, 1993).

Gann, Pamela B. Abandoning Marital Status as a Factor in Allocating Income Tax Burdens, 59 Tex. L. Rev. 1 (1980).

Gardner, Howard. Cracking Open the IQ Box, The Am. Prospect (Winter 1994).

Garrett, Geoffrey. Partisan Politics in the Global Economy (New York: Cambridge Univ. Press, 1998).

Gladieux, Lawrence E., and Arthur M. Hauptman. The College Aid Quandary: Access, Quality, and the Federal Role (Washington, D.C.: Brookings Institution, 1995).

Glazer, Sarah. Head Start, 3 Cong. Q. 289 (1993).

Glendon, Mary Ann. Rights Talk (New York: Free Press, 1991).

Goldscheider, Frances K., and Linda J. Waite. New Families, No Families? (Berkeley: Univ. of California Press, 1991).

Gottschalk, Peter. Inequality, Income Growth, and Mobility: The Basic Facts, 11 J. Econ. Persp. 21 (Spring 1997).

Gould, Stephen Jay. Curveball, The New Yorker (Nov. 28, 1994).

Graetz, Michael J. The Decline (and Fall?) of the Income Tax (New York: W. W. Norton, 1997).

———. The Troubled Marriage of Retirement Security and Tax Policies, 135 U. Pa. L. Rev. 851 (1987).

———. To Praise the Estate Tax, Not to Bury It, 93 Yale L. J. 259 (1983).

Graetz, Michael J., and Deborah H. Schenk. 1997 Supplement to Federal Income Taxation (Westbury, N.Y.: Foundation Press, 1997).

———. Federal Income Taxation, 3d ed. (Westbury, N.Y.: Foundation Press, 1995).

Gravelle, Jane G. The Economic Effects of Taxing Capital Income (Cambridge: MIT Press, 1994).

———. Behavioral Responses to Proposed High-Income Tax Rate Increases: An Evaluation of the Feldstein-Feenberg Study, 59 Tax Notes 1097 (1993).

Greenstein, Robert. Looking at the Details of the New Budget Legislation: Social Program Initiatives Decline Over Time While Upper-Income Tax Cuts Grow, CBPP (Aug. 12, 1997).

Gustafson, Charles H., Robert J. Peroni, and Richard C. Pugh. Taxation of International Transactions (St. Paul, Minn.: West, 1996).

Hadfield, Gillian K. Households at Work: Beyond Labor Market Policies to Remedy the Gender Gap, 82 Geo. L. J. 89 (1993).

Hall, Robert E. Intertemporal Substitution in Consumption, 96 J. Pol. Econ. 339 (1988).

Hall, Robert E., and Alvin Rabushka. The Flat Tax (Stanford, Calif.: Hoover Institution Press, 1995).

Handbook of U.S. Labor Statistics: Employment, Earnings, Prices, Productivity, and Other Labor Data (Lanham, Md.: Bernan Press, 1997).

Handler, Joel F., and Yeheskel Hasenfeld. We the Poor People (New Haven: Yale Univ. Press, 1997).

Harrington, James. The Commonwealth of the Oceana; and, A System of Politics (J. G. A. Pocock, ed.) (Cambridge: Cambridge Univ. Press, 1992).

Haveman, Robert. Starting Even (New York: Simon and Schuster, 1988).

Haveman, Robert, and Barbara Wolfe. The Determinants of Children's Attainments, 33 J. Econ. Lit. 1829 (1995).

———. Succeeding Generations (New York: Russell Sage Foundation, 1994).

Henshaw, Stanley K. Teenage Abortion and Pregnancy Statistics by State, 29 Fam. Plan. Persp. 115 (1997).

Herrnstein, Richard, and Charles Murray. The Bell Curve: Intelligence and Class Structure in American Life (New York: Free Press, 1994).

Hershey, Alan M., and LaDonna Pavetti. Turning Job Finders into Job Keepers, 7 The Future of Children 75 (1997).

Hochschild, Jennifer L. The New American Dilemma: Liberal Democracy and School Desegregation (New Haven: Yale Univ. Press, 1984).

Holden, Karen C. Social Security and the Economic Security of Women. In Social Security in the Twenty-First Century 91 (Eric R. Kingson and James H. Schulz, eds.) (New York: Oxford Univ. Press, 1997).

Holmes, Stephen, and Cass Sunstein. The Costs of Rights (New York: W. W. Norton, 1998).

Holtz-Eakin, Douglas. The Uneasy Case for Abolishing the Estate Tax, 51 Tax L. Rev. 495 (1997).

Hotz, V. Joseph, Susan W. McElroy, and Seth G. Sanders. The Impacts of Teenage Childbearing on the Mothers and the Consequences of Those Impacts for Government. In Kids Having Kids 55 (Rebecca A. Maynard, ed.) (Washington, D.C.: Urban Institute Press, 1997).

Hout, Michael. More Universalism, Less Structural Mobility: The American Occupational Structure in the 1980s, 93 Am. J. Soc. 1358 (1988).

Ibbotson Associates. Stocks, Bonds, Bills, and Inflation: 1997 Yearbook, Market Results for 1926–1996 (Chicago: R. G. Ibbotson Associates, 1997).

IRS (Internal Revenue Service). Statistics of Income Bulletin, Selected Historical and Other Data (Spring 1997).

International Monetary Fund. Balance of Payments Statistics Yearbook, vol. 48 (Washington, D.C.: International Monetary Fund, 1997).

Jargowsky, Paul A. Poverty and Place: Ghettos, Barrios, and the American City (New York: Russell Sage Foundation, 1997).

Jencks, Christopher. Rethinking Social Policy: Race, Poverty, and the Underclass (Cambridge: Harvard Univ. Press, 1992).

Jensen, Erik M. The Apportionment of "Direct Taxes": Are Consumption Taxes Constitutional? 97 Col. L. Rev. 2334 (1997).

Johnson, Calvin. Apportionment of Direct Taxes: The Glitch in the Center of the Constitution, Wm. and Mary Bill of R. J. (1998).

JCT (Joint Committee on Taxation). U.S. Congress, General Explanation of Tax Legislation Enacted in 1997 (JCS-23–97), reprinted in 97 TNT 245-65 (LEXIS) (Dec. 17, 1997).

———. Methodology and Issues in Measuring Changes in the Distribution of Tax Burdens (JCS-7–93) (June 14, 1993).

Kasarda, John D. The Severely Distressed in Economically Transforming Cities. *In* Drugs, Crime, and Social Isolation (Adele V. Harrell and George E. Peterson, eds.) (Washington, D.C.: Urban Institute Press, 1992).

Katz, Michael B. The Undeserving Poor (New York: Pantheon Books, 1989).

Kaus, Mickey. The "It-Matters-Little" Gambit. *In* The Bell Curve Wars 130 (Steven Fraser, ed.) (New York: Basic Books, 1995).

———. The End of Equality (New York: Basic Books, 1992).

Keenan, Maureen, and Jeffrey B. Curry. Individual Income Tax Returns, 1994: Early Tax Estimates, 14 Statistics of Income Bulletin 9 (Fall 1995).

Kelman, Mark, and Gillian Lester. Jumping the Queue: An Inquiry into the Legal Treatment of Students with Learning Disabilities (Cambridge: Harvard Univ. Press, 1997).

Kennickell, Arthur B., Martha Starr-McCluer, and Annika E. Sunden. Family Finances in the U.S.: Recent Evidence from the Survey of Consumer Finances, Federal Reserve Bulletin 1 (Jan. 1997).

Kennickell, Arthur B., and R. Louise Woodburn. Consistent Weight Design for the 1989, 1992, and 1995 scfs (preliminary draft working paper, Board of Governors of the Federal Reserve System) (Aug. 1997).

Kessler, Denis, and Andre Masson. Bequest and Wealth Accumulation: Are Some Pieces of the Puzzle Missing? 3 J. Econ. Persp. 141 (1989).

Kingson, Eric R., and James H. Schulz. Should Social Security Be Means-Tested? *In* Social Security in the Twenty-First Century 41 (Kingson and Schulz, eds.) (New York: Oxford Univ. Press, 1997).

Klein, William A. A Proposal for a Universal Personal Capital Account, Institute for Research on Poverty Working Paper No. 422–77 (1977).

Korenman, Sanders, and Jane E. Miller. Effects of Long-Term Poverty on Physical Health of Children in the National Longitudinal Survey of Youth. *In* Consequences of Growing Up Poor 70 (Greg J. Duncan and Jeanne Brooks-Gunn, eds.) (New York: Russell Sage Foundation, 1997).

Kotlikoff, Laurence J. Generational Accounting (New York: Free Press, 1993).

———. Intergenerational Transfers and Savings, 2 J. Econ. Persp. 41 (1988).

Kronman, Anthony. Talent-Pooling, 23 Nomos 58 (New York: Atherton Press, 1981).

Ladd, Helen F. Spatially Targeted Economic Development Strategies: Do They Work? 1 Cityscape 193 (1994).

Langbein, John H. The Twentieth-Century Revolution in Family Wealth Transmission, 86 Mich. L. Rev. 722 (1988).

Lav, Iris J. The Final Tax Bill: Assessing the Long-Term Costs and the Distribution of Tax Benefits, cbpp (Aug. 1, 1997).

Lehman, Carrie. Dividend Deals Tempt Alaskans to Empty Newly Padded Pockets, Alaska J. Com., p. 1 (Sept. 29, 1997).

Levy, Frank. Dollars and Dreams: The Changing American Income Distribution (New York: Russell Sage Foundation, 1987).

Longman, Phillip J., and Amy Graham. The Cost of Children, U.S. News and World Rep. (Mar. 30, 1998).

Lyotard, Jean-François. The Postmodern Condition (Minneapolis: Univ. of Minnesota Press, 1984).

MacCurdy, Thomas. Work Disincentive Effects of Taxes: A Reexamination of Some Evidence, 82 Am. Econ. Rev. 243 (1992).

Madison, Kristin. Using the Survey of Income and Program Participation to Value Lifetime Transfers, Yale Univ., unpublished ms. (Nov. 21, 1997).

Mahony, Rhona. Kidding Ourselves: Breadwinning, Babies, and Bargaining Power (New York: Basic Books, 1995).

Marcia, James. Ego Identity: Research Review. *In* Kenneth Hoover, The Power of Identity: Politics in a New Key 85 (Chatham, N.J.: Chatham House, 1997).

Mashaw, Jerry L., and Theodore R. Marmor. The Great Social Security Scare, The Am. Prospect 29 (Nov.–Dec. 1996).

Mayer, Susan E. What Money Can't Buy: Family Income and Children's Life Chances (Cambridge: Harvard Univ. Press, 1997).

Mayer, Susan E., and Christopher Jencks. Poverty and the Distribution of Material Hardship, 24 J. Human Resources 88 (1989).

McCaffery, Edward J. Taxing Women (Chicago: Univ. of Chicago Press, 1997).

————. The Uneasy Case for Wealth Transfer Taxation, 104 Yale L. J. 283 (1994).

————. Slouching Towards Equality: Gender Discrimination, Market Efficiency, and Social Change, 103 Yale L. J. 595 (1993).

McIntosh, C. Allison. Recent Pronatalist Policies in Western Europe. *In* Below-Replacement Fertility in Industrial Societies 318 (Kingsley Davis, Mikhail S. Bernstam, and Rita Ricardo-Campbell, eds.) (New York: Population Council, 1987).

McKeon, Richard. The Basic Works of Aristotle (New York: Random House, 1941).

McMurrer, Daniel P., Mark Condon, and Isabel V. Sawhill. Intergenerational Mobility in the United States, The Urban Inst. (May 1997).

McMurrer, Daniel P., and Isabel V. Sawhill. Getting Ahead: Economic and Social Mobility in America (Washington, D.C.: Urban Institute Press, 1998).

Meade, Sir James. Efficiency, Equality, and the Ownership of Property (London: George Allen and Unwin, 1964).

Menchik, Paul L. Inter-Generational Transmission of Inequality: An Empirical Study of Wealth Mobility, 46 Economica 349 (1979).

Metcalf, Gilbert E. Life-Cycle Versus Annual Perspectives on the Incidence of a Value-Added Tax. *In* Tax Policy and the Economy, vol. 8, 45 (James M. Poterba, ed.) (Cambridge: NBER and MIT Press Journals, 1994).

Mincy, Ronald B. The Underclass: Concept, Controversy, and Evidence. *In* Confronting Poverty: Prescriptions for Change 109 (Sheldon Danziger, Gary Sandefur, and Daniel H. Weinberg, eds.) (New York: Russell Sage Foundation; Cambridge: Harvard Univ. Press, 1994).

Mincy, Ronald B., and Hillard Pouncy. Paternalism, Child Support Enforcement, and Fragile Families. *In* The New Paternalism 130 (Lawrence Mead, ed.) (Washington, D.C.: Brookings Institution, 1997).

Mirrlees, James A. An Exploration in the Theory of Optimum Income Taxation, 38 Rev. Econ. Stud. 175 (1971).

Mitchell, Olivia S., James M. Poterba, and Mark J. Warshawsky. New Evidence on the Money's Worth of Individual Annuities, NBER Working Paper No. 6002 (Apr. 1997).

Modigliani, Franco. The Role of Intergenerational Transfers and Life Cycle Saving in the Accumulation of Wealth, 2 J. Econ. Persp. 15 (1988).

Moffitt, Robert A. Incentive Effects of the U.S. Welfare System: A Review, 30 J. Econ. Lit. 1 (1992).

Moffitt, Robert A., and Mark Wilhelm, Taxation and the Labor Supply of the Affluent, unpublished ms. (Apr. 1998).

Moon, Marilyn. Are Social Security Benefits Too High or Too Low? In Social Security in the Twenty-First Century 62 (Eric R. Kingson and James H. Schulz, eds.) (New York: Oxford Univ. Press, 1997).

Moynihan, Daniel P. Maximum Feasible Misunderstanding: Community Action in the War on Poverty (New York: Free Press, 1969).

Mullins, Ina V. S., et al. NAEP 1992 Trends in Academic Progress (Washington, D.C.: U.S. Department of Education, National Center for Education Statistics, 1994).

Munnell, Alicia H. The Couple Versus the Individual Under the Federal Personal Income Tax. In The Economics of Taxation 247 (Henry J. Aaron and Michael J. Boskin, eds.) (Washington, D.C.: Brookings Institution, 1980).

Newman, Katherine S. Declining Fortunes: The Withering of the American Dream (New York: Basic Books, 1993).

NICHD Early Child Care Research Network. Poverty and Patterns of Child Care. In Consequences of Growing Up Poor 100 (Greg J. Duncan and Jeanne Brooks-Gunn, eds.) (New York: Russell Sage Foundation, 1997).

Nozick, Robert. Anarchy, State, and Utopia (New York: Basic Books, 1974).

O'Brien, J. Patrick, and Dennis Olson. The Alaska Permanent Fund and Dividend Distribution Program, 18 Pub. Fin. Q. 139 (1990).

OECD (Organisation for Economic Cooperation and Development). Revenue Statistics 1965–1996 (Paris: OECD, 1997).

————. Jobs Study: Investment, Productivity, and Employment (Paris: OECD, 1995).

————. Taxation and Household Saving (Paris: OECD, 1994).

————. Taxation of Net Wealth, Capital Transfers, and Capital Gains of Individuals (Paris: OECD, 1988).

Offe, Claus. Towards a New Equilibrium of Citizens' Rights and Economic Resources? In Societal Cohesion and the Globalising Economy 81 (Paris: OECD, 1997).

OMB (Office of Management and Budget), Budget of the U.S. Government, Fiscal Year 1998, Historical Tables (1997).

Okin, Susan M. Justice, Gender, and the Family (New York: Basic Books, 1989).

Okun, Arthur. Equality and Efficiency: The Big Tradeoff (Washington, D.C.: Brookings Institution, 1975).

Oliver, Melvin L., and Thomas M. Shapiro. Black Wealth / White Wealth (New York: Routledge, 1995).

Orfield, Gary. Money, Equity, and College Access, 62 Harv. Ed. Rev. 337 (Fall 1992).

Orfield, Gary, and Susan E. Eaton. Dismantling Desegregation: The Quiet Reversal of *Brown v. Board of Education* (New York: New Press, 1996).

Orshansky, Mollie. Commentary: The Poverty Measure, 51 Soc. Sec. Bulletin 22 (1988).

Pahl, Jan. Money and Marriage (Houndmills, Basingstoke, Hampshire: Macmillan, 1989).

Paine, Thomas. Agrarian Justice (1797). *In* Collected Writings of Thomas Paine 396 (Eric Foner, ed.) (New York: Library of America, 1995).

Parfit, Derek. Reasons and Persons (Oxford: Clarendon Press, 1984).

Parrish, Thomas B., et al. Disparities in Public School Spending 1989–1990 (Washington, D.C.: U.S. Department of Education, National Center for Education Statistics, 1995).

Pateman, Carole. The Patriarchal Welfare State. *In* Democracy and the Welfare State 231 (Amy Gutmann, ed.) (Princeton, N.J.: Princeton Univ. Press, 1988).

Pechman, Joseph A. Tax Reform: The Rich and the Poor (Washington, D.C.: Brookings Institution, 1989).

Phelps, Edmund S. Rewarding Work (Cambridge: Harvard Univ. Press, 1997).

Poterba, James M. The Estate Tax and After-Tax Investment Returns, NBER Working Paper No. 6337 (Dec. 1997a).

———. The History of Annuities in the United States, NBER Working Paper No. 6001 (Apr. 1997b).

Radin, Margaret. Contested Commodities (Cambridge: Harvard Univ. Press, 1996).

Randolph, William C., and Diane L. Rogers. The Implications for Tax Policy of Uncertainty About Labor-Supply and Savings Responses, 48 Nat'l Tax J. 429 (1995).

Rapaczynski, Andrzej, and Roman Frydman. Privatization in Eastern Europe: Is the State Withering Away? (Budapest and New York: Central European Univ. Press, 1994).

Ratner, Sidney. American Taxation: Its History as a Social Force in Democracy (New York: W. W. Norton, 1942).

Rawls, John. A Theory of Justice (Cambridge: Belknap Press, 1971).

Reischauer, Robert D. The Size and Characteristics of the Underclass. Paper presented at the annual meeting of the Association for Public Policy Analysis and Management, Bethesda, Md. (1987).

Reno, Virginia P. Strong Support but Low Confidence: What Explains the Contradiction? *In* Social Security in the Twenty-First Century 178 (Eric R. Kingson and James H. Schulz, eds.) (New York: Oxford Univ. Press, 1997).

Report of the 1994–1996 Advisory Council on Social Security (1996).

Rich, Kim. Dividend Days: Alaskans Go on Shopping Spree, Anchorage Daily News, p. D1 (Oct. 10, 1997).

Ricketts, Erol R., and Isabel V. Sawhill. Defining and Measuring the Underclass. 7 J. Pol'y Analysis and Measurement 316 (1988).

Rosen, Harvey S. Public Finance, 3d ed. (Homewood, Ill., and Boston: Richard D. Irwin, 1992).

Ross, Jane L., and Melinda M. Upp. Treatment of Women in the U.S. Social Security System, 1970–1988, 56 Soc. Sec. Bull. 56 (Fall 1993).

Ruggles, Patricia. Drawing the Line (Washington, D.C.: Urban Institute Press, 1990).

Sandel, Michael. Democracy's Discontent (Cambridge: Belknap Press, 1996).

———. Liberalism and the Limits of Justice (New York: Cambridge Univ. Press, 1982).

Sandmo, Agnar. The Effects of Taxation on Savings and Risk-Taking. In Handbook of Public Economics 265 (Alan J. Auerbach and Martin Feldstein, eds.) (Amsterdam and New York: North-Holland, 1985).

Sass, Steven A., and Robert K. Triest. Social Security: How Social and Secure Should It Be? In Social Security Reform: Conference Proceedings 29 (Boston: Federal Reserve Bank of Boston, June 1997).

Scarbrough, William H. Who Are the Poor? A Demographic Perspective. In Child Poverty and Public Policy 55 (Judith A. Chafel, ed.) (Washington, D.C.: Urban Institute Press, 1993).

Sen, Amartya K. Inequality Reexamined (New York: Russell Sage Foundation; Cambridge: Harvard Univ. Press, 1992).

Senesky, Sarah. Parental Income as a Measure of Childhood Privilege, Yale Univ., unpublished ms. (May 21, 1998).

Shafik, Nemat. Making a Market: Mass Privatization in the Czech and Slovak Republics, 23 World Dev. 1143 (1995).

Shaviro, Daniel. The Minimum Wage, the Earned Income Tax Credit, and Optimal Subsidy Policy, 64 U. Chi. L. Rev. 405 (1997).

Sidgwick, Henry. Methods of Ethics (Chicago: Univ. of Chicago Press, 1906).

Silver, Harry. The Privatization of Public Housing in Great Britain. In Privatization and Its Alternatives (William T. Gormley, Jr., ed.) (Madison: Univ. of Wisconsin Press, 1990).

Skocpol, Theda. The GI Bill and U.S. Social Policy Past and Future, 14 Soc. Phil. and Pol'y 95 (1997).

Slemrod, Joel, and Jon Bakija. Taxing Ourselves (Cambridge: MIT Press, 1996).

Smith, Judith R., et al. Parental Employment and Children. In Indicators of Children's Well-Being (Robert M. Hauser, Brett V. Brown, and William R. Prosser, eds.) (New York: Russell Sage Foundation, 1997).

Smith, Rogers. Civic Ideals (New Haven: Yale Univ. Press, 1997).

Social Security Administration. Soc. Sec. Bull., Annual Statistical Supplement (1997).

Solon, Gary. Intergenerational Income Mobility in the United States, 82 Am. Econ. Rev. 393 (1992).

Sowell, Thomas. Ethnicity and IQ. In The Bell Curve Wars 70 (Steven Fraser, ed.) (New York: Basic Books, 1995).

Staudt, Nancy C. Taxing Housework, 84 Geo. L. J. 1571 (1996).

Steuerle, C. Eugene, and Jon M. Bakija. Retooling Social Security for the Twenty-First Century (Washington, D.C.: Urban Institute Press, 1994).

Stranahan, Susan Q. Alaska: It's Cold and There Aren't Many Women, but . . . , 150 Time 22 (Oct. 20, 1997).

Sturm, Susan, and Lani Guinier. The Future of Affirmative Action: Reclaiming the Innovative Ideal, 84 Cal. L. Rev. 953 (1996).

Taylor, Charles. Sources of the Self (Cambridge: Harvard Univ. Press, 1989).

Tobin, James. Raising the Incomes of the Poor. In Agenda for the Nation 77 (Kermit Gordon, ed.) (Washington, D.C.: Brookings Institution, 1968).

Unger, Roberto. What Should Legal Analysis Become? (London and New York: Verso, 1996).

U.S. Bureau of the Census. Poverty in the U.S.: 1996 (Current Population Reports, P60–198) (1997a).

———. Statistical Abstract of the United States, 117th ed. (1997b).

———. Asset Ownership of Households: 1993, Current Population Reports, P70–47 (1993a).

———. Who Can Afford to Buy a House in 1993? Current Housing Reports, H121/97–1 (1993b).

U.S. Department of Education. Fiscal Year 1998 Congressional Action, at http://www.ed.gov/offices/OUS/Budget98/98main.html (1998).

———. National Center for Education Statistics, Access to Post-Secondary Education for the 1992 High School Graduates (Washington, D.C.: U.S. GPO, Oct. 1997a).

———. National Center for Education Statistics, Digest of Education Statistics (Washington, D.C.: U.S. GPO, 1997b).

———. National Center for Education Statistics, Profile of Undergraduates in American Postsecondary Institutions (Washington, D.C.: U.S. GPO, 1990).

U.S. Department of Health and Human Services. National Center for Health Statistics, Vital Statistics of the United States 1992, vol. 2, Mortality, part A (1996).

U.S. Department of Justice. Statistical Yearbook of the Immigration and Naturalization Service (Washington, D.C.: U.S. GPO, 1996).

U.S. Department of Labor. Bureau of Labor Statistics, Consumer Price Index: All Urban Consumers (CPI-U), ftp://146.142.4.23/pub/special.requests/cpiai.txt (May 14, 1998).

———. Bureau of Labor Statistics, Employment and Earnings (Jan. 1993).

U.S. Department of the Treasury. Integration of the Individual and Corporate Tax Systems (Washington, D.C., 1992).

U.S. House of Representatives, Committee on Ways and Means. 1998 Green Book: Background Material and Data on Programs Within the Jurisdiction of the Committee on Ways and Means (Washington, D.C.: U.S. GPO, 1998).

———. 1996 Green Book: Background Material and Data on Programs Within the Jurisdiction of the Committee on Ways and Means (Washington, D.C.: U.S. GPO, 1996).

———. 1993 Green Book: Background Material and Data on Programs Within the Jurisdiction of the Committee on Ways and Means (Washington, D.C.: U.S. GPO, 1993).

Van Parijs, Philippe. Real Freedom for All (Oxford: Oxford Univ. Press, 1995).

————. Introduction: Competing Justifications of Basic Income. *In* Arguing for Basic Income: Ethical Foundations for a Radical Reform (Van Parijs, ed.) (London: Verso, 1992).

Walzer, Michael. Spheres of Justice (New York: Basic Books, 1983).

Warren, Alvin C., Jr. How Much Capital Income Taxed Under an Income Tax Is Exempt Under a Cash-Flow Tax? 51 Tax L. Rev. 1 (1996).

————. American Law Institute, Federal Income Tax Project: Integration of the Individual and Corporate Income Taxes, Reporter's Study of Corporate Tax Integration (1993).

Washington, Valora, and Ura J. O. Bailey. Project Head Start: Models and Strategies for the Twenty-First Century (New York: Garland, 1995).

Weicher, John. The Distribution of Wealth: Increasing Inequality? (Washington, D.C.: American Enterprise Institute, 1996).

Whitney, Craig R. The World: Europe Isn't Divided in Its Joblessness, New York Times, sec. 4, p. 4 (Mar. 31, 1997).

Wilhelm, Mark. Revenue Estimates and Distributional Analysis for "The Stakeholder Society" (unpublished ms., 1998).

Williams, Joan. Is Coverture Dead? Beyond a New Theory of Alimony, 82 Geo. L. J. 2227 (1994).

Wilson, William J. When Work Disappears (New York: Alfred A. Knopf, 1996).

Wolff, Edward N. Recent Trends in the Size Distribution of Household Wealth, 12 J. Econ. Persp. 131 (Summer 1998).

————. Top Heavy: The Increasing Inequality of Wealth in America and What Can Be Done About It (New York: New Press, 1996).

World Bank. Averting the Old-Age Crisis (Oxford: Oxford Univ. Press, 1994).

Young, Beth Aronstam, et al. The Social Context of Education. *In* Condition of Education 1997 (Washington, D.C.: U.S. Department of Education, 1997).

Zelenak, Lawrence. Marriage and the Income Tax, 67 S. Cal. L. Rev. 339 (1994).

Zelizer, Viviana. The Social Meaning of Money (New York: Basic Books, 1994).

Ziliak, James P., et al. Accounting for the Decline in AFDC Caseloads: Welfare Reform or Economic Growth, Institute for Research on Poverty Discussion Paper No. 1151–97 (Nov. 1997).

# Index